A Universe From Someone

A Universe From Someone

Essays on Natural Theology

Peter S. Williams

Foreword by
J.P. Moreland

WIPF & STOCK · Eugene, Oregon

A UNIVERSE FROM SOMEONE
Essays on Natural Theology

Copyright © 2022 Peter S. Williams. All rights reserved. Except for brief quotations in critical publications or reviews, no part of this book may be reproduced in any manner without prior written permission from the publisher. Write: Permissions, Wipf and Stock Publishers, 199 W. 8th Ave., Suite 3, Eugene, OR 97401.

Wipf & Stock
An Imprint of Wipf and Stock Publishers
199 W. 8th Ave., Suite 3
Eugene, OR 97401

www.wipfandstock.com

PAPERBACK ISBN: 978-1-6667-0292-7
HARDCOVER ISBN: 978-1-6667-0293-4
EBOOK ISBN: 978-1-6667-0294-1

AUGUST 24, 2022 8:23 AM

This book is dedicated to
everyone in the Renal Department
at Queen Alexandra Hospital, Portsmouth,
and most especially to my mother, Linda J. Williams,
in celebration of her living donation of a kidney to my father,
Stephen H. Williams,
on November 2nd 2021.

Arguments do not compel our assent. They merely appeal for it.
—Brian Leftow, *Great Thinkers on Great Questions*.

Contents

Foreword by J. P. Moreland | ix

Preface: Autobiographically Framed Reflections on Natural Theology | xi

1 This House Believes that God is not a Delusion | 1
2 The Existence of God | 8
3 In Defence of Theism | 13
4 Can Moral Objectivism Do Without God? | 19
5 A Universe From Someone: Against Lawrence M. Krauss's *A Universe From Nothing: Why There Is Something Rather Than Nothing* | 35
6 A Brief Introduction to and Defence of the Modern Ontological Argument | 51
7 A Beginner's Guide to the Theistic Argument from Desire | 57
8 Natural Theology and Science in Contemporary Apologetic Context: An Overview | 65

Appendix A: Four Dozen Key Resources on Apologetics and Natural Theology in an Age of Science | 95

Appendix B: Recommended Resources | 104

Bibliography | 113

Foreword

In the fall of 1966, I went to the University of Missouri to begin a four-year adventure in studying chemistry. I loved the sciences, and found chemistry to involve an integrative combination of mathematics, physics and distinctively chemical concepts and properties. I enjoyed it so much that in 1970 I graduated with honors in physical chemistry. I had also received a full fellowship to complete a Ph.D. in nuclear chemistry from the University of Colorado. Since my sophomore year in high school, my aim had been to be a university professor and researcher in chemistry, and the door was now opened to achieving that goal.

However, a funny thing happened to me along the way: In November of 1968, I came to believe that God exists, the New Testament documents are historically reliable, the claims of Jesus were accurate and true, and based on the evidence, I placed my trust in Jesus and became his apprentice. Without a doubt, it was the best decision of my life and, as of this writing, I have been his follower for fifty-three years. Note carefully the role of evidence and reason in my conversion. For me, faith is trust or confidence in what we have reason to believe is true. Since I had always been a curious person who loved intellectual pursuits, it became quite natural for me to continue that approach to life, and during my entire sojourn as a Jesus-follower, knowing why I believe what I believe has been at the core of my development.

When I became a Christian in 1968, there were some very good books defending the existence of God, but to be honest, they were quite few in number. Little did I know at the time that somewhere around the 1980s, an explosion of high-level academic defenses of theism, particularly, biblical theism, was to break out. And a steady stream of such works has continued to flow from a growing number of Christian thinkers' pens, both at a popular and scholarly level. This has all been great news for us Christians. But is has generated a problem: Given such a wide array of writings, how is one to stay on top of the literature and aware of the recent issues and options being debated?

This is where Peter S. Williams's timely and excellent book *A Universe from Somewhere* enters the picture. In my opinion, it is the top work currently available that (1) provides an insightful overview of the re-emergence of (especially Christian) natural theology for the last seventy-five years or so; (2) offers a readable, but quite substantive, presentation of updated versions of the key arguments that have constituted this re-emergence. Along the way, Williams offers new development of important, but less popular arguments in natural theology. As if that were not enough, the well-selected, large, annotated bibliography is alone worth the price of the book.

Williams knows the literature well and he has well-developed skills in taking hard material and making it accessible to a wide audience in an engaging way. I am so thankful for this important book. Read it and get the bigger picture of what's been going on in debates about God's existence.

J.P. Moreland
Distinguished Professor of Philosophy,
Talbot School of Theology, Biola University, USA,
and co-editor of the *Blackwell Companion to Natural Theology*.

Preface

Autobiographically Framed Reflections on Natural Theology

I have faith *in* God; that is, I give my trusting allegiance to God.¹ I also believe *that* God exists. On the assumption that beauty is an objective value,² the God in whom I believe and trust can be defined as being not only unsurpassably beautiful, but as having a necessarily existing essential nature that exhibits the beauty of having "the greatest possible array of compossible [i.e. possible together] great-making properties."³ Moreover, I believe this God to be the very same Trinitarian God⁴ revealed in and through the Bible, "the the God of Abraham, the God of Isaac, and the

---

1. See YouTube Playlist, "Nature of Faith;" McKaughan and Howard-Snyder, "Faith;" McKaughn, "Value of Faith and Faithfulness;" Howard Snyder, "Does Faith Entail Belief?" Pojman, "Faith Without Belief?" Pruss, "Christian Faith and Belief;" Himma, "Christian Faith Without Belief;" Swinburne, *Faith and Reason*, Second Edition. On the interpretation of Heb 11:6 (a topic discussed in some of the above sources), see: Williams, "Hebrews 11 and Faith;" Hartley, "Reassessment Of The Translation 'God Exists,'" 289–230.

2. See: YouTube Playlist, "Beauty;" Cowen and Spiegel, *Love Of Wisdom*, Chapter Nine; DeWeese and Moreland, *Philosophy Made Slightly Less Difficult*, Second Edition, Chapter Seven; Groothuis, *Truth Decay*; Lewis, *Abolition of Man*; Taliaferro, *Aesthetics*; Tallon, "The Theistic Argument from Beauty;" Williams, *Faithful Guide to Philosophy*, Chapter Fourteen; Williams, *I Wish I Could Believe in Meaning*, Chapter Six.

3. Morris, *Our Idea of God*, 37.

4. See: YouTube Playlist, "The Trinity;" Williams, "Sermon: Revelation 1:1–8;" Copan, "Is the Trinity a Logical Blunder?" Craig, "Doctrine of the Trinity;" Hasker, "Objections to Social Trinitarianism;" Williams, "Understanding the Trinity."

God of Jacob" (Exod 3:6) who is also "the God and Father of our Lord Jesus Christ" (1 Pet 1:3).[5] Finally, I believe that the case for God's existence is stronger than the case against.[6] The focus of the present volume is upon the *positive* case for believing that God exists.

I've been pondering questions about God's existence for a long time. As a three-year-old, I surprised my mother by stopping in the middle of a road crossing to ask her: "If God made everything, who made God?" She doesn't remember her response, though it presumably satisfied me enough at the time to get me out of the road! Of course, the answer to my question is that (by definition) God is not the sort of thing that needs to be made. To assume that if God exists then something had to have made God is to assume that each and every thing that exists (including God) must be the sort of thing that needs to be made to exist, and is thus to affirm the existence of an actually infinite regress of causes. On the contrary, God is the uncaused cause, the non-contingent cause of contingent reality.[7] Perhaps my early interest in the nature of God's existence explains the intellectual satisfaction I would find grappling with the cosmological argument in my teens (through reading philosophers like F.C. Copleston, Norman L. Geisler, J.P. Moreland, Bruce Reichenbach and Dallas Willard).[8]

Having been born (in September 1974) to Christian parents who raised me within the community of a Baptist Church in the south-coast English city of Portsmouth, my spiritual maturation was (and is) a process of ratcheting understanding and ongoing re-commitment within "the faith that God has once for all given to his people" (Jude 1:3, CEV). My parents were both science teachers who encouraged me to think about everything, not least the relationship between science and theology,[9] so I didn't take

---

5. On the latter point, see: Williams, *Getting at Jesus*.

6. See: O'Leary-Hawthorn, "Arguments for Atheism;" Shalkowski, "Atheological Apologetics." For some responses specific to the "problem of evil" objection to theism, see: YouTube Playlist, "The Problem of Evil;" Craig, *On Guard*, Chapter Seven; Williams, *Faithful Guide to Philosophy*, Chapter Seventeen. On the so-called "Hiddenness of God" argument for atheism, see: Evans, *Natural Signs and Knowledge of God*, especially Chapter Six.

7. See: Williams, "Who Made God?"

8. See: YouTube Playlist, "Cosmological Arguments for God;" Beck, "God's Existence;" Willard, "Language, Being, God;" Beck, *Does God Exist?*, Chapter Two; Russell and Copleston, "Debate on the Existence of God;" Geisler, *Christian Apologetics*; Moreland, *Scaling the Secular City*; Rasmussen, "Argument for a Supreme Foundation;" Sadowsky, "Endless Regress of Causes?" Reichenbach, *Cosmological Argument*.

9. See: YouTube Playlist, "Christianity and Science;" Williams, "Christian Worldview

Christianity lightly. I knew other people have different worldviews. Moreover, my parents had taught me to play chess by the time I was five, which probably encouraged my capacity for logical thought.

Getting familiar with chess pieces at c. fourteen months old, January/February 1976.

My mother began reading C.S. Lewis's *Narnia* books to me when I was five, and I was reading them for myself by *Prince Caspian* at six or seven. As I matured, I absorbed much of Lewis's non-fiction, beginning with the handful of volumes in my parent's book collection, including *Mere Christianity*, *The Problem of Pain*, and *Miracles*. Together with other books from the same source, especially Keith Ward's *The Battle for the Soul*, my interest in philosophy was kindled.[10]

At sixth-form college in the early 1990s I studied A Levels in English Literature, Music, and Classical Civilization. The latter subject introduced me to ancient Greek literature (including Plato's *Apology*) and stoked my interest in philosophy to the point that I wrote my dissertation on the influence of polytheistic and monotheistic worldviews upon the development of "scientific" thought in Greek culture.

I was further stimulated to explore the intellectual dimension of faith by a friend from college. A student of the natural sciences as well as an

---

and Science in Apologetic Perspective: Introduction;" Koons, "Science and Theism;" Lennox, *God's Undertaker*, Second Edition; Pearcey and Thaxton, *Soul of Science*; Ratzsch, *Science and Its Limits*; Williams, *Faithful Guide to Philosophy*, Chapter Sixteen.

10. The "other books" included Hawthorne's *Windows on Science and Christian Faith*; Pine-Coffin's translation of *Saint Augustine's Confessions*; and Ramm's *The Christian View of Science and Scripture*.

excellent musician, David Bacon was "a bright cookie." Together, we helped lead the college Christian Union, and formed a band (mainly playing covers of Pink Floyd). Having studied at Cambridge University, Dr. Bacon is now a Senior Lecturer and Reader in Cosmology at the University of Portsmouth, and a fellow congregant of the Church of England.

University

When I went to Cardiff University in 1993, it was to study a joint degree in English Literature and Music. However, as a humanities student, I had to take three subjects in the first year, and chose philosophy as my third course. Here I discovered part of the University that actively invited rational discourse about the factuality and significance of God's existence or non-existence. While some of my teachers were atheists (e.g. Professor Christopher Norris, whom I'd later debate on God's existence), I was taught Philosophy of Religion by an agnostic, and my personal tutor—Professor Michael Durrant (1934–2018)[11]—was a Christian.

Professor Durrant served as Head of Cardiff University's Department of Philosophy from May to September 1987 and Head of the Philosophy Section of Cardiff's School of English Studies, Journalism, and Philosophy until 1991. He was a member of the Executive Committee of the British Society for the Philosophy of Religion at its inception, and a founder-member and first President of the European Society for the Philosophy of Religion. As well as being my personal tutor, the pipe-smoking Professor (who spent some of his spare time as a church organist) taught my lecture course on Aristotle, and served as President of the Student Philosophical Society that I and some coursemates established. I recall Professor Durrant lecturing from memory, often with his eyes closed, and even from a recumbent position on the desk at the head of the lecture room!

---

11. See: "Obituaries: Michael Durrant."

PREFACE

My room in my first-year halls of residence (University Hall) at Cardiff University in 1993. Yes, that is a CD/Audio-Cassette player on my desk, next to my extremely high-tech electronic word-processor.

Playing a grand piano in the music department at Cardiff University.

During my first year at Cardiff, I experienced a growing frustration with the postmodernism of the English Literature department at that time, a frustration that bled in two directions. On the one hand, I found an outlet for enjoying creative writing in my philosophy assignments. For example, I wrote an essay on Aristotle's distinction between primary and secondary matter in the form of a dialogue between a man and a Sphinx, conducted entirely in iambic pentameter. On the other hand, I wrote what was basically a philosophy essay for my Literature course, critiquing French atheist philosopher and literary critic Roland Barthes's rejection of authorial intent.

The Resurrection of the Author

Barthes's "death of the author" was a self-contradictory rejection of objective meaning, both in literary texts and "the world as text" authored by God:

> We know now that a text is not a line of words releasing a single 'theological' meaning (the 'message' of the Author-God) . . . Once the Author is removed, the claim to decipher a text becomes quite futile. To give a text an Author is to impose a limit on that text, to furnish it with a final signified . . . writing ceaselessly posits meaning ceaselessly to evaporate it, carrying out a systematic exemption of meaning. In precisely this way literature (it would be better from now on to say writing), by refusing to assign a 'secret', an ultimate meaning, to the text (and to the world as text), liberates what may be called an anti-theological activity, an activity. that is truly revolutionary since to refuse to fix meaning is, in the end, to refuse God and his hypostases—reason, science, law.[12]

Barthes's "death of the author" was the application to literature of the existential philosophy that shrouds the acceptance of an objective nihilism with the subjective meanings of supposedly self-made people. The obvious question here is, did Barthes *intend* or *mean* to communicate this philosophy to his readers?

If removing the author renders any claim to decipher what a text signifies "quite futile," it necessarily renders quite futile any claim—even a claim on the part of a text's author—that one has *mis*interpreted what a text signifies. But as William Lane Craig wryly comments: "nobody adopts a Postmodernist view of literary texts when reading the labels on a medicine bottle or a box of rat poison!"[13]

If denying God's existence means denying that "the world as text" has an objective meaning (the kind of meaning that is discovered rather than invented), it follows that the only way to coherently affirm that the world has an objective meaning is to affirm the existence of God as its "Author." This is one justification for Mortimer J. Adler's statement that: "More

---

12. Barthes, "Death of the Author," 142–48.
13. Craig, "Resurrection of Theism."

consequences for thought and action follow the affirmation or denial of God than from answering any other basic question."[14] In other words—as atheist philosophers such as Friedrich Nietzsche, Bertrand Russell and Jean-Paul Sartre recognized—the question of God's existence is not a question of merely academic interest, but a question of existential import.[15] Indeed, if we embrace a properly basic rational intuition of the meaningfulness of reality, we can reverse Barthes's argument into an argument for theism (see "A Beginner's Guide to the Theistic Argument from Desire" in this volume).

During a Q&A time with our lecturers at the end of the first-year literature course, I asked for a response to a quotation that I thought skewered the claim of postmodern hermeneutics to "see through" authorial intent and objective meaning:

> You cannot go on seeing through things for ever. The whole point of seeing through something is to see something through it. It is good that the window should be transparent, because the street or garden beyond it is opaque. How if you saw through the garden too? It is no use trying to see through first principles. If you see through everything, then everything is transparent. But a wholly transparent world is an invisible world. To "see through" all things is the same as not to see.[16]

In reply, one of the lecturers asked who had written the passage in question. An interesting question given the supposed "death of the author!" This being the case, I should have responded that the origin of the argument was irrelevant to its cogency. Instead, I disclosed that the passage came from C.S. Lewis's *The Abolition of Man* (which was originally published in 1943, and which *National Review* chose as the seventh entry in their list of the "100 Best Nonfiction Books of the Twentieth Century"[17]). With this authorial information now in hand, my lecturer proceeded to ignore my application of Lewis' argument to postmodern hermeneutics in favor of dismissing *The Abolition of Man* as a work authored in and to a society seeking certainty on account of the Second World War. This *ad*

---

14. Adler, *Great Books of the Western World*, 561.

15. See: Evans, *Despair*; Nietzsche, "Parable of the Madman;" Russell, "Free Man's Worship;" Sartre, "Existentialism is a Humanism;" Williams, *I Wish I Could Believe In Meaning*.

16. Lewis, *Abolition of Man*, 48.

17. Lewis, *Abolition of Man*. See: Aeschliman, *Restoration of Man*, third edition; Mosteller and Anacker, ed.'s. *Contemporary Perspectives on C.S. Lewis'* The Abolition of Man; Ward, *After Humanity*.

hominem attack upon the supposed authorial intent of Lewis' work not only constituted a genetic fallacy (attacking the source rather than the content of the argument) but contradicted the professed rejection of authorial intent!

Looking back, the whole situation puts me in mind of this passage from theologian D.A. Carson's book *The Gagging of God*:

> A few years ago I was teaching an evening course on hermeneutics ... I was trying to set out both what could be learned from the new hermeneutic, and where the discipline was likely to lead one astray. In particular, I was insisting that true knowledge is possible, even to finite, culture-bound creatures. A doctoral student from another seminary ... quietly protested that she did not think I was escaping from the dreaded positivism of the nineteenth century. Deeper appreciation for the ambiguities of language, the limits of our understanding, the uniqueness of each individual, and the social nature of knowledge would surely drive me to a more positive assessment of the new hermeneutic. I tried to defend my position, but I was quite unable to persuade her. Finally, in a moment of sheer intellectual perversity on my part, I joyfully exclaimed, "Ah, now I think I see what you are saying. You are using delicious irony to affirm the objectivity of truth." The lady was not amused. "That is exactly what I am not saying," she protested with some heat, and she laid out her position again. I clasped my hands in enthusiasm and told her how delighted I was to find someone using irony so cleverly in order to affirm the possibility of objective knowledge. Her answer was more heated, but along the same lines as her first reply. I believe she also accused me of twisting what she was saying. I told her I thought it was marvelous that she should add emotion to her irony, all to the purpose of exposing the futility of extreme relativism, thereby affirming truth's objectivity. Not surprisingly, she exploded in real anger, and accused me of a lot of unmentionable things. When she finally cooled down, I said, rather quietly, "But this is how I am reading you." Of course, she saw what I was getting at immediately, and sputtered out like a spent candle ... My example was artificial, of course, since I only pretended to read her in a certain way, but what I did was sufficient to prove the point I was trying to make to her. "You are a deconstructionist," I told her, "but you expect me to interpret your words aright. More precisely, you are upset because I seem to be divorcing the meaning I claim to see in your words from your intent. Thus, implicitly you affirm the link between text and authorial intent. I have never read a deconstructionist who would be pleased if a reviewer misinterpreted his or her work: thus in practice deconstructionists

implicitly link their own texts with their own intentions . . ." . . . in the real world, for all the difficulties there are in communication from person to person . . . we still expect people to say more or less what they mean (and if they don't, we chide them for it), and we expect mature people to understand what others say, and represent it fairly. The understanding is doubtless never absolutely exhaustive and perfect, but that does not mean the only alternative is to dissociate text from speaker, and then locate all meaning in the reader or hearer.[18]

Towards the end of the Q&A session, one of our lecturers told us that if we wanted to enjoy reading literature, we didn't need to *study* English Literature, just to read it. I thought she had a good point.

The Philosophical Turn

Walking towards the University library after the English Literature Q&A session had ended, I met a member of the philosophy faculty. They encouraged me to "come and join" the philosophers because they were "more sensible" than the English department! At the end of my first year, I followed his advice (and that of the tutor who marked my first-year essays) and switched to a single honors degree in philosophy.[19]

---

18. Carson, *Gagging of God*, 101–3 [Kindle location].

19. I'd come too late to music (I studied GCSE Music in my final year at Secondary School) to have the performance grades on multiple instruments required to progress with composition past the first year at Cardiff, which was the aspect of the course that most interested me. I had reached Grade 7 on the flute, and continued playing for many years. Later still, I returned to composing, as described in Appendix II of Williams, *Apologetics in 3D*, and as you can hear via my website's "Composing" page at www.peterswilliams.com/composing/.

PREFACE

The library at Cardiff University (on the right) on the way to philosophy lectures in 1993.

Although I embarked upon philosophical study as a theist, I was willing to change my mind should I meet a strong enough case for doing so. I didn't come across one then and I haven't since. On the contrary, the more I studied philosophy—including that of atheists such as A.J. Ayer, J.L. Mackie, Michael Martin, Kai Nielson and Bertrand Russell—the more I came to appreciate the breadth and strength of the case for theism. As David Bradshaw reports:

> The practice of natural theology goes back to Xenophanes and Anaximander and was developed in elaborate detail by Plato and Aristotle. It has a long and complex history stretching from antiquity through the Middle Ages and modern philosophy, one that was by no means brought to an end (as is sometimes supposed) by Hume and Kant. Although it went into eclipse in the first half of the twentieth century, owing to the dominance of phenomenology on the Continent and of positivism and ordinary language philosophy in the Anglophone world, it came roaring back with the revival of metaphysics that began in the 1960s. Today natural theology is a flourishing enterprise that includes a wide range of argument types and strategies, some of them drawing from classical sources and many others of more recent vintage.[20]

Talking of positivism, the anti-metaphysical philosophy of "[the] Vienna Circle, an influential group of scientifically oriented philosophers

20. Bradshaw, "Introduction" in *Natural Theology in the Eastern Orthodox Tradition*, 2. On Hume's critique of natural theology, see: Sennett and Groothuis, ed.'s. *In Defence Of Natural Theology*. See also Geivett and Habermas, *In Defence of Miracles*. On Kant, see: Geisler, *Christian Apologetics*, 5–6, 13.

who flourished in Vienna from the early 1920s to the mid-1930s,"[21] A.J. Ayer's classic but self-refuting positivist polemic *Language, Truth and Logic* was a set text in my first year at Cardiff. I'm not sure if this was meant as an example of how to do philosophy, or an example of how not to do it, since philosophers had long since pointed out that Ayer's attempt to confine linguistic meaning to statements that were either true by definition or empirically verifiable was neither true by definition nor empirically verifiable.

Despite the collapse of verificationism (which even Ayer went on to repudiate), atheist Kai Nielson, in his 1988 debate against J.P. Moreland, put all his philosophical eggs into arguing that definite descriptions such as "God is the maker of heaven and earth" and "The being transcendent to the world on whom all things depends and who depends on nothing himself" are "so problematic and so obscure that it turns out that we don't know what we are talking about when we use them."[22]

Commenting on the debate, philosopher Dallas Willard observed that Nielson's approach looked "awfully like warmed over Logical Positivism with superficial disclaimers"[23] and argued that "The overly-simple quasi-positivist models which, it seems to me, lie back of Nielson's remarks surely cannot do justice to the actual performances of language."[24]

In the debate itself, Moreland replied to Nielson that,

> It seems to me that it's possible to have ostensive knowledge of God. It's also possible to have knowledge of him as you infer a cause to explain a set of effects. I would further say that . . . miraculous acts of God could be baptismal events, to use Kripke's phrase, and meanings associated with those events . . . could be passed through salvation history in a way similar to a Kripkian ancestral chain view of reference. So . . . I believe that God-talk makes sense through ostentation, through the fact that [we have] been visited by Jesus of Nazareth, through a very similar kind of meaning as is used in science, and through analogy with myself as I reflect upon my own faculties and form a conception of God as a being who has intellect, emotion, and will.[25]

---

21. Edwards, "Behaviorism." Nancy R. Pearcey and Charles B. Thaxton explain that according to positivists, "progress in science consists in its 'emancipation' from the confining fetters of religion and metaphysics." *Soul of Science*, xi, see also 46–49.

22. Nielsen, "No! A Defence of Atheism," 51.

23. Willard, "Language, Being, God."

24. Willard, "Language, Being, God."

25. Moreland, "A Christian's Rebuttal," 59. On Jesus of Nazareth, see: Williams,

Moreover, just as D.A. Carson argued that we "can understand what others say" despite the fact that our understanding is "never absolutely exhaustive and perfect," so Moreland argued that,

> Most people know very well what "God" means, and they use it to refer, even if they cannot give you a complete theory of reference and meaning to explain this. There is no philosophical topic of interest wherein philosophers are in universal agreement regarding how we talk about it or what its definition is. No philosopher to my knowledge has given a universally accepted definition of "knowledge." I couldn't for the life of me define "history." I'm not sure I could define "love;" I'm not sure that I could define to everyone's satisfaction what a number is. And I couldn't define to everyone's satisfaction what God is nor how I refer to any of these entities. Nonetheless, it does seem reasonable that I could know something about these things, whether or not I could give an exhaustive treatment of how those terms get meaning. We can know them truly without knowing them exhaustively.[26]

As the Cambridge University philosopher A.C. Ewing argued in his 1973 book *Value and Reality*, "There are a number of intermediate degrees between a perfectly clear definite concept and no concept at all... It may be argued that the suggestion that there is such a being [as God] is groundless, but hardly that it has no meaning at all."[27] In the end, as William Lane Craig concluded, "Nielsen fails to prove... that the concept 'God' is any more problematic than theoretical entities in science..."[28]

I *devoured* the 1993 published form of this debate, being particularly impressed by the incisive debate review contributed by William Lane Craig, and by Dallas Willard's now classic essay "Language, Being, God, and the Three Stages of Theistic Evidence."[29]

Superseding Scientism

William Lane Craig describes how, during the 1950s and 60s:

Getting at Jesus.
26. Moreland, "Christian's Rebuttal," 59.
27. Ewing, *Value and Reality*, 31.
28. Craig, "Defence of Rational Theism," 158.
29. See: Moreland and Nielson et al, *Does God Exist?* Willard, "Language, Being, God." Moreland's *Scaling the Secular City: A Defence of Christianity* (Baker, 1987) was a major early influence on my philosophical thinking.

The overwhelmingly dominant mode of thinking was scientific naturalism. Physical science was taken to be the final, and really only, arbiter of truth. Metaphysics—that traditional branch of philosophy which deals with questions about reality which are beyond science (hence, the name "*meta*-physics," *i.e.*, "beyond physics")—had been vanquished, expelled from philosophy like an unclean leper . . . Any problem that could not be addressed by science was simply dismissed as a pseudo-problem.[30]

Whereas verificationism attributes the determination of linguistic *meaning* (outside of purely definitional truths) to empirical verifiability, the related epistemology (that is, theory of knowledge) of "scientism" attributes exclusive rights over *knowledge* and/or *rational belief* to empirical verification. Whilst verificationism is an all-but-dead philosophy today, scientism is alive and kicking in contemporary culture.[31]

For example, leading neo-atheist and evolutionary biologist Richard Dawkins proclaims that "the only good reason to believe that something exists is if there is real evidence that it does . . . it always comes back to our senses, one way or another."[32] Likewise, neo-atheist chemist Peter Atkins affirms:

> I stand by my claim that the scientific method is the only means of discovering the nature of reality, and although its current views are open to revision, the approach, making observations and comparing notes, will forever survive as the only way of acquiring reliable knowledge.[33]

Neo-atheist philosopher and physicist Victor J. Stenger complained that: "critics accuse New Atheism of 'scientism,' which is the principle that science is the only means that can be used to learn about the world and humanity. They cannot quote a single new atheist who has said that."[34] Yet Stenger himself defined science as "belief in the presence of

---

30. Craig, "Resurrection of Theism."

31. For an introduction to and critique of scientism, see: YouTube Playlist, "Scientism;" Deane, "Is Science the Only Means for Acquiring Truth?" Moreland, *Scientism and Secularism*; Trigg, *Does Science Undermine Faith?*, Chapter One; West, ed. *Magician's Twin*.

32. Dawkins, *Magic of Reality*, 16, 19.

33. Atkins, *Being*, xiii.

34. Stenger, *New Atheism*, 238–39.

supportive evidence,"[35] affirming that "faith is belief in the absence of supportive evidence,"[36] that "Science . . . does not require nor does it use any metaphysics"[37] and that "reason is just the procedure by which humans ensure that their conclusions are consistent with the theory that produced them and with the data that test those conclusions,"[38] such that "Being rational just means that when you talk about some subject, the words you use are well defined and the statements you make are self-consistent."[39] In other words, Stenger held that while philosophical reason checks the *coherence* of propositions (to show if they might be true), it is only if there is (sufficient) "supportive evidence" (i.e. non-metaphysical, empirical data) for a proposition that belief in the truth of that proposition can be considered "scientific" rather than being a matter of blind faith. Sounds like scientism to me.

Of course, the scientistic demand that *rational belief must be justified by empirical evidence* is self-contradictory, in that it can't be justified by empirical evidence, and in that it entails an infinite regress that can't be satisfied (since the demand requires evidence for the existence and reliability of one's evidence, and so on *ad infinitum*). It's also open to obvious counter-examples (e.g. metaphysical, moral and aesthetic knowledge).

On this last point I'm happy to agree with neo-atheist philosopher Sam Harris, who contradicts scientism (along with his own book's central thesis, that science can deal with morality) when he admits in *The Moral Landscape* that:

> Science cannot tell us why, *scientifically*, we should value [human] well-being . . . the demand for *radical* justification leveled by the moral skeptic could not be met by science. Science is defined with reference to the goal of understanding the processes at work in the universe. Can we justify this goal scientifically? Of course not . . . What evidence could prove that we should value evidence?[40]

No *empirical* evidence of what is the case could justify believing that we "should" value evidence in the moral sense of "having an objective obligation" to do so; but the non-empirical, phenomenological evidence of

---

35. Stenger, *New Atheism*, 15.
36. Stenger, *New Atheism*, 45.
37. Stenger, *New Atheism*, 21.
38. Stenger, *New Atheism*, 15.
39. Stenger, *New Atheism*, 71.
40. Harris, *Moral Landscape*, 37.

moral experience does justify such a belief.[41] As atheist philosopher Mary Midgely warned: "Physical science . . . is not a separate, supreme champion outclassing history or philosophy. It has no private line to reality."[42]

Indeed, as philosopher of science Del Ratzsch points out, "science cannot validate either scientific method itself or the presuppositions of that method . . . Those who claim either that science is competent for dealing with all matters" or that science is the only legitimate method for dealing with any matter are seriously confused."[43] After all, there are second order philosophical questions about first order scientific issues, questions about science and the significance of scientific ideas, such that scientists have philosophical disagreements that can't be settled on scientific grounds but which affect how they do science. Furthermore, however detailed and accurate our scientific descriptions of physical realities become, such descriptions can't explain *why physical reality has the fundamental structure it has* or *why any physical reality described by that structure exists at all*. In other words, science makes metaphysical assumptions and raises metaphysical questions that require metaphysical answers. In my own view, as in the view of such leading lights of the scientific revolution as Kepler and Newton, the best understanding of those assumptions, and the best answers to many of those questions, make reference to God.

Science presupposes that the natural world isn't an illusion. Science presupposes that the natural world exhibits a rational order. However, it also presupposes that this rational order cannot simply be deduced from first principles, so that observation and experiment are useful activities. Science presupposes that human cognitive and sensory faculties are both generally reliable; and it presupposes that there are knowable objective values of truth, goodness, and even beauty. These presuppositions are all at home within the Judeo-Christian worldview. After all, as Stephen C. Meyer explains: "modern science was specifically inspired by the conviction that the universe is the product of a rational mind who . . . designed the human mind to understand it."[44] Indeed, sociologist of science Steve Fuller concedes that:

41. See: Beckwith and Koukl, *Relativism*; Williams, *Faithful Guide to Philosophy*, Chapter Eight.

42. Midgley, *Are You An Illusion?*, 6.

43. Ratzsch, *Science and Its Limits*, 93.

44. Meyer, *Return of the God Hypothesis*, 24. See: YouTube Playlist, "Theological Roots of Science;" Chapman, *Slaying the Dragons*; Grant, *History of Natural Philosophy*; Hannam, *Genesis of Science*; Keas, *Unbelievable*; Peterson, *Flat Earths and Fake Footnotes*.

> While I cannot honestly say that I believe in a divine personal creator, no plausible alternative has yet been offered to justify the pursuit of science as a search for the ultimate systematic understanding of reality . . . science . . . makes sense only if there is an overall design to nature that we are especially well-equipped to fathom, even though most of it has little bearing on our day-to-day animal survival. Humanity's creation in the image of God . . . provides the clearest historical rationale for the rather specialised expenditure of effort associated with science.[45]

As Fuller intimates, the assumption that rational thought can penetrate through *what works* in terms of survival to *what's true about reality* isn't merely an assumption that's at home within a theistic worldview, but an assumption ill at ease with a naturalistic worldview.[46]

Arguments About Morality

Since the verification principle applies to moral propositions as well as to propositions about God, the collapse of verificationism opened up the metaphysical debate between moral subjectivists (also known as moral relativists) and moral objectivists.[47] This debate overlaps with the debate over scientism, because knowledge of objective moral facts lies beyond the reach of science,[48] such that belief in moral facts that are knowable requires the rejection of scientism. As James Davidson Hunter and Paul Nedelisky explain:

> When it began, the quest for a moral science sought to discover the good. The new moral science has abandoned that quest and now, at best, tells us how to get what we want . . . Today's moral scientists no longer look to science to discover moral truths, for they believe there is nothing there to discover. As they see it, there are no such things as prescriptive moral or ethical norms; there are no moral "oughts" or obligations; there is no ethical good, bad, or objective value of any kind. Their view is . . . a kind of moral nihilism . . . In the end, as these thinkers see it, the "good" is a social

---

45. Fuller, *Dissent Over Descent*, 9, 70.

46. See: Beck, "God's Existence;" Williams, *Faithful Guide to Philosophy*, Chapter Twelve; Williams, *C.S. Lewis vs. the New Atheists*, Chapter Four.

47. See: Harman and Thomson, *Moral Relativism And Moral Objectivity*.

48. For a critique of Sam Harris' muddled claims to the contrary, see Williams, *C.S. Lewis vs. the New Atheists*, 153–60. See also: Hunter and Nedelisky, *Science and the Good*.

engineering project, the foundation of which is an unmitigated, though rarely acknowledged metaphysical scepticism.[49]

Many atheists—e.g., Friedrich Nietzsche, Jean-Paul Sartre, Paul Kurtz and J.L. Mackie (whose 1977 book *Ethics: Inventing Right and Wrong* was a set text in my undergraduate days)—argue that the existence of God is a prerequisite (or at least the best explanation) for the existence of objective moral values, so that the subjectivity (and hence relativity) of morality is entailed (or at least implied) by the truth of atheism. Joel Marks, Professor Emeritus of Philosophy at the University of New Haven, takes this position, explaining that his atheism leads him to reject moral objectivism:

> the religious fundamentalists are correct: without God, there is no morality. But they are incorrect, I still believe, about there being a God. Hence, I believe, there is no morality . . . In sum, while theists take the obvious existence of moral commands to be a kind of proof of the existence of a Commander, i.e., God, I now take the non-existence of a Commander as a kind of proof that there are no Commands, i.e., morality.[50]

Conversely, many theists agree with such atheistic colleagues that the existence of God is a prerequisite (or at least the best explanation) for the existence of objective moral values, but use this premise in the service of natural theology by arguing for moral objectivism. My own sympathies are firmly on the side of both moral objectivism and the meta-ethical moral argument built upon such objectivism.[51]

According to John Cottingham: "the increasing consensus among philosophers today is that some kind of objectivism of truth and of value is correct . . ."[52] Unsurprisingly, philosophers who accept moral objectivism whilst remaining atheists reject the traditional atheistic belief that atheism

---

49. Hunter and Nedelisky, *Science and the Good*, xv, 21.

50. Joel Marks, "Amoral Manifesto."

51. See: YouTube Playlist, "Moral Argument For God;" Kreeft, "Refutation of Moral Relativism;" Beckwith, "Why I Am Not a Moral Relativist;" Baggett and Walls, *Good God*; Beck, *Does God Exist?*, Chapter Four; Beckwith and Koukl, *Relativism*; Copan, "God, Naturalism, and the Foundations of Morality;" Copan, "Hume and the Moral Argument;" Evans, *Natural Signs and Knowledge of God*, Chapter Five; Garcia and King, ed.'s, *Is Goodness without God Good Enough?* Owen, "Why Morality Implies the Existence of God;" Williams, *Outgrowing God?*, Chapter Four; Williams, *Faithful Guide to Philosophy*, Chapter Eight; Williams, *Case For God*, Chapter Two.

52. Cottingham, "Philosophers Are Finding Fresh Meanings in Truth, Goodness and Beauty."

entails moral subjectivism. My essay "Can Moral Objectivism Do Without God?" (which forms Chapter Four of this book) engages this trend by interacting with atheist and moral objectivist Russ Schafer-Landau.

Neutralizing Methodological Naturalism

In the nineteenth century, the French empiricist philosopher Auguste Compt (1798–1857) "insisted that science properly practiced could make no reference to divine action to explain any events or phenomena."[53] Subsequent thinkers have sometimes expanded Compt's rule to exclude from science reference to any intelligence that might be suspected of being irreducibly mental. Hence the U.S. *National Academy of Science* asserts that: "The statements of science must invoke only natural things and processes."[54] This "methodologically naturalistic" conception of science remains prevalent amongst scientists, though it is controversial among philosophers of science.[55]

Inferring the activity of "intelligence" as the best explanation for empirical data within archaeology, cryptography, forensic science, or the search for extra-terrestrial intelligence, is an avowedly scientific venture, even if a philosopher might argue—perhaps correctly—that the intelligence in question is best conceived in terms of substance dualism (a subject to which we will return). In the same way, inferring the activity of "intelligence" as the best explanation for empirical data within biology or cosmology should count as a scientific venture, whether the intelligence in question appears to be an immanent extra-terrestrial intelligence that a philosopher might think of in terms of a naturalism-busting substance dualism, or a transcendent intelligence best conceptualized in equally naturalism-busting metaphysical terms. As philosopher of science Bruce L. Gordon writes:

> When generating scientific conclusions in cryptography or forensics, the design inference is not controversial. The sticking point is with the philosophical issue of methodological naturalism. What happens if the design inference, applied to certain natural

53. Meyer, *Return of the God Hypothesis*, 53.

54. *Teaching about Evolution*, 2.

55. See: YouTube Playlist, "Scientific Status of Intelligent Design Theory;" Gordon, "Is Intelligent Design Science?" Larmer, "Science, Methodological Naturalism, and Question-Begging;" Meyer, "Sauce For The Goose;" Monton, "Is Intelligent Design Science?" Moreland, *Scientism and Secularism*, Chapter Eleven; Moreland, "Design and the Nature of Science;" Plantinga, "Should Methodological Naturalism Constrain Science?"

phenomena, yields the conclusion that there is an intelligent cause that might transcend our universe? There seems to be an illegitimate double standard operative in barring such a conclusion when design inferences are otherwise scientifically acceptable.

Atheist and theoretical physicist Sean Carroll warns that "methodological naturalism, while deployed with the best of intentions by supporters of science, amounts to assuming part of the answer ahead of time. If finding truth is our goal, that is just about the biggest mistake we can make."[56] Likewise, atheist philosopher of science Bradley Monton argues that:

> If science really is permanently committed to methodological naturalism, it follows that the aim of science is not generating true theories. Instead, the aim of science would be something like: generating the best theories that can be formulated subject to the restriction that the theories are naturalistic . . . science is better off without being shackled by methodological naturalism . . .[57]

Strictly speaking, a methodological refusal to allow evidentially supported design inferences to count as "science" *if and when the inferred intelligence is most plausibly interpreted in irreducibly mental terms* means either (a) refusing to follow the evidence where it leads, or (b) excluding study of the relevant empirical data from "science" and thus from "scientific" institutions.[58] The latter option entails a willingness to transfer resources to some "non-scientific" institution (which we might call an institution of "natural philosophy") in order to understand the truth about the relevant aspect of physical reality on the basis of empirical evidence! It seems to me that such a move is pragmatically less appealing than simply recognizing that "science" just *is* "natural philosophy," a first-order discipline demarcated by its object of study and its intellectual goals (to rationally explain and/or predict as much as we can about physical reality), rather than by its adherence to "methodological naturalism." As J.P. Moreland argues: "The most important thing about a scientific theory . . . is that it explains things."[59]

In any event, given that scientism is false, Thomas Nagel is surely right when he observes that "a purely semantic classification of a hypothesis or

56. Carroll, *Big Picture*, quoted in "Intelligent Design and Methodological Naturalism."
57. Monton, "Is Intelligent Design Science?," 2, 9–10.
58. See: Kojonen, "Methodological Naturalism and the Truth Seeking Objection."
59. Moreland, "Intelligent Design and the Nature of Science," 57.

its denial as belonging or not to science is of limited interest to someone who wants to know whether the hypothesis is true or false."[60]

The Collapse of Verificationism and the Renaissance of Natural Theology

Basil Mitchell observes that,

> the Logical Positivist movement started as an attempt to make a clear demarcation between science and common sense on the one hand, and metaphysics and theology on the other. But work in the philosophy of science convinced people that what the Logical Positivists had said about science was not true, and, by the time the philosophers of science had developed and amplified their accounts of how rationality works in science, people discovered that similar accounts applied equally well to the areas which they had previously sought to exclude, namely theology and metaphysics.[61]

As Craig explains:

> The collapse of this Verificationism was perhaps the most important philosophical event of the twentieth century. Its downfall meant a resurgence of metaphysics, along with other traditional problems of philosophy which Verificationism had suppressed. Accompanying this resurgence came something altogether unanticipated: a renaissance of Christian philosophy.[62]

So startling was this renaissance that *Time*, which had famously used its cover to ask "Is God Dead?" in 1966, ran a cover story entitled "Modernizing the Case for God" in 1980:

> In a quiet revolution in thought and argument that hardly anyone could have foreseen only two decades ago, God is making a comeback. Most intriguingly, this is happening not among theologians or ordinary believers—most of whom never accepted for a moment that he was in any serious trouble—but in the crisp, intellectual circles of academic philosophers, where the consensus had long banished the Almighty from fruitful discourse.
>
> Now it is more respectable among philosophers than it has been for a generation to talk about the possibility of God's

---

60. Nagel, *Secular Philosophy and the Religious Temperament*, 48.
61. Mitchell, "Reflections on C.S. Lewis," 19.
62. Craig, "Does God Exist?"

existence. The shift is most striking in the Anglo-American academies of thought, where strict forms of empiricism have reigned ... A.J. Ayer, on behalf of logical positivism, decreed that "all utterances about the nature of God are nonsensical." The accepted wisdom was that the only valid statements were those verifiable through the senses. Today even atheistic philosophers agree that Ayer's rigid rule is inadequate to deal with human experience.[63]

Moreover, as Craig also notes:

> The renaissance of Christian philosophy has not been merely defensive ... it has also been accompanied by a resurgence of interest in natural theology ... All of the traditional arguments for God's existence, such as the cosmological, teleological, moral, and ontological arguments, not to mention creative, new arguments, find intelligent and articulate defenders on the contemporary philosophical scene.[64]

Science and Natural Theology

The philosophical resurgence of interest in natural theology began around the same time that scientists were making a series of breakthroughs in our understanding of the physical universe, breakthroughs that gave added impetus to reflection upon cosmic and biological origins.

For example, while "few physicists and astronomers at the beginning of the twentieth century doubted the infinite age of the universe,"[65] the cosmic background radiation discovered in 1964 by American physicist Arno Penzias and radio-astronomer Robert Wilson solidified the "Big Bang" model of a finite cosmic past advanced in 1927 by Belgian physicist (and Catholic priest) Georges Lemaître. This development made its way into philosophical discussion via William Lane Craig's *The Kalam Cosmological Argument* (1979).[66]

63. Time, "Modernizing the Case for God."
64. Craig, "Resurrection of Theism."
65. Meyer, *Return of the God Hypothesis*, 73.
66. See: Hackett, *Resurrection of Theism* (a major influence upon Craig); Craig, *Kalam Cosmological Argument*; Copan and Craig, ed's. *Kalam Cosmological Argument: Volume One* and *The Kalam Cosmological Argument: Volume Two*. See also: Cerebral Faith, "Why The Divisibility Of Time Is Irrelevant To The Kalam Cosmological Argument;" Meyer, *Return of the God Hypothesis*; Williams, "A Christian Worldview and Science in Apologetic Perspective: Cosmos;" Williams, "ELF 2022: Can We Believe In God In An

The significance of the scientific picture of a cosmic beginning can be measured by the impact it had upon Antony Flew (1923–2010), whom philosopher Craig J. Hazen called "arguably the world's foremost philosophical atheist."[67] In 1992 Flew admitted to being "embarrassed by the contemporary cosmological consensus . . . that the universe had a beginning."[68] He recognized that the Big Bang's description of cosmic history was in tension with the naturalistically comfortable idea that the existence of the universe "without beginning," together with "whatever are found to be its most fundamental [physical] features," should be accepted as our "explanatory ultimates."[69] Flew conceded that "it is certainly neither easy nor comfortable to maintain this position in the face of the Big Bang story."[70] In 2004, Flew publicly announced his intellectual conversion to a belief in God (though not to belief in any particular divine revelation), in part because "There does seem to be a reason for a First Cause."[71]

Then again, beginning with atheist astrophysicist Fred Hoyle's 1953 prediction of a finely tuned resonance state in the carbon 12 atomic nucleus (later verified and known as "the Hoyle state"), scientists have come to recognize that the existence of life, and most especially of "embodied conscious agents (ECAs)"[72] like ourselves (observers able to "significantly interact with each other"[73] and to "develop scientific technology and discover the universe"[74]) depends upon a staggering degree of cosmic (as well as more local[75]) "fine tuning." Over and above the laws of nature themselves, there are two aspects to this fine tuning:

> When the laws of nature are expressed as mathematical equations, you find appearing in them certain . . . unchanging quantities, like the force of gravity, the electromagnetic force, and the subatomic

---

Age Of Science? Big Bang Cosmology And God;" Williams, *Faithful Guide to Philosophy*, Chapter Five.

67. Flew in Hazen, Habermas and Flew, "Pilgrimage from Atheism to Theism."
68. Flew in *Cosmos, Bios, Theos*, 241.
69. Flew in Hazen et al, "Pilgrimage from Atheism to Theism."
70. Flew in *Cosmos, Bios, Theos*, 241.
71. Flew in Hazen et al, "My Pilgrimage from Atheism to Theism."
72. Holder, *Ramified Natural Theology in Science and Religion*, 56.
73. Collins, "Anthropic Fine-Tuning: Three Approaches," 173–91.
74. Collins, "Anthropic Fine-Tuning: Three Approaches," 173–91.
75. See: Denton, *Nature's Destiny*; Gonzalez and Richards, *Privileged Planet*; Ward and Brownlee, *Rare Earth*; Waltham, *Lucky Planet*.

weak force. These unchanging quantities are called constants. The values of these constants are not determined by the laws of nature . . . Depending on the values of those constants, universes governed by the same laws of nature will look very different . . . In addition to the constants, there are . . . initial conditions on which the laws of nature operate . . . An example would be the amount of thermodynamic disorder (or entropy) in the early universe . . . Now what scientists have been surprised to discover is that these constants and quantities must fall into an extraordinarily narrow range of values if the universe is to be life-permitting.[76]

To give just a few examples:

The force of gravity is so finely tuned that an alteration in its value by even one part out of 10^{50} would have prevented a life-permitting universe. Similarly, a change in the value of the so-called cosmological constant, which drives the acceleration of the universe's expansion, by as little as one part in 10^{120} would have rendered the universe life-prohibiting . . . the odds of the universe's initial low entropy condition's existing by chance is on the order of one chance out of $10^{10(123)}$ . . .[77]

Multiplying together the odds of these constants and quantities *all* falling by chance within the specification provided by the narrow, life-permitting and/or ECA-permitting range of values, gives an improbability that's beyond astronomical![78] Hence cosmic fine-tuning appears to be an example of specified complexity that is best explained by the activity of intelligence.[79]

Reflecting upon the evidence for cosmic fine tuning, agnostic cosmologist Paul Davies recognizes that: "the impression of design is

---

76. Craig, *Does God Exist?*, 44–45.

77. Craig, *Does God Exist?*, 45.

78. Roger Trigg reports the estimate "that there are 30 constants in basic physics and modern cosmology that must be fine-tuned for the emergence of life." – *Does Science Undermine Faith?*, 25.

79. See: Williams, "Christian Worldview and Science in Apologetic Perspective: Cosmos;" Williams, "Cosmic Fine Tuning;" Williams, *Outgrowing God?*, Chapter 9. See also: YouTube Playlist, "Cosmic Fine Tuning;" Robin Collins' Fine-Tuning Website; Collins, "Argument from Physical Constants;" Collins, "Exploration of the Fine-Tuning of the Universe;" Collins, "Teleological Argument;" Gordon, "Balloons on a String;" Holder, *God, The Multiverse, And Everything*; Holder, *Big Bang, Big God*; Løkhammer, "The Fine-Tuning Argument;" Lewis and Barnes, *A Fortunate Universe*; Meyer, *Return of the God Hypothesis*; Moreland and Craig, *Philosophical Foundations*, second edition, 493–500.

overwhelming."[80] Atheist philosopher of science Bradley Monton reflects that the fine-tuning argument:

> doesn't stop me from being an atheist, but I don't have any completely definitive objections to it – and I have problems with all the objections that are presented as completely definitive . . . This is why I consider the fine-tuning argument to be somewhat plausible.[81]

Even neo-atheist Christopher Hitchens once commented that: "At some point, certainly, we [Neo-Atheists] are all asked which is the best argument you come up against from the other side. I think every one of us picks the fine-tuning one as the most intriguing . . . It's not a trivial [argument]. We all say that."[82]

The philosophical impact of the scientific discovery of cosmic fine tuning can be seen in a fascinating turn of events that followed my debate about God's existence with Norwegian agnostic philosopher Professor Einar Bøhn, which took place at the Norwegian University of Science and Technology in Trondheim in 2018 (see Chapter Four of this volume for my opening speech).[83] During the period allotted for interaction with audience questions after the formal debate, an atheist student objected to the fine tuning argument that I'd presented. Professor Bøhn promptly stepped in to defend the argument as being worthy of serious attention. He used philosopher John Leslie's analogy, of a man sentenced to execution by firing squad who survives when every member of the squad misses him, to show that although we wouldn't exist to be surprised by cosmic fine tuning if no finely tuned cosmos existed, this fact does nothing to explain why a finely tuned cosmos exists. The fact that the sentenced man wouldn't exist to be surprised if the firing squad hadn't missed him doesn't explain *why* they missed him. The fact that an event is a pre-condition of its being observed doesn't explain the occurrence of the event in question. Moreover, Professor Bøhn used Leslie's analogy to argue that fine-tuning does naturally

---

80. Davies, *Cosmic Blueprint*, 203.
81. Monton, *Seeking God in Science*, 86.
82. Hitchens, "Christopher Hitchens Makes a Shocking Confession."
83. An audio recording of this debate is available from my podcast: "Debate: Does God Exist? Peter S. Williams vs. Einar Bohn at the Norwegian University of Science and Technology in Trondheim." With respect to Professor Bøhn's comments about simplicity, see: Flannagan, "Is Naturalism Simpler than Theism?"

suggest an explanation framed in terms of intentionality, *if one thinks that life is something special*.

In the same year that Hoyle predicted the resonance state in the carbon 12 nucleus (i.e. 1953), Francis Crick and James Watson announced their discovery of the three-dimensional, double helical structure of DNA.[84] In 1958, Crick theorized that "the sequence specificity of amino acids in proteins derives from a prior specificity of arrangement in the nucleotide bases on the DNA molecule,"[85] which "functioned just like alphabetic letters in an English text or binary digits in software or a machine code."[86] A series of experiments in the 1960s established that the sequential arrangement of amino-acids that determine the folding and thus the function of proteins is indeed encoded within the rungs of the twisting DNA ladder. Since the 1960s, it has therefore been apparent that, as origin-of-life researcher Bernd-Olaf Küppers observed: "The problem of the origin of life is clearly basically equivalent to the problem of the origin of information."[87] This problem poses a significant challenge to the naturalistic/materialistic worldview.[88] As William Lane Craig comments:

> Most of us were probably taught . . . that life originated in the so-called primordial soup by chance chemical reactions, perhaps fuelled by lightning strikes. All of these old, chemical origin of life scenarios have broken down and are now rejected by the scientific community. Today there are a plethora of competing, speculative theories with no consensus on the horizon.[89]

Indeed, to quote atheist philosopher Thomas Nagel:

> the origin of life remains, in light of what is known about the huge size, the extreme specificity, and the exquisite functional precision of the genetic material, a mystery – an event . . . to which no significant probability can be assigned on the basis of what we know of the laws of physics and chemistry.[90]

---

84. See: Pray, "Discovery of DNA Structure and Function."
85. Meyer, *Signature in the Cell*, 101.
86. Meyer, *Signature in the Cell*, 100.
87. Küppers, *Information and the Origin of Life*, 170–72.
88. See: Davies, *Origin of Life*; Nagel, *Mind and Cosmos*.
89. Craig in Caruso ed., *Science and Religion: 5 Questions*, 36.
90. Nagel, "Dawkins and Atheism."

PREFACE

Starting with scientist-philosopher Michael Polanyi's 1967 paper "Life Transcending Physics and Chemistry,"[91] the scientific recognition that information lies at the root and heart of biology has formed the basis for increasingly sophisticated arguments against reductive explanations of life in terms of chance and/or physical necessity, and for the need to incorporate an appeal to intelligence into any causally adequate explanation of organic life.[92] As philosopher of science Stephen C. Meyer argues:

> Experience shows that large amounts of specified complexity (especially in codes and languages) invariably originate from an intelligent source – from a mind or personal agent. Since intelligence is the only known cause of specified information (at least starting from a nonbiological source), the presence of specified information-rich sequences in even the simplest living systems points definitely to the past existence and activity of a designing intelligence.[93]

Not only is complex and functionally specified information[94] an essential aspect of life with respect to the production of proteins considered individually, but of the many "irreducibly complex" molecular machines composed of multiple interacting protein parts upon which the functions of cells depend,[95] and of the different cell-types and arrangements that specify different basic body-plans.[96] In other words, organic life turns out to be a matter of interdependent, hierarchically nested information. And

---

91. Polanyi, "Life Transcending Physics and Chemistry," 54–69.

92. See: YouTube Playlist, "Origin of Life;" Meyer, "DNA and the Origin of Life;" Abel, *Primordial Prescription*; Bracht, "Natural Selection as an Algorithm;" Abel, ed., *The First Gene*; Johnson, *Programming of Life*; Klinghoffer ed., *Signature of Controversy*; Overman, *A Case Against Accident and Self-Organization*; Meyer, *Return of the God Hypothesis*; Meyer, *Signature in the Cell*; Pullen, *Intelligent Design or Evolution?* Tan and Stadler, *Stairway To Life*; Thaxton, et al., *Mystery Of Life's Origin*; Williams, *Outgrowing God?*

93. Meyer, *Signature in the Cell*, 343.

94. See: YouTube Playlist, "Specified Complexity;" Dembski, "Specification;" Meyer, "Intelligent Design in the Origin of Life;" Dembski and Wells, *Design of Life*, Chapter Seven.

95. See: YouTube Playlist, "Irreducible Complexity;" Behe, "Irreducible Complexity: Obstacle to Darwinian Evolution;" Dembski, "Irreducible Complexity Revisited;" Behe, *Darwin's Black Box*, 10th anniversary edition; Behe, "Appendix: Clarifying Perspective;" Behe, "Appendix C: Assembling the Bacterial Flagellum;" Behe, *Mousetrap for Darwin*; Dembski, *No Free Lunch*; Dembski and Wells, *Design of Life*.

96. See: Meyer, *Darwin's Doubt*; Klinghoffer ed., *Debating Darwin's Doubt*.

while there is a philosophical gap between an argument for "intelligent design" and an argument for design *by God*, the former obviously offers grist to the mill of arguments within the purview of natural theology that seek to bridge this gap.[97]

The discovery of fine tuning within physics and biology laid the foundations for a renaissance of design arguments in science and philosophy, adding to the evidence that supports the case for thinking that we inhabit "a universe from Someone."[98] Bradley Monton notes that "intelligent design" arguments (in combination with the Kalam cosmological argument): "make me less certain of my atheism that I would be had I never heard the arguments."[99] He admits: "I think that there is some evidence for an intelligent designer, and in fact, I think that there is some evidence that that intelligent designer is God."[100] As Fred Hoyle commented in 1982:

> A common sense interpretation of the facts suggests that a super-intellect has monkeyed with physics, as well as with chemistry and biology, and that there are no blind forces worth speaking about in nature. The numbers one calculates from the facts seem to me so overwhelming as to put this conclusion almost beyond question.[101]

Thinking About Mind

The rediscovery of metaphysics precipitated by the fall of verificationism included a revitalization of interest in the philosophy of mind. Under the positivist paradigm of philosophical behaviorism, which was popular in the middle of the twentieth century, talk about "mind" was held to be ultimately translatable into talk about physical behavior caused by a physical response to physical stimuli. As philosopher C.E.M. Joad explained in his 1942 *Guide to Modern Thought*, according to the behaviorists:

---

97. See: Williams, "A Christian Worldview and Science in Apologetic Perspective: Cosmos;" Williams, "A Christian Worldview and Science in Apologetic Perspective: Bios (b) Intelligent Design Theory;" Williams, *Outgrowing God?*, Chapters Seven and Nine; Meyer, *Return of the God Hypothesis*.

98. See: YouTube Playlist, "Introduction to Intelligent Design Theory."

99. Monton, *Seeking God in Science*, 39.

100. Monton, *Seeking God in Science*, 39. See also: Luskin, "Interview With Bradley Monton."

101. Hoyle, "Universe: Past and Present."

a living organism must in the last resort be presumed to be of the same character as an automatic machine. It will, that is to say, only "behave" in so far as it is caused to do so by a specific stimulus; and this stimulus must be a physical stimulus. It is the object of the Behviourist, therefore, to describe all behaviour in terms of responses to stimuli.[102]

On the positivist philosophy of the Vienna Circle that lay behind behaviorism, "All sentences about reality must be measurable; and if you cannot measure something then it does not exist."[103] Hence Rudolph Carnap asserted that: "All sentences of psychology describe physical occurrences, namely, the physical behaviour of humans and other animals."[104] To give an example from Gilbert Ryle:

> If we now raise the epistemologist's question, "How does a person find out what mood he is in?" we can answer that . . . he does not groan "I feel bored" because he has found out that he is bored . . . Rather, somewhat as the sleepy man finds out that he is sleepy by finding that, among other things, he keeps on yawning, so the bored man finds out that he is bored, if he does find this out, by finding that among other things he glumly says to others and to himself "I feel bored" . . .[105]

However, as Rem B. Edwards reports: "First-person self-knowledge based on direct introspective experience has been a great obstacle to the acceptance of behaviorism."[106] A.C. Ewing makes this point with a vivid example:

> In order to refute such views I shall suggest your trying an experiment. Heat a piece of iron red-hot, then put your hand on it, and note carefully how you feel. You will have no difficulty in observing that it is quite different from anything which a psychologist could observe, whether he considered outward behavior or you brain processes . . . The behaviorists pride themselves on being empiricist, but in maintaining their view they are going clean contrary to experience. We know by experience what feeling pain is

---

102. Joad, *Guide to Modern Thought*, 53.
103. Latham, *Enigma of Consciousness*, 13.
104. Carnap, *Psychology in Physical Language*, quoted by Latham, *Enigma of Consciousness*, 9.
105. Ryle, *Concept of Mind*, 102–3.
106. Edwards, "Behaviorism: II. Philosophical Issues."

like and we know by experience what the physiological reactions to it are, and the two are quite unalike.[107]

Moreover, as Edwards points out: "Purposive acts, like trying to persuade psychologists that behavior is the only proper subject matter of psychology, cannot be redescribed as nonpurposive behaviors without losing essential meaning..."[108]

According to behaviorism, a thought just is a piece of physical behavior, a bodily event caused by physical stimuli; but as Joad argued: "it would be meaningless to ask whether a bodily event, for example, the state of my blood pressure or the temperature of my skin, was true. These are things which occur and are real; they are facts. But they are not and cannot be true, because they do not assert anything other than themselves."[109] In contemporary philosophical parlance, Joad is pointing out that physical behavior lacks the intrinsic "aboutness," "intentionality" or "ofness" that characterizes the "directedness of a mental state towards its object."[110] As atheist philosopher and one-time clinical neuroscientist Raymond Tallis acknowledges: "Intentionality... points in the direction opposite to causation... it is incapable of being accommodated in the materialistic world picture as it is currently constructed."[111] Consequently, on the hypothesis that behaviorism is true, no one could actually believe that behaviorism is true, because no one could have a mental state that was *about* behaviorism. In other words, along with any physicalist account of the mind, behaviorism is self-contradictory.[112]

American philosopher of science Carl Hempel announced his defection from behaviorism in 1966, declaring that: "In order to characterize... behavioral patterns, propensities, or capacities... we need not only a suitable behavioristic vocabulary, but psychological terms as well."[113] George Graham reports that: "Contemporary psychology and philosophy largely

---

107. Ewing, *Fundamental Questions of Philosophy*, 101–2.
108. Edwards, "Behaviorism: II. Philosophical Issues."
109. Joad, *Guide To Philosophy*, 535.
110. Moreland, *Recalcitrant Imago Dei*, 91.
111. Tallis, *Aping Mankind*, 359.
112. For more on this and other aspects of "the argument from reason," see: Willard, "Knowledge And Naturalism;" Menuge, *Agents Under Fire*; Moreland, *Recalcitrant Imago Dei*, 91–95; Reppert, *C.S. Lewis' Dangerous Idea*; Williams, *Faithful Guide to Philosophy*, Chapter Twelve; Williams, *C.S. Lewis vs. the New Atheists*, Chapter Four.
113. Hemple, *Philosophy of Natural Science*, 110.

share Hempel's conviction that the explanation of behavior cannot omit invoking a creature's representation of its world."[114] As Charles Taliaferro observes:

> generally, philosophers have come to abandon the project of eliminating consciousness. The denial of our mental life simply flies in the face of every waking moment. The subsequent philosophical task has been to explain, rather than to explain away, consciousness.[115]

Of course, many philosophers assume that a creature's subjective "representation of its world" must ultimately be explained, if not explained away, in terms that are consistent with a materialistic worldview. As William Lycan observes: "few theorists question the eventual truth of materialism in some form, but many see a deep principled difficulty for the materialist in giving a plausible account of consciousness."[116] This is what David Chalmers famously dubbed "the hard problem of consciousness"[117] in 1995; and as Chalmers would admit,[118] the contemporary situation in consciousness studies remains as described by Anthony O'Hear:

> Evolutionary biology and psychology can give partial accounts of particular mental functions . . . But these explanations, such as they are, assume that we do have consciousness, thought and experience . . . What they do not explain . . . is how consciousness, thought and experience can be produced by material processes at all. The most we can do is to correlate these mental phenomena with brain activity. But however fine-grained these accounts get, they do nothing to solve the basic enigma, which is how mental states and experience can emerge from physical matter . . .[119]

When I was introduced to the philosophy of mind by Dr. Alessandra Tanesini at Cardiff University, the subject was dominated by discussion of mind-brain identity and functionalism, theories of mind that appeared fundamentally mistaken to me in their rejection of mind-body dualism.[120]

114. Graham, "Behaviorism."
115. Taliaferro, "Where Do Thoughts Come From?," 156–7.
116. Lycan, quoted by Iredale, "Putting Descartes Before the Horse," 40.
117. Chalmers, "Facing up to the Problem of Consciousness," 207.
118. See: Chalmers, "Hard Problem of Consciousness."
119. O'Hear, *Philosophy*, 87.
120. See: YouTube Playlist, "Mind-Body Dualism, Free Will and Related Issues;" Taliaferro, *Consciousness and the Mind of God*; Williams, *Faithful Guide to Philosophy*,

PREFACE

By 1998 naturalistic philosopher of mind John Heil was reporting that "in recent years, dissatisfaction with materialist assumptions has led to a revival of interest in forms of dualism."[121] More recently, there has been a revived interest in various forms of Panpsychism, predicated upon a naturalistic rejection of both strong physicalism and substance dualism.[122] Still, much contemporary philosophy of mind continues to find itself torn between the acknowledgement of subjective realities (such as incorrigible and mentally unified phenomenal experiences, and mental intentionality) on the one hand, and the assumption that the mental must ultimately be explained in physical terms lacking such subjectivity and intentionality on the other hand. Yet, as atheist Julian Baggini admits: "we do not have a rational explanation for how consciousness can be produced in physical brains."[123]

For many scholars and lay-people alike, mind-body physicalism isn't a conclusion supported by evidence, but a deduction from their pre-commitment to materialism. As philosopher Michael Lockwood revealed:

> I count myself a materialist . . . I take consciousness to be a species of brain activity. Having said that, however, it seems to me evident that no description of brain activity of the relevant kind, couched in the currently available language of physics . . . is remotely capable of capturing what is distinctive about consciousness. So glaring, indeed, are the shortcomings of all the reductive programmes currently on offer, that I cannot believe that anyone with a philosophical training, looking dispassionately at these programmes, would take any of them seriously for a moment, were it not for the deep-seated conviction that . . . *something* along the lines of what the reductionists are offering *must* be true.[124]

Those whose thinking isn't constrained by the same conviction might find something persuasive in theistic arguments to the effect that while "it is hard to see how finite consciousness could result from the rearrangement

---

Chapter Eleven.

121. Heil, *Philosophy of Mind*, 53. See: Göcke, ed. *After Physicalism*; Koons and Bealer, ed.'s., *Waning of Materialism*.

122. See: Mind Matters, "Dr. Angus Menuge: Models of Consciousness (Part II);" Moreland, *Consciousness and the Existence of God*, Chapter Six; Robinson, "Qualia, Qualities, and Our Conception of the Physical World."

123. Baggini, *Atheism*, 77.

124. Lockwood, "Consciousness and the Quantum World," *Consciousness*, 447.

of brute matter; it is easier to see how a conscious Being could produce finite consciousness."[125]

Moving Onwards and Upwards

Towards the end of my time at Cardiff, an unravelling romantic relationship led me into what a flat-mate who studied psychology recognized as depression. Soon after my finals, the relationship in question ended, leading to a Summer of selective serotonin reuptake inhibitors (SSRIs) and sessions with a Christian Counsellor. Despite my trying personal circumstance, I graduated with a "2:1" degree just a few marks off a "First," and was accepted onto a one year taught MA in Philosophy at Sheffield University, where my studies encompassed the Philosophy of Mind, of Time, and of Religion.

I recall writing about the contingency form of the cosmological argument whilst taking in the view over the landscape beyond Sheffield as seen from high up in the modernist architecture of the Arts Tower, with its constantly moving paternoster lifts.[126]

(Left) The Arts Tower, University of Sheffield, viewed from almost due East on Bolsover Street in 2013, https://en.wikipedia.org/wiki/File:Arts_Tower_S_2013.jpg. (Right) Paternoster lift in the Arts Tower, University of Sheffield. Top floor, https://en.wikipedia.org/wiki/File:Paternoster_Arts_Tower_2013.jpg.

125. Moreland, "Physicalism, Naturalism and the Nature of Human Persons," 225. See also: Moreland, *Consciousness and the Existence of God*; Williams, *Faithful Guide to Philosophy*, Chapter Twelve.

126. See: "Arts Tower."

Alongside my taught courses, I attended a study group that worked its way through Aristotle's famous "Five Ways" of arguing for God.[127] I also served on the Committee of the Joint Chaplaincy Society, which stretched the boundaries of my ecclesiology, and through which I discovered solace in some close friendships as I continued my slow trek out of depression.

From Sheffield, I went to the University of East Anglia (UEA) in Norwich, where I wrote an interdisciplinary MPhil thesis cashing out perfect being theology in terms of the classical transcendental values of truth, goodness and beauty. Parts of my thesis were inspired by Mortimer J. Adler's defence of the objectivity of the transcendental values, a taped lecture by Norman L. Geisler on "The Issue of Beauty," and Alvin Plantinga's *Warrant and Proper Function* (Oxford, 1993).

My primary supervisor was atheist philosopher Nicholas Everett, but he spent some time away during my sojourn in Norwich (I think he was teaching abroad), leaving me with a stand-in supervisor who, as a Wittgensteinian, wasn't supportive of my project. During my oral thesis defence, Dr. Everett ended up "going to bat" for me against his colleague's criticism of my essentially Anselmian project!

I remember Professor Everett phoning me with the news that my thesis had been passed "subject to minor correction." The correction in question was the deletion of a single footnote. I got the distinct impression that this requirement hadn't been imposed by him . . . To save me the effort and expense of having to reprint and resubmit my manuscript, Dr. Everett offered to apply some tip-ex to the offending footnote on my behalf. As this merely meant not saying something I believed, rather than saying something I didn't believe, I accepted his offer with thanks.

Beside my studies at Norwich, I helped lead the Christian Union and the Anglican Theological Society. The latter was set up by the Anglican chaplain, the Revd. Dr. Garth Barber, an astrophysicist and cosmologist who would discuss his research with me. Somehow, I also found time to hang out with friends, to participate in a short published debate on God's existence with the American atheist philosopher Michael Martin (in the pages of *The Philosopher's Magazine*[128]), and to write my first book—*The Case For God* (Monarch, 1999). Quantum physicist turned theologian

---

127. See: Aquinas, "Five Ways;" Kreeft, "Thomistic Cosmological Argument;" Copleston, "Commentary on the Five Ways," 86–93.

128. See: "Is There a Personal God?."

PREFACE

Revd. Dr. John Polkinghorne KBE FRS (1930–2021)[129] described this volume as "A scrupulous and wide-ranging survey of the arguments for the existence of God . . ."[130]

Playing flute in a worship band in the Chaplaincy church on campus at UEA, in Norwich.

From Being a Student to Working with Students

After UEA, I spent three years as a student pastor at Holy Trinity, a Church of England congregation in Leicester, before moving to Southampton to spend about fifteen years working with a (now defunct) Christian educational charity called the Damaris Trust. My role included presenting, and eventually producing and training a team of presenters for "Philosophy and Ethics" conferences aimed at upper year school students. Our conferences aimed to equip participants with the critical thinking tools to think for themselves about their worldview by exploring questions about logic, the meaning of life and/or moral responsibility.

Though Damaris I found myself teaching Norwegian students from Gimlekollen College in Kristiansand on their annual UK study tour, and then in Norway as well. I became an "Assistant Professor in Communication and Worldviews" and Gimlekollen became part of NLA University

---

129. See: McGrath, "John Polkinghorne (1930–2021)."

130. From Dr. Polkinghorne's endorsement on the front cover of *The Case For God* (Monarch, 1999).

College. Today, I regularly lecture on philosophical topics including logic, the philosophy of science and natural theology.

Exploring The God Question

In sum, philosophical exploration of "the God question" and its worldview ramifications has been a consistent theme in my life and work. This is a topic of perennial interest that I've been privileged to write about in various books and journals, and to speak about and/or debate not only around the United Kingdom, but also in Norway and Finland, in Eastern Europe (in Bulgaria, Hungry, Poland and Romania), in Greece, and even in Australia.

> On a speaking trip to Athens in 2013, I visited the sixth-century B.C. Theatre of Dionysus, at the foot of the Parthenon, where the classical Greek plays I'd read in Classical Civilization back in college had originally been performed.

It seems to me that most theistic arguments try to formalize, and so rationally and explicitly motivate, the recognition of relationships between God and creation. Each relationship uncovered adds to our understanding of God. Many of these relationships are intuitively perceived (as being at least plausible) by most people.

In this context I note with appreciation C. Stephen Evans's appropriation of Thomas Reid's concept of "natural signs" to articulating a nuanced understanding of the link between phenomenologically grounded intuitions and natural theology. For example, in discussing the cosmological argument, Evans suggests that:

> The perception of the world as contingent, as something that might never have been, is closely linked to the contrasting notion of something that lacks this character, something whose existence is in some way impervious to non-existence . . . a reality that has a deeper and firmer grasp on existence than the things we see around us.[131]

Intuition plays a key role in philosophy, and so in all intellectual pursuits. As C.S. Lewis observed: "You cannot produce rational intuition by argument, because argument depends upon rational intuition. Proof rests upon the unprovable which just has to be 'seen.'"[132] This is one reason (contra the "New Atheists") it doesn't do to see reason and faith—taking the latter in the sense of *trust* and *allegiance*—as opposed to one-another by nature. Rationality requires faith. However, faith should be exercised wisely. While some intuitions (e.g. intuitions of the basic laws of logic, or of one's own existence) are indubitable, others carry varying degrees of *prima facie* warrant, such that "if one carefully reflects on something, and a certain viewpoint intuitively seems to be true, then one is justified in believing that viewpoint in the absence of overriding counterarguments (which will ultimately rely on alternative intuitions)."[133]

From childhood, I found it natural to trust the *prima facie* appearance of my irreducibly first-person experience, the appearance that I was an embodied but more than bodily self, and that I had a degree of freedom that connected to a moral responsibility to think and to judge and to act well according to the interlinked objective values of truth, goodness and beauty (and their parasitical shadows of falsehood, evil and ugliness). It also seemed to me that I was part of a whole world of selves and other objects of intricate complexity and grandeur that had some meaningful purpose. And I found it natural to believe that behind all of this stood the reality of a God. Now, I realize that (beyond indubitable intuitions) such appearances are the beginning of a philosophical conversation, rather than the end of the discussion. Nevertheless, I think it's important to recognize that this is where the conversation begins, and that the ensuing discussion proceeds on the basis of a principled credulity.

131. Evans, *Natural Signs and Knowledge of God*, 62, 63.
132. Lewis, "Why I am not a Pacifist," 67.
133. Moreland and Craig, *Philosophical Foundations*, 422.

Of course, "an appeal to intuitions does not rule out the use of additional arguments that add further support to that appeal;"[134] and I think the arguments for accepting the above description of reality are stronger than those against—as Thomas Nagel reminds us, "Philosophy has to proceed comparatively."[135] Concerning ultimate reality, I think there are sound and mutually re-enforcing cases against naturalism/materialism[136] and for theism.[137]

Indeed, there's a far broader range of theistic arguments than most people realize. In his bestselling book *The God Delusion*, Richard Dawkins devotes just *thirty-seven pages* to rejecting just *ten* theistic arguments. Alvin Plantinga once presented a paper outlining "a couple of dozen or so" theistic arguments.[138] Not that I'd endorse *every* argument suggested by Plantinga's paper, but the point stands. Moreover, theistic arguments come in "families" that deal with the same general theme (e.g. axiological arguments deal with value, cosmological arguments deal with causality) in different ways, e.g., appealing to different premises and/or using different argumentative forms.

When making a theistic argument, there is often a trade-off to be made between *accessibility* (brevity, informality, being intuitively convincing, lack

134. Moreland and Craig, *Philosophical Foundations*, 422.

135. Nagel, *Mind and Cosmos*, 127.

136. See: YouTube Playlist, "Problems with Materialism/Metaphysical Naturalism;" Craig and Moreland, ed.'s, *Naturalism*; Dennett and Plantinga, *Science and Religion*; Goetz and Taliaferro, *Naturalism*; Moreland, *Recalcitrant Imago Dei*; Menuge, *Agents Under Fire*; Nagel, *Mind and Cosmos*; Reppert, *C.S. Lewis' Dangerous Idea*; Swinburne, *Mind, Brain, and Free Will*; Williams, *Faithful Guide to Philosophy*.

137. See: YouTube Playlist, "Natural Theology;" YouTube Playlist, "Debating God;" Beck, "God's Existence;" Craig, "Five Arguments for God;" Evans, "The Mystery of Persons and Belief in God;" Kreeft and Tacelli, "Twenty Arguments For God's Existence;" Plantinga, "Two Dozen (Or So) Arguments for God;" Swinburne, "Evidence for God;" Willard, "Language, Being, God;" Beck, *Does God Exist*? Copan, "The Naturalists Are Declaring the Glory of God;" Copan and Taliaferro, ed.'s, *Naturalness of Belief*; Copan and Moser, ed.'s. *Rationality of Theism*; Craig, *Does God Exist*? Geivett and Sweetman, ed.'s. *Contemporary Perspectives on Religious Epistemology*; Meyer, *Return of the God Hypothesis*; Moreland, *Consciousness and the Existence of God*; Moreland and Craig, *Philosophical Foundations*, second edition; Moreland and Craig, ed.'s, *Blackwell Companion To Natural Theology*; Sennett and Groothuis ed.'s, *In Defence Of Natural Theology*; Swinburne, *Existence of God*, second edition; Walls and Dougherty, ed.'s, *Two Dozen (Or So) Arguments For God*; Williams, *Outgrowing God*? Williams, *Faithful Guide to Philosophy*; Williams, *C.S. Lewis vs the New Atheists*.

138. Plantinga, "Two Dozen (Or So) Arguments for God." See: Walls and Dougherty, ed.'s, *Two Dozen (Or So) Arguments For God*.

of dependence upon specialized knowledge) and *robustness* (e.g., explicit logical validity, dependence upon the detailed explanation of specialized knowledge). I hope that this collection strikes a balance that will serve to introduce a robust cumulative case for God in a way that is accessible to interested non-specialists.

I have added contextual explanations in the footnotes at the start of each of the following chapters, which are presented here with occasional, generally minor revisions and/or additions, if any, relative to the originals. Chapters Four, Six, Eight, and the appendix were previously published in *Theofilos*—a Nordic peer reviewed journal devoted to the study of theology, philosophy, culture and neighboring disciplines[139]—and are republished here with permission.

Concluding Thoughts

Two things have particularly struck me in writing this preface. The first is how so many highly influential ideologies promulgated by atheists, from verificationism and philosophical behaviorism to modernistic scientism and postmodern death-of-the-author hermeneutics, are self-contradictory. It suggests that there's a measure of truth to the hyperbolic witticism (widely attributed to G.K. Chesterton) that: "When men stop believing in God they don't believe in nothing; they believe in anything."[140] The second is how the twentieth-century revival of metaphysics coincided and combined with a string of important discoveries in science (from discoveries pointing to the Big Bang and Cosmic Fine Tuning, to the discovery that functionally complex information lies at the core of life) to produce a renaissance in natural theological arguments for thinking that, far from being a universe from nothing, as atheistic naturalists affirm, ours is in fact *a universe from someone*. In the words of philosopher Robert T. Lehe:

> The classical "proofs" of the existence of God are widely assumed to have been decisively discredited since the days of Hume and

---

139. *Theofilos* was first established in 2009 as a popular journal of apologetics, and then re-established and officially recognized as a peer-reviewed academic journal from 2012. It was transformed into an *open access* journal in 2020. *Theofilos* publishes papers written in Norwegian, Swedish, Danish or English. See: https://theofilos.no/.

140. According to Ratcliffe ed., *Oxford Essential Quotations* (fourth edition), this saying is "Widely attributed to G.K. Chesterton, although not traced in his works; first recorded as 'The first effect of not believing in God is to believe in anything' in Emile Cammaert's *Chesterton: The Laughing Prophet* (1937)."

PREFACE

Kant, but they have made a comeback in the last half of the twentieth century. There has been a resurgence of Christian philosophy since the 1960s, which has benefitted from scientific developments in the last hundred years that seem to be consistent with the idea that the universe was created by a supremely powerful, intelligent being.[141]

I'd like to close this preface by offering thanks to,

- Professor William Lane Craig, for his inspirational example, and for partnering with me at the Cambridge Union in 2011.
- Dr. Lars Dahle, Associate Professor in Systematic Theology and Christian Apologetics at NLA University College (Kristiansand, Norway), and chief editor of *Theofilos*.
- My colleagues at Campus Kristiansand of NLA University College in Norway (www.nla.no/en/).
- Everyone involved in the 2018 Veritas Symposium on Natural Theology in an Age of Science and the subsequent special edition of *Theofilos* that I had the honor of guest editing.
- Gavin Matthews and the Solas Centre for Public Christianity (www.solas-cpc.org/).
- Professor J.P. Moreland, for his inspirational example, and for writing the foreword.
- Everyone at Wipf and Stock.
- All those who have facilitated my speaking and publishing on the existence of God.
- My church small-group, for their encouragement and prayers.
- Last but not least, thanks go to my parents for their constant love and support.

Peter S. Williams,
Spring 2022.

---

141. Lehe, *God, Science, and Religious Diversity*, [Kindle loc. 1506].

1

This House Believes that God is not a Delusion[1]

According to the *Diagnostic and Statistical Manual of Mental Disorders* (DSM-IV 2000, 765) a delusion is:

> A false belief based on incorrect inference about external reality that is firmly sustained despite what almost everyone else believes and despite what constitutes incontrovertible and obvious proof or evidence to the contrary. The belief is not one ordinarily accepted by other members of the person's culture or subculture (e.g., it is not an article of religious faith) . . .[2]

---

1. This is the speech I made at the Cambridge Union in 2011, when I had the honor of being paired with American philosopher, theologian, and apologist Professor William Lane Craig in defending the motion "This house believes that God is not a Delusion" against atheists Andrew Copson (Chief Executive of Humanists UK) and Cambridge University philosopher Dr. Arif Ahmed. Having decided I would open for the motion (leaving Craig the task of thinking on his feet in response to the opposition), my draft was revised in light of comments from Craig and iterated with him until we were both happy with it. On the day, we carried the motion by fourteen votes.

A video of the debate is available on YouTube: www.youtube.com/watch?v=s5N5SvkPhME.

You can read my analysis of the whole debate online: www.bethinking.org/does-god-exist/god-is-not-a-delusion-debate/2-debate-analysis.

"The Case for Christian Theism: The Reasonable Faith UK Tour," a documentary about Craig's 2011 Speaking Tour of England, includes additional "behind-the-scenes" coverage of the Cambridge Union event: www.youtube.com/watch?v=vCa9WQBrARc.

2. "Delusion," *Stanford Encyclopedia of Philosophy*.

Unfortunately for our opponents, theism *is* an article of religious faith that *is* ordinarily accepted by people in our culture but which *isn't* necessarily inferred from external reality. Hence it is *by definition* not a delusion! While we forego this purely definitional victory, it does seem fair to note that since the opposition claim that theism isn't merely intellectually mistaken, but *delusory*, they thereby shoulder the burden of offering "incontrovertible and obvious proof" for the non-existence of God. Since we don't know of any "incontrovertable" disproof of God, rather than attack *straw men* at this point, we'll simply argue for theism; for *if theism is true, it can't be a delusion*. Permit me to sketch three arguments for God.

1) A Moral Argument

1. If god does not exist, then objective moral values do not exist.
2. At least one objective moral value exists.
3. Therefore, god exists.

It's important not to confuse this argument with the false claim that we must *believe* in God in order to *know* or to *do* the right thing.

What does it mean to say that moral values are objective? Suppose one person thinks the sun goes around the earth, and another thinks the opposite. In this case, we know the earth goes around the sun. Those who believe otherwise, *however sincerely*, are wrong. Moreover, coming to know that the earth goes around the sun is a matter of *discovering* truth, not *inventing* it. Moral objectivism says that ethics is about *discovering* moral truths, truths that exist even if we fail to discern them. According to moral objectivism there are genuine moral disagreements; and the observation that people sometimes hold different moral opinions just shows that our moral *beliefs* can be either correct or incorrect *according to the moral facts of the matter*.

So, are there any objective moral facts? Those who point to the reality of evil as the basis for an argument against God certainly think so; for nothing can be objectively evil if there are no objective values.

John Cottingham reports that "the increasing consensus among philosophers today is that some kind of objectivism of . . . value is correct . . ."[3] For example, atheist Peter Cave (chair of The Humanist Philosophers' Group of the British Humanist Association) defends moral objectivism by appealing to his intuitions:

3. Cottingham, "Truth, Goodness and Beauty."

whatever sceptical arguments may be brought against our belief that killing the innocent is morally wrong, we are more certain that the killing is morally wrong than that the argument is sound . . . Torturing an innocent child for the sheer fun of it is morally wrong.[4]

The properly basic moral intuition that torturing innocent children for fun is wrong isn't undermined by the existence of the psychopath who enjoys torturing children. By the principle of credulity, torturing an innocent child for fun clearly isn't *merely* something that stops the child functioning normally (an empirical observation), or *merely* something we dislike because of our evolutionary history, or *merely* something our society has decided to discourage. Rather, torturing an innocent child for fun is *objectively wrong*. So *at least one thing is objectively wrong*. Therefore, *moral subjectivism is false*.

Some moral intuitions are specific (e.g. It's evil to use children to clear mine fields, as was done in the Iran/Iraq war) and some are general (e.g. it's always right to choose the lesser of two evils). Of course, our intuitions *could* be mistaken; but *this very admission* of fallibility *presupposes moral objectivism*; for if moral subjectivism were true, no moral claims could be mistaken! As atheist Russ Shafer-Landau argues: "subjectivism's . . . picture of ethics as a wholly conventional enterprise entails a kind of moral infallibility for individuals or societies . . . This sort of infallibility is hard to swallow."[5]

Finally, if moral objectivism were false it couldn't be true that we objectively *ought* to consider arguments against objectivism, or that we *ought* to consider them fairly: Knowing this, we see the impossibility of justifying subjectivism, for to embrace an argument for subjectivism would be to take the self-contradictory position that: (a) there are no objective moral values, but that (b) we objectively *ought* to accept subjectivism!

Therefore, the second premise of the moral argument seems secure. Turning to the first premise, many *atheists* acknowledge that "if god doesn't exist, then objective moral values don't exist." For example, Jean-Paul Sartre wrote that he found it,

> extremely embarrassing that God does not exist, for there disappears with Him all possibility of finding values in an intelligible

---

4. Cave, *Humanism*, 146.
5. Shafer-Landau, *Whatever Happened to Good and Evil?*, 16–17.

heaven. There can no longer be any good *a priori*, since there is no infinite and perfect consciousness to think it.[6]

An objective moral value is a transcendent ideal that prescribes and obligates behaviour; but an ideal implies a mind, a prescription requires a prescriber and an obligation is contingent upon a person. As H.P. Owen argues:

> On the one hand [objective moral] claims transcend every human person . . . On the other hand . . . it is contradictory to assert that impersonal claims are entitled to the allegiance of our wills. The only solution to this paradox is to suppose that the order of [objective moral] claims . . . is in fact rooted in the personality of God.[7]

2) A Cosmological Argument

The Leibnitzian cosmological argument builds upon the "principle of sufficient reason":

1. Everything that exists has an explanation of its existence, either in the necessity of its own nature or in an external cause.
2. The universe exists.
3. Therefore the universe has an explanation of its existence.
4. If the universe has an explanation of its existence, that explanation is God.
5. Therefore, the explanation of the universe's existence is God.

Since the universe obviously exists, non-theists must deny premises 1 or 4 to rationally avoid God's existence.

Many philosophers think that Premise 1—the principle of sufficient reason—is self-evident: Imagine finding a translucent ball on the forest floor whilst hiking. You'd naturally wonder how it came to be there. If a fellow hiker said, "It just exists inexplicably. Don't worry about it!" you wouldn't take him seriously. Suppose we increase the size of the ball so it's as big as the planet. That doesn't remove the need for explanation. Suppose it were the size of the universe. Same problem.

Premise 4—"If the universe has an explanation of its existence, that explanation is God"—is synonymous with the standard atheistic claim that

---

6. Sartre, *Existentialism Is a Humanism*, 28.
7. Owen, "Morality Implies the Existence of God," 648.

if God doesn't exist, then the universe has no explanation of its existence. The only other alternative to theism is to claim the universe has an explanation *in the necessity of its own nature*. But this is a *very* radical step and we can't think of any contemporary atheist who takes it. After all, it's coherent to imagine a universe made from a wholly different collection of quarks than the collection that actually exists; but such a universe would be a different universe, so universes clearly don't exist necessarily.

Suppose I ask you to loan me a certain book, but you say: "I don't have a copy right now, but I'll ask my friend to lend me his copy and then I'll lend it to you." Suppose your friend says the same thing to you, and so on. Two things are clear. First, if the process of asking to borrow the book goes on *ad infinitum*, I'll never get the book. Second, if I get the book, the process that led to me getting it can't have gone on *ad infinitum*. Somewhere down the line of requests to borrow the book, someone *had* the book *without having to borrow it*. Likewise, argues Richard Purtill, consider any contingent reality:

> the same two principles apply. If the process of everything getting its existence from something else went on to infinity, then the thing in question would never [have] existence. And if the thing has . . . existence then the process hasn't gone on to infinity. There was something that had existence without having to receive it from something else . . .[8]

A necessary being explaining all physical reality can't itself be a physical reality. The only remaining possibilities are an abstract object or an immaterial mind. But abstract objects are causally impotent. Therefore, the explanation of the physical universe is a necessarily existent, transcendent mind.

3) An Ontological Argument

As the "greatest possible being" God is *by definition* a necessary being. A necessary being is *by definition* a being that must exist if its existence is possible. Hence we argue:

1. If it is possible that God exists, then God exists.
2. It is possible that God exists.
3. Therefore, God exists.

---

8. Purtill, quoted by Taliaferro, *Contemporary Philosophy of Religion*, 358–59.

A "great-making property" is any property that (a) *endows its bearer with some measure of objective value and which* (b) *admits of a logical maximum*. A sock isn't more valuable than you because it's smellier than you; and however smelly a sock we imagine, it's always possible to imagine a smellier one. Smelliness isn't a great-making property. On the other hand, *power* is a great-making property, one that has a logical maximum in the quality of being "omnipotent." Likewise, *necessary being* is the maximal instantiation of a great-making property. Even if Kant was right to argue that saying something "exists" doesn't add to our knowledge of its properties, to say that something "exists necessarily" certainly *does* add to our knowledge of its properties. Hence most philosophers agree that if God's existence is even possible, then, as a necessary being, he must exist.

Unlike "the tooth fairy" God couldn't just happen not to exist *despite his existence being possible*. To deny the existence of the tooth fairy, one needn't claim that its existence is impossible. However, to deny the existence of God one *must* make the *metaphysically stronger claim* that his existence is *impossible*. But the claim that God exists clearly isn't on a *par* with the claim that there exists a round square! Many atheists acknowledge that the idea of God is coherent. Indeed, atheist Richard Carrier warns that arguments for thinking otherwise are

> not valid, since any definition of god (or his properties) that is illogical can just be revised to be logical. So in effect, Arguments from Incoherence aren't really arguments for atheism, but for the reform of theology.[9]

Moreover, humans exhibit non-maximal degrees of great-making properties (such as power, knowledge and goodness), and this supports the hypothesis that *maximal degrees* of great-making properties can co-exist over the hypothesis that they cannot.

Finally, the moral and cosmological arguments, by confirming various aspects of the theistic hypothesis, provide independent grounds for thinking that the crucial second premise of the ontological argument is more plausible than its denial.

---

9. Carrier, *Sense and Goodness Without God*, 276.

Conclusion

In conclusion, to show that belief in God is a delusion, the opposition must both rebut our cumulative case for theism and offer "incontrovertible and obvious proof" of God's non-existence. Until and unless they accomplish these goals, I recommend the motion to the house.

Addressing the Cambridge Union in 2011 (photograph by Jan Craig).

2

The Existence of God[1]

My opening speech will offer a cumulative case of four arguments for theism.

1) A Moral Argument

Coming to know that the earth goes around the sun was a matter of *discovering* truth, not *inventing* it. Moral objectivism says that ethics is about *discovering* moral truths that exist even if we fail to discern them. According to moral objectivism there are genuine moral disagreements; and the observation that people sometimes hold different moral opinions just shows that our moral *beliefs* can be either correct or incorrect *according to the moral facts of the matter*.

Are there any moral facts? Those who point to the reality of evil as the basis for an argument against God certainly think so; for nothing can be objectively evil if there are no objective values. Hence atheist philosopher Peter Cave defends moral objectivism by appealing to his intuitions about evil:

> Whatever sceptical arguments may be brought against our belief that killing the innocent is morally wrong, we are more certain

---

1. This is the opening speech from my debate with atheist philosopher Professor Christopher Norris at Cardiff University in February 2013. A video of the debate, which was jointly organized by the University's Christian Union and Atheist Society, is available on YouTube: www.youtube.com/watch?v=wWhkJZw4inY.

that the killing is morally wrong than that the argument is sound . . .[2]

The properly basic intuition that torturing innocent children for fun is wrong isn't undermined by the existence of the psychopath who enjoys torturing children. By the principle of credulity, torturing an innocent child for fun clearly isn't *merely* something that stops the child functioning normally (an empirical observation), or *merely* something we dislike because of our evolutionary history, or *merely* something our society has decided to discourage. Rather, torturing an innocent child for fun is *objectively wrong*. So *at least one thing is objectively wrong*. Therefore, *moral objectivism is true*.

Of course, my moral intuition *could be wrong*; but *this very admission of fallibility presupposes moral objectivism*; for if moral subjectivism were true, no moral claims could be objectively false. As atheist Russ Shafer-Landau argues: "subjectivism's . . . picture of ethics . . . entails a kind of moral infallibility for individuals or societies . . . This sort of infallibility is hard to swallow."[3]

Finally, if moral objectivism were false it couldn't be true that we objectively *ought* to consider arguments against objectivism, or that we *ought* to consider them fairly: Knowing this, we see that to embrace an argument for subjectivism would be to take the self-contradictory position that: (a) there are no objective moral values, but that (b) we objectively *ought* to accept subjectivism!

Many atheists argue that *if* God doesn't exist, *then* objective moral values don't exist. For example, Jean-Paul Sartre said he found it:

> extremely embarrassing that God does not exist, for there disappears with Him all possibility of finding values in an intelligible heaven. There can no longer be any good *a priori*, since there is no infinite and perfect consciousness to think it.[4]

An objective moral value is a transcendent ideal that prescribes and obligates behaviour; but an ideal implies a mind, a prescription requires a prescriber and an obligation demands a person. As H.P. Owen argues:

> On the one hand [objective moral] claims transcend every human person . . . On the other hand . . . it is contradictory to assert that impersonal claims are entitled to the allegiance of our wills. The

---

2. Cave, *Humanism*, 146.
3. Shafer-Landau, *Whatever Happened to Good and Evil?*, 16–17.
4. Sartre, "Existentialism Is a Humanism," 28.

only solution to this paradox is to suppose that the order of [objective moral] claims ... is in fact rooted in the personality of God.[5]

It's important not to confuse this argument with the false claim that one must *believe* in God in order to *know* or to *do* the right thing. The moral argument is concerned with moral ontology and not moral epistemology.

2) The Argument from Reason

Atheist Sam Harris affirms that "our logical, mathematical, and physical intuitions have not been designed by natural selection to track the Truth."[6] Likewise, Patricia Churchland holds that

> Boiled down to essentials, a nervous system enables the organism to succeed in the four F's: feeding, fleeing, fighting, and reproducing. The principal chore of nervous systems is to get the body parts where they should be in order that the organism may survive ... Truth ... definitely takes the hindmost.[7]

But if truth "takes the hindmost" on naturalism, how can Harris and Churchland be confident about their naturalism? As atheist Thomas Nagel concedes: "the reliance we put on reason implies a belief that ... the basic methods of reasoning we employ are not merely human but belong to a more general category of *mind*."[8] That is, our rationally inescapable cognitive confidence is at odds with naturalism, but stands in a mutually supporting relationship with theism.

3) A Fine-Tuning Argument

Neither complexity without specificity, nor specificity without complexity compels us to infer design. However, if you saw a poem written out in alphabet fridge magnets, you'd infer design. Such a pattern is both specified *and* sufficiently improbable to merit a design inference on the grounds that "in all cases where we know the causal origin of ... specified complexity, experience has shown that intelligent design played a causal role."[9] This

---

5. Owen, "Morality Implies the Existence of God," 648.
6. Harris, *Moral Landscape*, 66.
7. Churchland, quoted by Plantinga, *Where the Conflict Really Lies*, 315.
8. Nagel, *Last Word*, 140.
9. Meyer, "Teleological Evolution."

observation becomes highly significant in light of Stephen Hawking's affirmation that for life to exist: "the initial state of the universe had to be set up in a very special *and* highly improbable way."[10]

4) A Cosmological Argument

Suppose I ask you to loan me a certain book, but you say: "I don't have a copy right now, but I'll ask my friend to lend me his copy and then I'll lend it to you." Suppose your friend says the same thing to you, and so on. Two things are clear. First, if the process of asking to borrow the book goes on *ad infinitum*, I'll never get the book. Second, if I get the book, the process that led to me getting it can't have gone on *ad infinitum*. Somewhere down the line of requests to borrow the book, someone *had* the book *without having to borrow it*. Likewise, argues Richard Purtill, consider any contingent reality:

> The same two principles apply. If the process of everything getting its existence from something else went on to infinity, then the thing in question would never [have] existence. And if the thing has . . . existence then the process hasn't gone on to infinity. There was something that had existence without having to receive it from something else . . .[11]

Atheist cosmologist Alexander Vilenkin recently affirmed that "All the evidence we have says that the universe had a beginning."[12] Big bang cosmology describes the evolution of the universe over a finite length of time, but it doesn't explain why the universe exists. Concerning this question, physicist Paul Davies observes:

> One might consider some supernatural force . . . as being responsible for the big bang, or one might prefer to regard the big bang as an event without a cause. It seems to me that we don't have too much choice. Either . . . something outside of the physical world [or] an event without a cause.[13]

---

10. Hawking and Milodinov, *Grand Design*, 130, 144.
11. Purtill, quoted by Taliaferro, *Contemporary Philosophy of Religion*, 358–59.
12. Vilenkin quoted by Grossman, "Death of the Eternal Cosmos," 7. See: Vilenkin, "Did the Universe Have a Beginning?"
13. Davies, "Birth of the Cosmos," 8–9.

A physical event is a *contingent* reality, and a contingent reality is contingent *upon something beyond itself*. Hence every physical event must have at least one cause—in a general sense of the term. Since the *first* physical event cannot depend upon a physical reality, the finitude of the past highlights the need for a non-contingent and therefore non-physical "first cause." That is:

1. There was a first physical event.
2. All physical events have at least one cause outside and independent of themselves.
3. Therefore, the first physical event had at least one cause outside and independent of itself.
4. The cause of the first physical event can't have been a physical cause.
5. Therefore, the first physical event had a non-physical cause.
6. It's impossible for everything to have a cause.
7. Therefore, there exists a first, uncaused, non-contingent and non-physical cause of physical reality.

Quantum mechanics doesn't provide a counter example to the second, causal premise. Even under the Copenhagen interpretation, quantum events happen against a backdrop of physical reality that causally conditions, even if it doesn't causally necessitate, the quantum events in question. Atheist philosopher Quentin Smith confirms that quantum considerations "at most tend to show that acausal laws govern the change of condition of particles . . . They state nothing about the causality or acausality of absolute beginnings . . ."[14]

Since the universe had a beginning, non-theists must either deny our causal premise or claim that every physical event *has a physical cause*. However, making an exception to our causal premise when it comes to the *first* physical event is *ad hoc*, whereas invoking the necessity of physical causation entails an infinite regress.

---

14. Smith, "Uncaused Beginning of the Universe," 50.

3

In Defence of Theism[1]

Most people agree with the Roman writer Cicero, who asked: "What could be more clear or obvious when we look up to the sky and contemplate the heavens, than that there is some divinity of superior intelligence?"[2] Such intuitive perceptions of divinity are properly basic beliefs grounded in experience, which means they're reasonable to accept in the absence of sufficient counter-evidence. Nevertheless, I will sketch a selection of arguments for belief in a supernatural creator.

Existential Desire

Consider the experience of Teresa Vining, who as a student began to doubt God's existence: "For some time there had been a gnawing uncertainty deep inside me . . . What if it is all a lie?"[3] When Teresa hit rock bottom she discovered some intuitions that countered her scepticism:

> There is no God, I told myself. This life is all there is . . . There is no real meaning, no basis for knowing what is right and what

---

1. This is the opening speech from my debate with Norwegian agnostic philosopher Professor Einar Bøhn, which took place in 2018 at the Norwegian University of Science and Technology, in Trondheim.

An audio recording of the debate is available from my podcast: "Debate: Does God Exist? Peter S. Williams vs. Einar Bohn at the Norwegian University of Science and Technology in Trondheim:" http://peterswilliams.podbean.com/mf/feed/e5dvj8/Trondheim_2018_Debate.mp3arguments-from-desire/.

2. Cicero, *De Natura Deorum*.

3. Vining, *Making Your Faith Your Own*, 11.

is wrong. It doesn't matter what we do or how we live . . . *No!* something deep inside of me screamed. It could not be true. I couldn't believe that life was just a sick joke with humans and their capacity for love, appreciation of beauty, and need for meaning as the pitiful punch line. That went against all my experience as a human being. There had to be *something* more! That night was the beginning of a new . . . search for truth in my life . . . because the one thing I *did* know after that night was that I couldn't believe this life is all there is.[4]

If the satisfaction of innate existential desires, such as those mentioned by Vining, requires God, then the intuition that life isn't "absurd" suggests that God exists. Indeed, "experience indicates that . . . natural desires are, in fact, good indicators that objects really exist to satisfy those desires."[5] At the very least, we should assume that no type of innate desire exists in vain until and unless we are shown otherwise.

Some people may profess a willingness to pay the price of affirming that life is "absurd," but this affirmation isn't easy to make or consistently sustain. As Andy Banister asks,

> What was it that possessed evolution . . . to equip us and us alone among the animal kingdom with desires not just for cake and copulation, but for value, meaning, purpose, and significance? If atheism is true, we are at best biological freaks, whose desires no more map onto reality than do those of a dyslexic cartographer . . . if atheism is *true*, not merely is there no meaning to which those desires connect, but the very fact that we have them at all would make us fundamentally irrational . . . deluded creatures . . . But if we are . . . *that* irrational, *that* demented, then we cannot trust *any* of our instincts, not one of our desires, none of our most cherished beliefs. Including our belief in cake, hope, meaning, or even atheism.[6]

Rationality

Atheist Sam Harris affirms that: "Our logical, mathematical, and physical intuitions have not been designed by natural selection to track the Truth."[7]

---

4. Vining, *Making Your Faith Your Own*, 12–13.
5. Habermas and Moreland, *Beyond Death*, 34.
6. Bannister, *Atheist Who Didn't Exist*, 185.
7. Harris, *Moral Landscape*, 66.

Atheist Patricia Churchland agrees that: "The principal chore of nervous systems is to get the body parts where they should be in order that the organism may survive . . . Truth . . . definitely takes the hindmost."[8] But if truth "takes the hindmost" on naturalism, how can naturalists be confident about the *truth* of naturalism or atheism? Indeed, while even the ability to think thoughts that are true or false about reality resists naturalistic explanation, human rationality fits within a theistic worldview.

Design

As Cicero observed, seeing letters arranged into a poem, we infer design. Such a pattern is both specified *and* sufficiently improbable to merit a design inference on the grounds that "in all cases where we know the causal origin of . . . specified complexity, experience has shown that intelligent design played a causal role."[9] The natural world exhibits many examples of specified complexity. For example, Stephen Hawking notes that for life to exist "the initial state of the universe had to be set up in a very special *and* highly improbable way."[10] The best explanation for this cosmic "fine tuning" is design.

Causation

Talking of "the initial state of the universe," big bang cosmology describes the expansion of the universe over a finite length of time, but it doesn't explain *why* the universe exists. A physical event is a *contingent* reality, and a contingent reality is by definition contingent *upon something beyond itself*. Hence every physical event must have at least one cause—in a general sense of the term. Since the *first* physical event cannot depend upon a physical reality, the fact that our universe had a beginning highlights the need for a non-physical and non-contingent cause.

Non-theists must either deny that a contingent thing is contingent upon something beyond itself, or else claim that *every physical event has a physical cause*. However, both denials are *ad hoc*, and invoking the necessity of physical causation entails an un-parsimonious and arguably impossible infinite regress, a regress that all of the available scientific evidence excludes.

---

8. Churchland, quoted by Plantinga, *Where the Conflict Really Lies*, 315.
9. Meyer, "Teleological Evolution."
10. Hawking and Milodinov, *Grand Design*, 130.

Moral Duty

Atheist Peter Cave defends the reality of objective moral duty by appealing to his intuitions about evil, explaining that,

> whatever sceptical arguments may be brought against our belief that killing the innocent is morally wrong, we are more certain that the killing is morally wrong than that the [skeptical argument] argument is sound . . .[11]

By the principle of credulity, killing an innocent child for fun clearly isn't *merely* something that stops the child functioning normally (an empirical observation), or *merely* something we dislike because of our evolutionary history, or *merely* something our society has decided to discourage. Rather, such an act is *objectively wrong*, something that we discover we are required and obligated not to do.

Of course, at least some of our moral intuitions *could be wrong*; but *this very admission* of fallibility *presupposes moral objectivism*, for if subjectivism were true, no moral claims could be objectively false. As atheist Russ Shafer-Landau argues: "subjectivism's . . . picture of ethics . . . entails a kind of moral infallibility for individuals or societies . . . This sort of infallibility is hard to swallow."[12]

Moreover, if moral subjectivism were true it couldn't be the case that we objectively *ought* to consider arguments for subjectivism, or that we *ought* to consider them fairly. Knowing this, we see that to accept any argument for subjectivism would be to take the self-contradictory position that: (a) there are no objective moral duties, but that (b) we objectively *ought* to accept subjectivism!

Objective moral duties are transcendent prescriptions that obligate our behaviour; but a prescription requires a prescriber and an obligation requires someone to whom we are obligated. Steven B. Cowan comments,

> it might be asked why objective moral values cannot simply exist as brute facts . . . The problem with this suggestion is that it cannot explain why moral values . . . would have anything whatsoever to do with us . . . Moral values prescribe behaviour . . . Moral values, understood objectively, bind our consciences, but why should moral values, if they are simply brute facts . . . bind my conscience?

---

11. Cave, *Humanism*, 146.
12. Shafer-Landau, *Whatever Happened to Good and Evil?*, 16–17.

> Moral prescriptions . . . make sense only if there is a moral prescriber . . .[13]

Or as H.P. Owen argues:

> The dictates of society cannot explain the absoluteness of the categorical imperative; but in so far as they are personal they have a superficial credibility . . . bare belief in an impersonal order of claims . . . does not provide the personal basis which their imperatival quality requires . . . On the one hand [objective moral] claims transcend every human person . . . On the other hand . . . it is contradictory to assert that impersonal claims are entitled to the allegiance of our wills. The only solution to this paradox is to suppose that the order of [objective moral] claims . . . is in fact rooted in the personality of God.[14]

Jesus

Finally, theism offers the best explanation of various historical facts about Jesus, a first-century Jew who not only laid claim to divinity (without appearing to be either a madman or a confidence trickster), but who pointed to his fulfilment of prophecy, including in his miracles and his resurrection from the dead, as signs that he was who he claimed to be.

Jewish scriptures written hundreds of years before the first century contain many predictions about the origins, actions and fate of the "messiah," including predictions it would have been impossible to fulfill by human manipulation, but which accurately describe Jesus. A conservative estimate of the odds of anyone fulfilling just twelve of these prophecies by chance would be one in 10^{12}—that's odds of a trillion to one! As Thomas V. Morris observes,

> A series of prophecies made by different people at different times and culminating in a single fulfilment by the life of so remarkable a person as Jesus cries out for an explanation . . . the most reasonable explanation is that God was involved in the prophecy and fulfilment . . .[15]

---

13. Cowan, "Question of Moral Values," 174.
14. Owen, "Morality Implies the Existence of God," 647–48.
15. Morris, *Making Sense of it All*, 166.

Historical evidence shows that Jesus died on a Roman cross, was buried in a tomb which was later found empty, and that individuals and groups of people subsequently had unexpected experiences in which they sincerely believed they interacted with a resurrected Jesus. It's important to note that,

> Jews had no belief in a dying, much less rising, Messiah. And Jewish beliefs about the afterlife prohibited anyone's rising from the dead *before* the resurrection at the end of the world. Nevertheless, the original disciples came to believe so strongly that God had raised Jesus from the dead that they were willing to die for the truth of that belief.[16]

The controversial question is how best to explain this generally accepted historical data. I would argue with N.T. Wright that, as long as one doesn't rule out miraculous explanations *a priori*, "all other explanations for why Christianity arose and took the shape it did are far less convincing as historical explanations than the one the early Christians themselves offer: that Jesus really did rise from the dead . . ."[17]

Conclusion

These arguments—from (1) desire, (2) rationality, (3) design, (4) causation, (5) duty and (6) Jesus—are just a sampling from dozens of arguments I think jointly validate the widespread perception that there exists a supernatural creator.

---

16. Craig, "Opening Speech" of the Craig-Hitchens Debate.
17. Wright, "Jesus' Resurrection and Christian Origins," 136–37.

4

Can Moral Objectivism Do Without God?[1]

The most discussed moral argument for God's existence is currently the argument concerning the ontological basis for objective moral values:
If God does not exist, objective moral values do not exist.
Objective moral values do exist.
Therefore, God exists.[2]
Although consistent atheists must avoid accepting both premises of this logically valid syllogism, it's not hard to find atheists who endorse either premise. Hence, this argument can be defended by quoting exclusively from atheists. After sketching a defence of both premises, and dealing with the frequent confusion between *epistemology* and *ontology* amongst its critics, this paper will focus upon defending the first premise against two objections from atheist Russ Shafer-Landau's otherwise excellent book *Whatever Happened to Good and Evil?* (Oxford, 2004).

Premise One: "If God does not exist, objective moral values do not exist'

Traditionally, atheists have acknowledged that God is a necessary condition of *objective* moral values (i.e. the sort of moral truths that are *discovered*

---

1. The original version of this paper appeared in Norwegian in the Forum section of Scandinavian apologetics journal *Theofilos*, vol. 3, nr. 2, 2011.
2. Craig, *God? A Debate*, 19. See also: Craig, *Reasonable Faith*, and Craig, *On Guard*.

rather than *invented* by humans and which are "valid and binding whether anybody believes in them or not").[3] For example:

- Jean-Paul Sartre: "when we speak of 'abandonment'—a favorite word of Heidegger—we only mean to say that God does not exist, and that it is necessary to draw the consequences of his absence right to the end. The existentialist is strongly opposed to a certain type of secular moralism which seeks to suppress God at the least possible expense. Towards 1880, when the French professors endeavoured to formulate a secular morality, they said . . . nothing will be changed if God does not exist; we shall rediscover the same norms of honesty, progress and humanity, and we shall have disposed of God as an out-of-date hypothesis which will die away quietly of itself. The existentialist, on the contrary, finds it extremely embarrassing that God does not exist, for there disappears with Him all possibility of finding values in an intelligible heaven. There can no longer be any good *a priori*, since there is no infinite and perfect consciousness to think it. It is nowhere written that 'the good' exists, that one must be honest or must not lie, since we are now upon the plane where there are only men. Dostoevsky once wrote: 'If God did not exist, everything would be permitted;' and that, for existentialism, is the starting point. Everything is indeed permitted if God does not exist, and man is in consequence forlorn, for he cannot find anything to depend upon either within or outside himself."[4]

- Paul Kurtz: "The central question about moral and ethical principles concerns their ontological foundation. If they are neither derived from God nor anchored in some transcendent ground, they are purely ephemeral."[5]

- Julian Baggini: "If there is no single moral authority [i.e. no God] we have to in some sense 'create' values for ourselves . . . [and] that means that moral claims are not true or false . . . you may disagree with me but you cannot say I have made a factual error."[6]

- Richard Dawkins: "The universe that we observe has precisely the properties we should expect if there is, at bottom, no design, no purpose

---

3. Craig, *God? A Debate*, 17.
4. Sartre, *Existentialism Is a Humanism*, 28.
5. Kurtz, *Forbidden Fruit*, 65.
6. Baggini, *Atheism*, 41–51.

[i.e. no God], *no evil, no good*, nothing but pitiless indifference."[7] Dawkins concedes: "It is pretty hard to defend absolutist morals on grounds other than religious ones."[8]

By distinguishing between various different properties of "the moral law," philosophers have put forward a variety of independent reasons to accept the first premise of the moral argument:

- *The argument from moral prescription:*

    Beyond its objectivity, what is sometimes called the "moral law" is not analogous to the scientific concept of physical "laws." When I trip up, falling is something I am *caused* to do, not something I am *obliged* to do! The "moral law," on the other hand, *prescribes* (but does not cause) actions that I am *obligated* to do or to refrain from doing. While I never fail to "obey" the "law" of gravity, I often fail to "do the right thing." A physical law describes what *is* the case, and can be used to predict what *will* be the case, but it doesn't *prescribe* what *ought* to be the case as does the "moral law." Now, as Francis J. Beckwith and Greg Koukl observe, "A command only makes sense when there are two minds involved, one giving the command and one receiving it."[9] If an objective moral law has the property of being a *command* that we receive, then there must be an objective, personal, moral *commander* beyond individual or collective humanity. As G.E.M. Anscombe affirmed concerning an objective moral law, "Naturally it is not possible to have such a conception unless you believe in God as a lawgiver; like Jews, Stoics, and Christians . . . you cannot be under a law unless it has been promulgated to you . . ."[10]

- *The argument from moral obligation:*

    Francis J. Beckwith observes how "our experience indicates that moral obligation . . . is deeply connected to our obligations *toward* other persons."[11] I have moral obligations, but since I can't be obligated by anything non-personal (e.g. the evolutionary history of my species), I must be obligated by something personal. Since there are

---

7. Dawkins, "God's Utility Function," 85, emphasis mine.
8. Dawkins, *God Delusion*, 232.
9. Beckwith and Koukl, *Moral Relativism*, 166.
10. Anscombe, "Modern Moral Philosophy," 31, 39.
11. Beckwith, "Right We Ought to Choose," 230.

objective moral obligations that transcend all finite persons (or groups thereof), there must therefore be a transcendent personal reality to whom we are most fundamentally obligated. As H.P. Owen argues:

> On the one hand [objective moral] claims transcend every human person . . . On the other hand we value the personal more highly than the impersonal; so that it is contradictory to assert that impersonal claims are entitled to the allegiance of our wills. The only solution to this paradox is to suppose that the order of [objective moral] claims . . . is in fact rooted in the personality of God.[12]

Richard Taylor agrees that the idea of a moral obligation or duty more important and binding than those imposed upon us by other individuals or by the state is only intelligible if we make reference to a person who transcends us all:

> A duty is something that is owed . . . But something can be owed only to some person or persons. There can be no such thing as duty in isolation . . . the idea of an obligation higher than this, and referred to as moral obligation, is clear enough, provided reference to some lawmaker higher . . . than those of the state is understood . . . This does give a clear sense to the claim that our moral obligations are more binding upon us than our political obligations . . . But what if this higher-than-human lawgiver is no longer taken into account? Does the concept of a moral obligation . . . still make sense? . . . the concept of moral obligation [is] unintelligible apart from the idea of God. The words remain, but their meaning is gone.[13]

- *The argument from moral ideals:*

    We appear to apprehend and to measure ourselves against a moral *ideal*. But it's hard to conceive of this ideal as an impersonal, abstract reality: "It is clear what is meant when it is said that a person is just; but it is bewildering when it is said that in the absence of any people, *justice* itself exists. Moral values seem to exist as properties of persons, not as mere [Platonic] abstractions . . ."[14] Hence A.E. Taylor argued that,

---

12. Owen, "Morality Implies The Existence Of God," 648.
13. Taylor, *Ethics, Faith, and Reason*, 83–84.
14. Moreland and Craig, *Foundations For A Christian Worldview*, 492.

were there no will in existence except the wills of human beings, who are so often ignorant of the law of right and so often defy it, it is not apparent what the validity of the law could mean. Recognition of the validity of the law thus seems to carry with it a reference to an intelligence which has not, like our own, to make acquaintance with it piecemeal, slowly and with difficulty, but has always been in full and clear possession of it, and a will which does not, like our own, often set it at nought, but is guided by it in all its operations.[15]

- *The argument from moral guilt*
  Beckwith argues that a non-personal ground of an objective moral law that transcends human subjectivity "is inadequate in explaining the guilt and shame one feels when one violates the moral law. For it is persons, not rules or principles, that elicit in us feelings of guilt and shame."[16] As Paul Copan asks: "Why should we feel guilt towards abstract moral principles?"[17] Since it would be inappropriate to feel guilt or shame before an abstract (impersonal) moral principle, and since it is appropriate to feel guilt and shame before the objective moral law, that moral law cannot be an abstract moral principle. In other words, objective moral values must be ontologically grounded in a transcendent *personality* before whom it is appropriate to feel moral guilt (its worth noting that the possibility of objective forgiveness for moral guilt is equally dependent upon the moral law having a personal ground).

These four arguments form a powerful cumulative case for the first premise of the moral argument.

Premise Two: "Objective moral values do exist"

Whilst no one who accept the first premise of the moral argument can consistently remain an atheist unless they reject the existence of objective moral values, as John Cottingham observes: "To everyone's surprise, the

---

15. Taylor, *Does God Exist?*, 107.
16. Beckwith, "Right We Ought to Choose," 230.
17. Copan, *True For You*, 62.

increasing consensus among philosophers today is that some kind of objectivism of truth and of value is correct...."[18]

For example, drawing upon the "principle of credulity," atheist Peter Cave argues that: "whatever sceptical arguments may be brought against our belief that killing the innocent is morally wrong, we are more certain that the killing is morally wrong than that the argument is sound... Torturing an innocent child for the sheer fun of it is morally wrong. Full stop."[19]

Indeed, to think that any argument against moral objectivism is compelling would be to embrace the self-contradictory position that (a) there are no objective moral values, and that (b) one objectively *ought* to accept subjectivism! As Margarita Rosa Levin comments in a related context,

> Even the enemies of objectivity rely on it ... the skeptic states a position that cannot possibly be sustained or rationally believed [because] he is in effect asking you not to apply his assertion to his own position, without giving any reason for exempting his own words from his own general claim. His position is futile and self-refuting; it can be stated, but it cannot convince anyone who recognizes its implications.[20]

Ontology not Epistemology

Writing in his *Gifford Lectures on Moral Values* And *The Idea Of God* (1921), W.R. Sorley describes and affirms moral objectivism:

> When I assert "this is good" or "that is evil," I do not mean that I experience desire or aversion, or that I have a feeling of liking or indignation. These subjective experiences may be present; but the judgment points not to a personal or subjective state of mind but to the presence of an objective value in the situation. What is implied in this objectivity? Clearly, in the first place, it implies independence of the judging subject. If my assertion "this is good" is valid, then it is valid not for me only but for everyone. If I say "this is good," and another person, referring to the same situation, says "this is not good," one or other of us must be mistaken... The validity of a moral judgment does not depend upon the person by whom the judgment is made... In saying that moral values belong to the nature of reality ... the statement implies an objectivity

---

18. Cottingham, "Truth, Goodness and Beauty."
19. Cave, *Humanism*, 146.
20. Levin, "Defence of Objectivity," 550, 558.

which is independent of the achievements of persons in informing their lives with these values, and is even independent of their recognising their validity. Whether we are guided by them or not, whether we acknowledge them or not, they have validity... objective moral value is valid independently of my will, and yet is something which satisfies my purpose and completes my nature...[21]

Since atheist philosopher Colin McGinn accepts the objectivity of moral value described by Sorley, he suggests that it is possible "to detach moral objectivity from any religious worldview—so that we do not need to believe in God in order to find morality both important and binding."[22] Here McGinn exhibits a common confusion, in that he conflates the argument for God as the ontological basis for objective moral values with the un-biblical epistemological claim that *belief* in God is a necessary condition of *knowing* the difference between right and wrong (cf. Rom 2:14–15). As J.P. Moreland and William Lane Craig caution:

> The question is *not*: Must we believe in God in order to live moral lives? There is no reason to think that atheists and theists alike may not live what we normally characterize as good and decent lives. Similarly, the question is *not*: Can we formulate a system of ethics without reference to God? If the non-theist grants that human beings do have objective value, then there is no reason to think that he cannot work out a system of ethics with which the theist would largely agree. Or again, the question is *not*: Can we recognize the existence of objective moral values without reference to God? The theist will typically maintain that a person need not believe in God in order to recognize, say, that we should love our children.[23]

Rather, as Paul Copan explains, the moral argument urges that although "*Belief* in God isn't a requirement for being moral... the *existence* of a personal God is crucial for a coherent understanding of objective morality."[24] In other words, although the non-theist can *do* the right thing because they *know* what the objectively right thing to do is, their worldview can't cogently provide *an adequate ontological account of* the objective moral values they know and obey.

---

21. Sorley, *Moral Values*, 93; *Idea of God*, 238-39.
22. McGinn, *Ethics, Evil and Fiction*, vii.
23. Moreland and Craig, *Foundations For A Christian Worldview*, 492.
24. Copan, *True For You*, 45.

A UNIVERSE FROM SOMEONE

Russ Shafer-Landau on Objective Values Without God

Atheist Russ Shafer-Landau does an excellent job of defending moral objectivism in his book *Whatever Happened to Good and Evil?* He writes,

> some moral views are better than others, despite the sincerity of the individuals, cultures, and societies that endorse them. Some moral views are true, others false, and my thinking them so doesn't make them so. My society's endorsement of them doesn't prove their truth. Individuals, and whole societies, can be seriously mistaken when it comes to morality. The best explanation of this is that there are moral standards not of our own making.[25]

Shafer-Landau acknowledges that many people think there is a connection between objective moral value and God:

> This includes theists, many of whom believe in God precisely because they believe in ethical objectivity, and see no way of defending this idea without God. But it also includes all those atheists who embrace moral [subjectivism], just because they believe that the only escape from it is through God, whom they reject.[26]

According to Shafer-Landau, the position of many atheists can thus be expressed in the following "argument from atheism" for moral subjectivism:

> Premise (1) Ethics is objective only if God exists.
> Premise (2) But God does not exist.
> (Conclusion) Therefore ethics isn't objective.[27]

As a case in point, the late J.L. Mackie acknowledged that objective moral values would be evidence for God:

> If we adopted moral objectivism, we should have to regard the relations of supervienence which connect values and obligations with their natural grounds as synthetic; they would then be in principle something that a god might conceivably create; and since they would otherwise be a very odd sort of thing, the admitting of them would be an inductive ground for admitting also a god to create them.[28]

25. Shaefer-Landau, *Whatever Happened to Good and Evil?*, viii.
26. Shaefer-Landau, *Whatever Happened to Good and Evil?*, 75.
27. See: Shafer-Landau, *Whatever Happened to Good and Evil?*, 75.
28. Mackie, *Miracle of Theism*, 118.

Mackie sidestepped the moral argument by embracing the "argument from atheism" and rejecting the objectivity of moral value: "If we adopted instead a subjectivist ... account of morality, this problem would not arise."[29] Unlike Mackie, Shafer-Landau isn't prepared to reject moral objectivism, so he rejects the other premise of the moral argument, saying that "both theists and atheists can (and should) reject"[30] the "argument from atheism".

On the one hand, since its second premise is "just an assertion of atheism,"[31] theists will naturally reject the argument from atheism:

> It may be that God really does not exist. But unless the atheist can provide compelling argument to that effect, then you theists out there are within your rights to reject the Argument from Atheism. And agnostics are pretty much in the same boat [because] they'll neither accept nor reject its second premise ... and so will refrain from endorsing its conclusion.[32]

On the other hand, Shafer-Landau thinks that *atheists* can and should reject the "argument from atheism." Since the "argument from atheism" is logically valid, and since Shafer-Landau accepts its atheistic second premise, he rejects its first premise (which amounts to denying the first premise of the moral argument). To justify this denial, Shafer-Landau tries to rebut what he mistakenly takes to be the *only* line of thought that ties moral objectivity to God's existence:

> In my experience, people tie objectivity to God because of a very specific line of thought. The basic idea is that all laws (rules, principles, standards, etc.) require a lawmaker. So if there are any moral laws, then these too require a lawmaker. But if these moral laws are objective, then the lawmaker can't be any one of us. That's just true by definition. Objectivity implies an independence from human opinion. Well, if objective moral rules aren't authorised by any one of us, then who did make them up? Three guesses. In a nutshell: all rules require an author. Objective rules can't be human creations. Therefore objective rules require a nonhuman creator. Enter God.[33]

---

29. Mackie, *Miracle of Theism*, 118.
30. Shaefer-Landau, *Whatever Happened to Good and Evil?*, 76.
31. Shaefer-Landau, *Whatever Happened to Good and Evil?*, 76.
32. Shaefer-Landau, *Whatever Happened to Good and Evil?*, 76.
33. Shaefer-Landau, *Whatever Happened to Good and Evil?*, 75–76.

Shafer-Landau thus reduces the premise that "If God does not exist, objective moral values do not exist" to the premise that "all laws require a lawmaker." Even if he can rebut the latter premise, it doesn't follow that he has rebutted the former premise; but let us examine each precondition of success in turn.

Shafer-Landau's Question-Begging Rebuttal of Premise One

Since the justification for the moral argument's first premise, according to Shafer-Landau, is the belief that "all laws require a lawmaker," he concludes that atheists,

> must either reject the existence of any objective laws, or reject the claim that laws require lawmakers. Since they can easily accept the existence of some objective laws (e.g. of physics or chemistry) they should deny that laws require authors.[34]

Of course, Shafer-Landau is correct when he says that "If you are an atheist, you do, in fact, believe that all objective laws lack a divine author."[35] But the question here is not what atheists *do* believe, but rather what they *can* and *should* believe. As a rebuttal to the premise "all laws require a lawmaker," the mere observation that atheists *believe* in the laws of physics without *believing* in a creator is lacking (obviously relevant theistic arguments are simply being ignored here).[36] The reason atheists believe in objective laws without a lawmaker is that atheists don't believe in an objective lawmaker: "Who made the second law of thermodynamics true? No one. If these laws are objective, then *we* certainly didn't create them. And if God doesn't exist, then, obviously, God didn't make them up either. No one did."[37] Here we clearly see that Shafer-Landau's rebuttal of the moral argument is *based upon the question-begging assumption that God does not exist*. Landau is offering "just an assertion of atheism,"[38] an assertion that theists and agnostics will naturally reject: "It may be that God really does not

---

34. Shaefer-Landau, *Whatever Happened to Good and Evil?*, 76.
35. Shafer-Landau, *Whatever Happened to Good and Evil?*, 77.
36. See: Foster, *Divine Lawmaker*; Pruss, "Leibnizian Cosmological Argument'; Craig, "Kalam Cosmological Argument"; Collins, "Exploration of the Fine-Tuning of the Universe"; Craig, *Reasonable Faith*, third edition; Gordon, "Balloons On A String."
37. Shafer-Landau, *Whatever Happened to Good and Evil?*, 77.
38. Shafer-Landau, *Whatever Happened to Good and Evil?*, 76.

exist. But unless the atheist can provide compelling argument to that effect, then you theists out there are within your rights to reject [this rebuttal]."[39] Shafer-Landau answers the moral argument like so:

> If objective ethical rules require God, that's because (i) rules require authors; (ii) therefore *objective* rules require non-human authors; (iii) therefore objective moral rules require a nonhuman author; and (iv) that must be God. Each of these steps follow naturally from the preceding one. Atheists reject the conclusion (iv). Therefore they should reject the initial claim that got them there: (i).[40]

Theists and agnostics will hardly be impressed by this mere "assertion of atheism."[41]

Equivocation is Illogical

Shafer-Landau sportingly allows the theist another move; namely, the claim that,

> normative laws—those that tell us what we *ought* to do, how we *should* behave—do require an author . . . Even if we concede the existence of scientific laws without lawmakers, we still need some reason to think that moral rules, which are obviously normative, are also authorless.[42]

Shafer-Landau questions any development of the moral argument based upon the distinction between normative and non-normative rules, since "The best reason for thinking that moral laws require an author is that all laws require an author. But that reason, as we've seen, is mistaken. What other reason could there be?"[43] Of course, his reason for rejecting the premise that all laws require an author is question-begging, so he's not off to a good start here. However, he does launch an independent counter-attack upon taking the *normative* nature of the moral law to be significant:

> Not all normative laws require lawmakers. For instance, the laws of logic and rationality are normative. They tell us what we ought

39. Shafer-Landau, *Whatever Happened to Good and Evil?*, 76.
40. Shafer-Landau, *Whatever Happened to Good and Evil?*, 77.
41. Shafer-Landau, *Whatever Happened to Good and Evil?*, 76.
42. Shafer-Landau, *Whatever Happened to Good and Evil?*, 77.
43. Shafer-Landau, *Whatever Happened to Good and Evil?*, 77.

to do. But no one invented them. If you have excellent evidence for one claim, and this entails a second claim, then you *should* believe that second claim. If you are faced with contradictory propositions, and you know that one of them is false, then you *must* accept the other. If you want just one thing out of life, then you *ought* to do what's necessary to achieve it . . .[44]

Unlike the example of the laws of nature, theists can agree with Shafer-Landau that no one, not even God, "invented" the laws of logic. However, when Shafer-Landau writes that "If you have excellent evidence for one claim, and this entails a second claim, then you *should* believe that second claim"[45] he equivocates between moral and pragmatic senses of the word "should." Logic *qua* logic has nothing to say about *what objectively ought to be the case morally speaking*. Logic can tell us that *if* we want to accept whatever conclusion is validly deducible from certain premises, *then* such-and-such is the conclusion that we should accept. But this is a pragmatic (if-then) "ought." Logic can't tell us that we have a *categorical moral obligation* to "be reasonable" or to value truth over falsehood. Why *not* agree with Nietzsche that "the falseness of a judgment is to us not necessarily an objection to a judgment . . . The question is to what extent it is life-advancing, life-preserving, species-preserving, perhaps even species-breeding"?[46] The fact that we can distinguish morality from logic shows that logic isn't normative *in the moral sense of the term*. As atheist Kai Nielsen acknowledges, "pure practical reason, even with a good knowledge of the facts, will not take you to morality."[47]

Shafer-Landau's Reductionist Strategy

Shafer-Landau's response to the moral argument is to *reduce* the premise that "if God does not exist, objective moral values do not exist" to the proposition that "all laws require a lawmaker," but his rebuttal of the latter claim begs the question. He then attempts to rebut the modified premise that "all *normative* laws require a lawmaker" by committing the fallacy of equivocation. But what of his overarching strategy of reducing the premise that "if

---

44. Shafer-Landau, *Whatever Happened to Good and Evil?*, 77.
45. Shafer-Landau, *Whatever Happened to Good and Evil?*, 77.
46. Nietzsche, *Beyond Good and Evil* (aphorism 4).
47. Nielsen, "Why Should I Be Moral?," 90.

God does not exist, objective moral values do not exist" to the premise that "all laws/normative laws require a lawmaker"?

First, although Shafer-Landau's reduction of the first premise is clearly in the same ballpark as *the argument from prescription*, it is at best "sitting on the bench." We must be careful to distinguish between positing a moral prescriber *as an explanation of the fact that objective moral norms are experienced as prescriptions*, and positing a moral prescriber *as an explanation of the objectivity of moral values*. While the moral argument posits God as the ontological "ground" of the existence of objective moral values *per se*, it doesn't employ the concept of prescription for this purpose. The problem with employing the notion prescription *in this way*, as Shafer-Landau points out, is that it gives the false impression that the moral law is *contingent* and *arbitrary*, in that (like gravity) it only exists because God *happens* to have created it (the terminology of a moral "law-giver" is especially susceptible to this misleading interpretation). Instead, the concept of moral prescription relates specifically to our experience of moral norms as facts *that prescribe our behaviour*. To put the argument from moral prescription another way (by replacing the terms in Shafer-Landau's own sketch of the moral argument):

> (i) a prescription requires a prescriber; (ii) therefore *objective* prescriptions require non-human prescribers; (iii) therefore objective moral prescriptions require a nonhuman moral prescriber; and (iv) that must be God.

Since Shafer-Landau admits that "Each of these steps follow naturally from the preceding one"[48] when the argument is framed in terms of rules and rule-givers, he ought to admit that each of these steps follows naturally from the preceding one now that we have simply replaced the terms.

Second, Shafer-Landau's reduction strategy simply ignores the premise-one-supporting arguments from *obligation*, *moral ideals* and *guilt* that we examined above. In effect, Shafer-Landau critiques a straw man.

Euthyphro Non Sequiter

In Plato's *Euthyphro* dialogue, Socrates asks: "Is what is holy holy because the gods approve it, or do they approve it because it is holy?"[49] This question

---

48. Shafer-Landau, *Whatever Happened to Good and Evil?*, 77.
49. Plato, *Collected Dialogues of Plato*, 178.

is often taken to entail that "God" is a redundant explanation for the objectivity of moral values. On the one hand, if we ground morality in God's commands, morality becomes arbitrary (if something good simply because God commands it, he could just have easily commanded the opposite). On the other hand, if we don't ground morality in God's commands, morality must be *independent of God's commands,* and thus (so it is frequently but mistakenly urged) *independent of God.* As Bertrand Russell argued:

> if you are quite sure there is a difference between right and wrong, you are then in this situation: is that difference due to God's fiat or is it not? If it is due to God's fiat, then for God himself there is no difference between right and wrong, and it is no longer a significant statement to say that God is good. If you are going to say, as theologians do, that God is good, you must then say that right and wrong have some meaning which is independent of God's fiat, because God's fiats are good and not bad independently of the mere fact that He made them. If you are going to say that, you will then have to say that it is not only through God that right and wrong came into being, but that they are in their essence logically anterior to God.[50]

Shafer-Landau uses the *Euthyphro* dilemma to argue that "ethical objectivists—even the theists among them—should insist on the existence of a realm of moral truths that have not been created by God."[51] I agree. To say that God "creates" moral truths by merely issuing *contingent* prescriptions entails the self-contradictory claim that *objective* moral truths are *contingent* and *arbitrary*. However, Shafer-Landau jumps from the need to reject the "arbitrary" horn of the *Euthyphro* dilemma to the conclusion that "even if you believe in God, you should have serious reservations about tying the objectivity of morality to God's existence."[52] Here we have a simple *non sequitur* that equivocates between (a) the conclusion that the objectivity of objective moral values is not grounded in God's *commands* and (b) the conclusion that the objectivity of objective moral values is not grounded in God's essential *nature*.

As has already been noted, we must distinguish between positing a transcendent moral prescriber *as an explanation for the prescriptive nature of objective moral norms*, and positing a transcendent person *as an*

---

50. Russell, *Why I Am Not A Christian*, 19..
51. Shafer-Landau, *Whatever Happened to Good and Evil?*, 79.
52. Shafer-Landau, *Whatever Happened to Good and Evil?*, 78.

explanation of the objective existence of moral values. While the moral argument posits *a personal God* to account for the existence of objective moral values *per se*, it doesn't employ the concept of God *qua* moral prescriber for *this* purpose. Rather: "God's commands are good, not because God commands them, but because God is *good*. Thus, God is not subject to a moral order outside of himself, and neither are God's moral commands arbitrary. God's commands are issued by a perfect being who is the source of all goodness."[53]

As Keith E. Yandell warns: "The Euthyphro argument nicely raises some issues, but it does not settle anything. There are alternatives in addition to the two that the Euthyphro argument considers. The argument would succeed only if there were not."[54] The *Euthyphro* dilemma destroys the "Divine Command Theory" according to which "actions are right because (and only because) God commands them."[55] Shafer-Landau is therefore right to say that "the best option for theists is to reject the Divine Command Theory;"[56] however, he is wrong to conclude from this that the moral argument is therefore unsound, because the moral argument simply doesn't depend upon "Divine Command Theory." As William Lane Craig observes,

> Plato himself saw the solution to this objection: you split the horns of the dilemma by formulating a third alternative, namely, God is the Good. The Good is the moral nature of God himself. That is to say, God *is* necessarily holy, loving, kind, just, and so on, and these attributes of God comprise the Good. God's moral character expresses itself towards us in the form of certain commandments, which become for us our moral duties. Hence God's commandments are not arbitrary, but necessarily flow from his own nature.[57]

This understanding of the relationship between God and goodness, which side-steps the *Euthyphro* dilemma, is called "essentialism" (because it sees goodness as part of God's ontological essence).

---

53. Beckwith, "Right We Ought to Choose," 232.
54. Yandell, "Theology, Philosophy, And Evil," 240.
55. Shafer-Landau, *Whatever Happened to Good and Evil?*, 80.
56. Shafer-Landau, *Whatever Happened to Good and Evil?*, 83.
57. Craig, *God, Are You There?*, 38–39.

Conclusion

While many atheists grant the existence of a connection between objective moral values and the existence of God, and therefore accept moral subjectivism, a significant number of contemporary atheists endorse moral objectivism. Atheists who endorse moral objectivism have to take issue with their fellow atheists over the first premise of the moral argument, despite the powerful cumulative case that supports it. Atheist Russ Shafer-Landau ably defends moral objectivism, and (unlike certain other atheists) he understands that the first premise of the moral argument is ontological rather than epistemological in character. However, in attempting to avoid the conclusion of the moral argument, Shafer-Landau attacks a straw man by begging the question, equivocating and drawing a *non sequitur* from a false dilemma.

5

A Universe From Someone

Against Lawrence M. Krauss's *A Universe From Nothing: Why There Is Something Rather Than Nothing* (Free Press, 2012)[1]

A Universe From Nothing: Why There Is Something Rather Than Nothing, by cosmologist Lawrence M. Krauss, has been lauded to the skies by fellow atheists such as A.C. Grayling, Sam Harris and Neil deGrasse Tyson. According to Richard Dawkins, "The title means exactly what it says. And what is says is devastating."[2] I agree that what this book says on the subject of why something exists rather than nothing (which isn't a lot) is devastating, but only to the intellectual credibility of Krauss and his supporters. Krauss spends most of his book redefining "nothing" in terms of increasingly incorporeal somethings (from "empty space" to reified "laws of physics") as if this justified the conclusion that literal nothingness could be the cause of the cosmos. That's like arguing that since its possible to live on less and less food each day it must be possible to live on no food.

Krauss admits that he is "not sympathetic to the conviction that creation requires a creator"[3] (a conviction he states is "at the basis of all of the

---

1. This paper was originally published online by www.bethinking.org, the apologetics website of the Universities and Colleges Christian Fellowship (UCCF). See: "A Universe From Someone" (2012): www.bethinking.org/is-there-a-creator/a-universe-from-someone-against-lawrence-krauss.
2. Dawkins, "Afterword," *Universe From Nothing*, 191.
3. Krauss, *Universe From Nothing*, xi.

world's religions"[4]—although this would come as a surprise to Buddhists who don't believe in God). It is of course true by definition that a *creation* requires a *creator* (to be a creator is to create a creation, and to be a creation is to be created by a creator). What Krauss *means* to say is that he isn't sympathetic to the idea that the cosmos is a creation, because that would entail a creator: "I can't prove that God doesn't exist, but I'd much rather live in a universe without one."[5] This sort of confusion is symptomatic of Krauss's dismissive attitude to philosophy, a self-confessed "intellectual bias"[6] that has led him to create a best-selling book riddled with red herrings, circumscribed by circular argumentation and undercut by self-contradiction.

Krauss acknowledges that "no one but the most ardent fundamentalists would suggest that each and every [material] object is . . . purposefully created by a divine intelligence . . ."[7] and that "many laypeople as well as scientists revel in our ability to explain how snowflakes and rainbows can spontaneously appear, based on simple, elegant laws of physics"[8] However, even giving maximum due to the inherent causal capacities of the natural world, there remains an open question: *why does the natural world exist?* Indeed, as Krauss acknowledges: "one can ask, and many do, 'Where do the laws of physics come from?'"[9] Pursuing this line of thought, Krauss acknowledges that "many thoughtful people are driven to the apparent need for First Cause, as Plato, Aquinas, or the modern Roman Catholic Church might put it, and thereby to suppose some divine being: a creator of all that there is . . ."[10] As Dallas Willard argues, "the dependent character of all physical states, together with the completeness of the series of dependencies underlying the existence of any given physical state, logically implies at least one self-existent, and therefore nonphysical, state of being."[11]

There are, of course, several independent versions of the "First Cause" or "cosmological" argument. The most relevant in the context of Krauss's book is clearly the Leibnitzian form of the argument, defended

---

4. Krauss, *Universe From Nothing*, xi.
5. Krauss, "Lawrence M. Krauss, on A Universe From Nothing."
6. Krauss in Harris, "Everything and Nothing."
7. Krauss, *Universe From Nothing*, xi.
8. Krauss, *Universe From Nothing*, xi.
9. Krauss, *Universe From Nothing*, xi.
10. Krauss, *Universe From Nothing*, xii.
11. Willard, "Three-Stage Argument for the Existence of God."

by contemporary philosophers such as Bruce R. Reichenbach[12], Richard Taylor[13] and William Lane Craig.[14] This type of argument might be put as follows:

1. Everything that exists has an explanation of its existence, either in the necessity of its own nature or in an external cause.
2. The universe exists.
3. Therefore the universe has an explanation of its existence.
4. If the universe has an explanation of its existence, that explanation is God.
5. Therefore, the explanation of the universe's existence is God.

Since this is a logically valid deductive argument, and since the universe obviously exists, non-theists must deny premises 1 or 4 to rationally avoid God's existence. However, many philosophers think that Premise 1 —a version of the "principle of sufficient reason"—is simply self-evident. Imagine finding a translucent ball on the forest floor while hiking. You'd naturally wonder how it came to be there. If a fellow hiker said, "It just exists inexplicably. Don't worry about it!" you wouldn't take him seriously. Suppose we increase the size of the ball so it's as big the planet. That doesn't remove the need for explanation. Suppose it were the size of the universe. Same problem. As for premise 4—"If the universe has an explanation of its existence, that explanation is God"—this is synonymous with the standard atheistic claim that if God doesn't exist, then the universe has no explanation of its existence. The only other alternative to theism is to claim the universe has an explanation of its existence *in the necessity of its own nature*. But this would be a *very* radical step (and I can't think of any contemporary atheist who takes it). After all, it's coherent to imagine a universe made from a wholly different collection of quarks/fields/strings than the collection that actually exists; but such a universe would be a different universe, so universes clearly don't exist necessarily. Indeed, Krauss invokes the possibility of other universes ("theorists have estimated that there are perhaps 10^{500} different possible consistent four-dimensional universes that could

---

12. See: Reichenbach, *Cosmological Argument*.
13. See: Taylor, "Cosmological Argument."
14. See: Craig, "Why Does Anything at All Exist?."

result from a single ten-dimensional string theory"[15]) and this possibility entails that universes doesn't exist by a necessity of their own nature.[16]

Suppose I ask you to loan me a certain book, but you say: "I don't have a copy right now, but I'll ask my friend to lend me his copy and then I'll lend it to you." Suppose your friend says the same thing to you, and so on. Two things are clear. First, if the process of asking to borrow the book goes on *ad infinitum*, I'll never get the book. Second, if I get the book, the process that led to me getting it can't have gone on *ad infinitum*. Somewhere down the line of requests to borrow the book, someone *had* the book *without having to borrow it*. Likewise, argues Richard Purtill, consider any contingent reality:

> The same two principles apply. If the process of everything getting its existence from something else went on to infinity, then the thing in question would never [have] existence. And if the thing has . . . existence then the process hasn't gone on to infinity. There was something that had existence without having to receive it from something else . . .[17]

A necessary being explaining all physical reality can't itself be a physical reality. The only remaining possibilities are an abstract object or an immaterial mind. But abstract objects (even granting their existence) are by definition causally impotent. Therefore, the explanation of the physical universe is a necessarily existent, transcendent mind.

In the face of the cosmological argument, Krauss reaches for the tired old objection at the top of the neo-atheist playbook:

> The declaration of a First Cause still leaves open the question, "Who created the creator?" After all, what is the difference between arguing in favour of an eternally existing creator verses an eternally existing universe without one?[18]

First, even supposing that the *deduction* (no mere "declaration") of a First Cause did leave open the secondary question of "who created the creator," this wouldn't provide any grounds upon which to object to the cosmological argument. The implicit assumption that an explanation can't

---

15. Krauss, *Universe From Nothing*, 134.

16. Calum Miller makes the same point in the context of his debate with Peter Atkins, http://dovetheology.com/apologetics/atkins/.

17. Purtill quoted by Taliaferro, *Contemporary Philosophy of Religion*, 358–59.

18. Krauss, *Universe From Nothing*, xii.

be the best explanation of a given data—set *unless one has available an explanation of the explanation* (and so on) clearly entails an actually infinite regress of explanations that can never be satisfied. Adherence to such a regressive explanatory assumption would make science impossible; which is one reason why the First Cause argument is justified in rejecting the notion of an actually infinite explanatory regress. Second, the First Cause argument *doesn't* leave open the secondary question of "who created the creator?" Krauss simply begs the question against the concept of an uncreated *First* Cause, a being that (unlike the physical universe) has an explanation of its existence in the necessity of its own nature.

Krauss goes on to conflate the contrast between caused realities on the one hand and the First Cause on the other hand with a vague contrast between an "an eternally existing universe" and "eternally existing creator" (Does Krauss mean to embrace the possibility of an actually infinite temporal regress for the cosmos? Is he mindful of current debates concerning the various models of God's relationship to time? One suspects not). Then he muddies the waters still further by noting that "an infinite regress of some creative force that begets itself . . . doesn't get us any closer to what it is that gives rise to the universe."[19] Of course such a kluge of incoherencies isn't going to help us here; but this kluge bears no relevant resemblance to the notion of an *uncaused* First Cause who created the universe a finite time ago!

Krauss objects that "Defining away the question [of origins] by arguing that the buck stops with God may seem to obviate the issue of infinite regression, but here I invoke my mantra: The universe is the way it is, whether we like it or not."[20] Note that "arguing that the buck stops with God" is *by definition* not a matter of merely "defining away the question" of origins. Arguing and defining are not synonymous activities. Note too that the first-cause argument *does* "obviate the issue of infinite regression." Note, finally, that Krauss's appeal to his mantra that "the universe is the way it is, whether we like it or not" is a disastrously misguided attempt to sidestep the logic of the cosmological argument by casting supposedly scientific aspersions upon logic!

In typical neo-atheist fashion, Krauss has little time for philosophy.[21] Krauss even states that: "the only knowledge we have is from experiments

19. Krauss, *Universe From Nothing*, xii.
20. Krauss, *Universe From Nothing*, xii.
21. See: Atkins vs. Craig, "Does God Exist?" and Enqvist vs. Craig, "Can the Universe

... the only knowledge we have about the world is empirical."[22] As atheist philosopher of science Massimo Pigliucci muses,

> I don't know what's the matter with physicists these days. It used to be that they were an intellectually sophisticated bunch, with the likes of Einstein and Bohr doing not only brilliant scientific research, but also interested, respectful of, and conversant in other branches of knowledge, particularly philosophy. These days it is much more likely to encounter physicists like Steven Weinberg or Stephen Hawking, who merrily go about dismissing philosophy for the wrong reasons, and quite obviously out of a combination of profound ignorance and hubris (the two often go together, as I'm sure Plato would happily point out). The latest such bore is Lawrence Krauss, of Arizona State University.[23]

Krauss's disrespect for philosophy undergirds and thus undermines his entire project. For example, he argues that while the question of ultimate origins "is usually framed as a philosophical or religious question, it is first and foremost a question about the natural world, and so the appropriate place to try and resolve it, first and foremost, is with science."[24] But this is to conflate all questions about the natural world with *scientific* questions about the natural world. In point of fact, there can be philosophical questions about the natural world, and the question of ultimate origins is one such. Trying to answer this philosophical question whilst side-lining philosophy leads to predictable results.

For example, and returning to Krauss's mantra, *of course* the universe "is the way it is, whether we like it or not." However, one of the ways in which the universe is ("whether we like it or not") is that *it conforms to the basic laws of logic*. One might desire a square-circle, one might very much like 1+1 to equal 7, but we know that the universe isn't going to oblige because these concepts are self-contradictory. Indeed, one cannot issue a denial of the proposition that "reality conforms to the basic laws of logic" without relying upon reality's conformity to the basic laws of logic in the very process of issuing one's denial. One certainly can't base such a denial on the claim that "The universe is the way it is, whether we like it or not"; for *this claim is itself simply a substitution of the logical law of the excluded*

Exist Without God?"

22. Krauss, "Unbelievable: Universe From Nothing?"
23. Pigliucci, "Lawrence Krauss."
24. Krauss, *Universe From Nothing*, xiii.

middle. To argue against the proposition that reality is logically coherent by appealing to the logically coherent statement that "the universe is the way it is, whether we like it or not" is logically incoherent.[25]

Krauss opines that "without science, any definition is just words."[26] After briefly bewailing the fate of our ancestors trying to talk before the invention of science, one might point out that Krauss has reinvented the wonky wheel of logical positivism (complete with its defunct verificationist theory of linguistic meaning) and that his claim that "without science, any definition is just words" falls foul of its own strictures. Such logical incoherence is one among many reasons why, as Bruce R. Reichenbach commented back in 1972: "The era is past when all metaphysical statements or arguments can simply be dismissed as silly or senseless, since they do not meet a preestablished criterion of verifiability."[27]

Krauss has been spotted in the embrace of verificationism before. Randy Everist observes that "the [March 2011] debate between Lawrence Krauss and William Lane Craig brought out some of the claims of scientism in the New Atheist community. In a way, it is highly reminiscent of logical positivism with A.J. Ayer and the old-line atheists of the early-to-mid twentieth century."[28] During the "Question and Answer" time Krauss stated that *"science does what it does, and it determines nonsense from sense by testing."*[29] An astonished Craig responded that Krauss:

> seems to hold to an epistemology which says that we should only believe that which can be scientifically proven, and . . . that itself is a self-contradictory position, because you can't scientifically prove that you should only believe that which can be scientifically proven. So when he says it "distinguishes sense from nonsense," that's old-line verificationism, isn't it, and positivism, which went out with the 30s and 40s. It's a self-defeating position.[30]

As Craig commented afterwards: "I am still amazed . . . when I enter into a debate with someone like a Lawrence Krauss, at how the epistemology

---

25. See: Craig, "Atheist Physicist's Repudiation of Logic."
26. Krauss, *Universe From Nothing*, xiv.
27. Reichenbach, *Cosmological Argument*, ix.
28. Everist, "Can Science Explain Everything?"
29. Krauss, debate with William Lane Craig, 2011.
30. Krauss, debate with William Lane Craig, 2011.

of old-time verificationism and logical positivism *still* casts its long shadow over Western culture."[31]

In the verificationist tradition Krauss complains that "religion and theology . . . muddy the waters . . . by focusing on questions of nothingness without providing any definition of the term based on empirical evidence"[32]—but of course *Krauss cannot provide any definition of this criterion of meaning based on empirical evidence*! Neither is Krauss's criterion of meaning tautologically true (in stark contrast to the tautological principle that "from nothing, nothing comes," to which Krauss objects). Thus Krauss falls foul of his failure to attend to philosophy when it comes to defining terms, and this failure turns the vast bulk of *A Universe From Nothing* into a wild goose chase in which he spends all but four pages (see 174–78) addressing questions *besides* the fundamental question of whether one can get a universe from nothing. As atheist scientist Jerry Coyne complains: "much of the book was *not* about the origin of the universe, but dealt with other matters, like dark energy and the like, that had already been covered in other popular works on physics. Indeed, much of Krauss's book felt like a bait-and-switch."[33] This objection slides off Krauss like water off a duck's back:

> Nothing upsets the philosophers and theologians who disagree with me more than the notion that I, as a scientist, do not truly understand "nothing." (I am tempted to retort here that theologians are experts in nothing.) "Nothing," they insist, is not any of the things I discuss. Nothing is "nonbeing," in some vague and ill-defined sense . . . But . . . surely "nothing" is every bit as physical as "something," especially if it is to be defined as the "absence of something." It then behoves us to understand precisely the physical nature of both these quantities. And without science, any definition is just words.[34]

Interviewed by fellow neo-atheist Sam Harris, Krauss embarrassingly asserts,

> the famous claim, "out of nothing, nothing comes" [is] spurious [because] science has made the something-from-nothing debate irrelevant. It has changed completely our conception of the very

---

31. Craig, "Sam Harris Debate (part 2)."
32. Krauss, debate with William Lane Craig 2011, xvi.
33. Coyne, "Alberts Pans Lawrence Krauss' New Book."
34. Krauss, debate with William Lane Craig 2011, xiii–xiv.

words "something" and "nothing." . . . "something" and "nothing" are physical concepts and therefore are properly the domain of science, not theology or philosophy.[35]

Unfortunately for Krauss, the famous claim that "out of nothing, nothing comes" (a claim that goes back to Parmenides of Elea in the fifth century B.C.) is clearly true *by definition*. To exist or to *be* is to be a something or other, having one or more properties. "Nothing," which is a term of universal negation, is "no thing"—i.e. not a something of any kind at all. "Nothing" does not have any properties (since there's nothing there to have any properties). By definition, then, "nothing" *doesn't have any properties capable of doing anything*—certainly not creating something. Hence, nothing can come "out of" (i.e. be caused by) nothing. Contra Krauss, there's nothing "vague and ill-defined" about this (and not even the self-contradictory verificationist criterion of meaning will avail Krauss at this juncture).

Furthermore, if Krauss means to deny the self-evident principle of sufficient reason and claim that things can just exist or pop into being with no cause or explanation of their existence, then he has abandoned serious metaphysics (indeed, he explicitly rejects metaphysics in the name of scientism). On such a theory there's literally no reason why the universe exists *rather than just a tea set* (and, contrary to empirical observation, no reason why tea sets don't fluctuate in and out of existence randomly for no reason at all)!

As for Krauss's claim that "surely 'nothing' is every bit as physical as 'something.'"—on the one hand this is so drastically idiosyncratic that one hardly knows where to begin; whereas, on the other hand, this claim reveals why A Universe From Nothing is a veritable school of red herrings. Faced with the philosophical question of ultimate origins, *Krauss simply changes the subject* to discuss the scientific question of how one natural thing (e.g. the big bang) might possibly have been caused by some other natural thing (e.g. a multi-verse). Krauss may complain that "religion and theology . . . muddy the waters . . . by focusing on questions of nothingness without providing any definition of the term based on empirical evidence"[36]—but any definition of nothing "based on empirical evidence" would be a definition of "nothing" that has nothing to do with the philosophical questions of why there is something rather than nothing, or whether or not the existence of an empirical realm entails or is best explained by a non-empirical

---

35. Krauss in Harris, "Everything and Nothing."
36. Krauss, *Universe From Nothing*, xvi.

(metaphysical) order of reality. Hence page 149 of *A Universe From Nothing* contains the candid admission that the kind of "nothing" Krauss has been discussing thus far is,

> the simplest version of nothing, namely empty space. For the moment, I will assume space exists, with nothing at all in it, and that the laws of physics also exist. Once again, I realise that in the revised versions of nothingness that those who wish to continually redefine the word so that no scientific definition is practical, this version of nothing doesn't cut the mustard. However, I suspect that, at the times of Plato and Aquinas, when they pondered why there was something rather than nothing, empty space with nothing in it was probably a good approximation of what they were thinking about.[37]

Of course, it's Krauss who is redefining terms here (moreover, the only way in which "something" and "nothing" could be "physical concepts," as Krauss claims, is on the assumption of a physicalist metaphysics—an assumption that makes Krauss's argument against the need for a Creator question begging). In what philosophers call "ordinary language" the poor student's fridge may indeed be "full of nothing," containing "nothing but empty space;" but it is extremely naïve to expect precise metaphysical debate to be conducted wholly in "ordinary language." As William E. Caroll writes: "The desire to separate the natural sciences from the alleged contamination of the 'word games' of philosophy and theology is not new; now, as always, it reveals an impoverished philosophical judgement."[38]

Every discipline (including science) has its own technical terminology with its own history of usage that needs to be understood by anyone who wishes to be part of the ongoing conversation within that discipline. Krauss's antipathy towards philosophy means that he blunders into the metaphysical debate about origins as an ill-prepared layperson. Krauss may "suspect that, at the times of Plato and Aquinas, when they pondered why there was something rather than nothing, empty space with nothing in it was probably a good approximation of what they were thinking about,"[39] but these suspicions are informed by his own anti-philosophical prejudice rather than by the historical facts. Aristotle wittily defined nothing as "what

---

37. Krauss, *Universe From Nothing*, 149.
38. Caroll, "Science of Nothing."
39. Krauss, *Universe From Nothing*, 149.

rocks think about."[40] The point being, of course, that rocks don't think about anything at all. Robert J. Spitzer notes that:

> Parmenides and Plato . . . use the term "nothing" to mean "nothing" (i.e. "that which there is no such thing as'). Nothing should not be thought to be a vacuum or a void (which is dimensional and orientable—where you can have more or less space); and it is certainly not a physical law. Inasmuch as the laws of physics have real physical effects, they must be considered to be something physical.[41]

Paul Copan reports,

> Augustine argued that since God alone is Being, he willed to exist what formerly did not exist. So he is not a mere shaper of formless and eternal primordial matter: "You did not work as a human craftsman does, making one thing out of something else as his mind directs . . . Your Word alone created [heaven and earth]."[42]

Likewise, when Thomas Aquinas writes about "nothing" in his "third way" argument he certainly seems to have the traditional concept of absolute nothingness in mind:

> That which does not exist begins to exist only through something already existing. Therefore if at one time nothing was in existence, it would have been impossible for anything to have begun to exist; and thus now nothing would be in existence—which is absurd.[43]

Indeed, *Krauss himself* refers elsewhere to "the classical ontological definition of nothing as 'the absence of anything' . . ."[44] Krauss admits on page 152 of *A Universe From Nothing* that "it would be disingenuous to suggest that empty space endowed with energy, which drives inflation, is really *nothing.*"[45] On page 172 Krauss acknowledges: "All of the examples I have provided thus far indeed involve creation of something from what one should be tempted to consider as nothing, but the rules for that creation, i.e.

---

40. Aristotle, quoted by Zacharias, *Can Man Live Without God*, 131.
41. Spitzer, "Metaphysics of Dr Stephen Hawking."
42. Copan, "Creatio Ex Nihilo A Post-Biblical Invention?."
43. Aquinas, quoted by Maydole, "Third Way Modalized."
44. Krauss, "Consolation of Philosophy."
45. Krauss, *Universe From Nothing*, 152.

the laws of physics, were pre-ordained. Where do the rules come from?"[46] Thus Stephen Hawking asks:

> Even if there is only one possible unified theory, it is just a set of rules and equations. What is it that breathes fire into the equations and makes a universe for them to describe? The usual approach of science of constructing a mathematical model cannot answer the questions of why there should be a universe for the model to describe. Why does the universe go to all the bother of existing?[47]

Hawking's question—sidestepped by Krauss (see 142, 172–74)—itself sidesteps the question of what ontology can be attributed to physical laws *in the supposed absence of any physical reality for them to describe or any mind/s to conceive of them*. Speaking as an atheist, Peter Atkins comments: "You have to realize that physical laws, which are summaries of observed behaviour, come into existence as a universe comes into existence . . ."[48]

By page 174 of *A Universe From Nothing* Krauss still hasn't gotten around to addressing the million dollar question: "I have focused on either the creation of something from preexisting empty space or the creation of empty space from no space at all . . . I have not addressed, directly, however . . . what some may view as the question of First Cause."[49] None of the venerable philosophers mentioned by Krauss would have mistaken any of his speculations about the cosmos arising from some pre-existent naturalistic reality or other as addressing what Leibniz called "the first question" of "why there exists something rather than nothing." Neither does Sam Harris, who in the course of an interview with Krauss commented:

> You have described three gradations of nothing—empty space, the absence of space, and the absence of physical laws. It seems to me that this last condition—the absence of any laws that might have caused or constrained the emergence of matter and space-time—really is a case of "nothing" in the strictest sense. It strikes me as genuinely incomprehensible that anything—laws, energy, etc.—could spring out of it.[50]

---

46. Krauss, *Universe From Nothing*, 172.
47. Hawking, *Brief History of Time*, http://en.wikiquote.org/wiki/Stephen_Hawking.
48. Atkins, "Does God Exist?"
49. Krauss, *Universe From Nothing*, 174.
50. Harris, "Everything and Nothing."

A UNIVERSE FROM SOMEONE

David Albert, an atheist philosopher of physics at Columbia University, is devastating in his review of *A Universe From Nothing*:

> The fundamental laws of nature . . . have no bearing whatsoever on questions of where the elementary stuff came from, or of why the world should have consisted of the particular elementary stuff it does, as opposed to something else, or to nothing at all. The fundamental physical laws that Krauss is talking about in *A Universe From Nothing* — the laws of relativistic quantum field theories — are no exception to this. The . . . elementary physical stuff of the world, according to the standard presentations of relativistic quantum field theories, consists (unsurprisingly) of relativistic quantum fields. And the fundamental laws of this theory . . . have nothing whatsoever to say on the subject of where those fields came from, or of why the world should have consisted of the particular kinds of fields it does, or of why it should have consisted of fields at all, or of why there should have been a world in the first place. Period. Case closed. End of story . . . Krauss seems to be thinking that these vacuum states amount to the relativistic-quantum-field-theoretical version of there *not being any physical stuff at all*. And he has an argument — or thinks he does — that the laws of relativistic quantum field theories entail that vacuum states are unstable. And that, in a nutshell, is the account he proposes of why there should be something rather than nothing. But that's just not right. Relativistic-quantum-field-theoretical vacuum states — no less than giraffes or refrigerators or solar systems — are particular arrangements of *elementary physical stuff*. The true relativistic-quantum-fieldtheoretical equivalent to there not being any physical stuff at all isn't this or that particular arrangement of the fields — what it is (obviously, and ineluctably, and on the contrary) is the simple *absence* of the fields! The fact that some arrangements of fields happen to correspond to the existence of particles and some don't is not a whit more mysterious than the fact that some of the possible arrangements of my fingers happen to correspond to the existence of a fist and some don't. And the fact that particles can pop in and out of existence, over time, as those fields rearrange themselves, is not a whit more mysterious than the fact that fists can pop in and out of existence, over time, as my fingers rearrange themselves. And none of these poppings . . . amount to anything even remotely in the neighborhood of a creation from nothing.[51]

---

51. Albert, "Origin of Everything."

In a telling display of intellectual hubris, Krauss publicly responded to Albert's review by saying "he is a philosopher not a physicist, so I discounted it"[52] (in point of fact, while David Albert is the Frederick E. Woodbridge Professor of Philosophy at Columbia University, he has a PhD in Theoretical Physics from Rockefeller University).

When Krauss finally turns his attention to the question the title of his book, he recognizes "two possibilities. Either . . . some divine being who is not bound by the laws or they arise by some less supernatural mechanism."[53] On the one hand, any naturalistic "mechanism" must involve some physical law or other (and thus, one would think, some physical reality described by that law), which provides nothing but a new way to raise the ultimate question of origins: "Why does this law exist?" On the other hand, if the "mechanism" Krauss has in mind is non-naturalistic, then Krauss is self-confessedly left with only one remaining option: *A Universe From Someone*. On the horns of this dilemma, Krauss's escape hatch is a self-contradictory attempt to use the authority of science to deny the authority of logic:

> The metaphysical "rule," which is held as an ironclad conviction by those with whom I have debated the issue of creation, namely that "*out of nothing nothing comes*," has no foundation in science.[54]

Indeed, none of the laws of logic (all of which science must presuppose on pain of incoherence) has a "foundation in science;" but so what? "Arguing that it is self-evident, unwavering, and unassailable [that 'from nothing, nothing comes']" alleges Krauss, represents "an unwillingness to recognize the simple fact that nature may be cleverer than philosophers or theologians."[55] Not at all! Rather, it represents a willingness to recognize the simple fact that logic is undeniable and that incoherent propositions are necessarily false. As William Lane Craig says: "If the alternative to theism is to deny logic, well, it seems to me that the non-theist is in really serious trouble there—they can never again say that theists are irrational for believing what we do."[56]

Grasping at one last logical straw (note that he thus engages in the double standard of holding theists to account by logic whilst exempting

---

52. Krauss in Brierley, "Universe From Nothing?"
53. Krauss, *Universe From Nothing*, 172.
54. Krauss, *Universe From Nothing*, 174.
55. Krauss, *Universe From Nothing*, 174.
56. Craig, "Can the Universe Exist Without God?"

atheism from the same duty), Krauss makes an objection that only serves to reveal his failure to grasp what is meant by the doctrine of creation "ex nihilo:"

> Those who argue that out of nothing nothing comes seem perfectly content with the quixotic notion that somehow God can get around this. But once again, if one requires that the notion of true nothingness requires not even the *potential* for existence, then surely God cannot work his wonders, because if he does cause existence from nonexistence, there must have been the potential for existence.[57]

Those who argue that "out of nothing nothing comes" are *not* content with the incoherent notion that "God can get around this." While true nothingness does of course require that not even the *potential* for existence exists (since any potential must be grounded in something actual), theists do *not* believe that God's creating the universe is an instance of something coming from nothing, since they do of course believe that God exists (necessarily) and that the potential for the existence of everything besides God exists *in God*.

Krauss is obviously labouring under the false impression that creation *ex nihilo* means "creation out of nothing," as if "nothing" were a sort of something somehow used by a non-existent God in the creation of the cosmos. However, to create *ex nihilo* is by definition not a matter of re-arranging pre-existing things, and certainly not of re-arranging a pre-existent "nothing," but rather of *arranging for there to be things* of some sort or other (beside God) *in the first place*. In other words, the doctrine of creation *ex nihilo* distinguishes between creating *by re-arranging pre-existent "stuff"* (e.g. the sort of creation envisaged by Plato for his "Demiurge"), and creating a new form of reality (like a universe) *without using pre-existing "stuff"* (e.g. Gen 1:1).[58] Philosophers call the second type of creation "*creatio ex nihilo*," meaning "creation [by a creator] not out of any pre-existing stuff." Belief in a necessarily existent being who grounds the potential for the existence of contingent things and who actualizes that potential via a freely chosen act of omnipotence is a logically coherent answer to the question of why the physical universe exists. Moreover, this answer is supported by the cosmological argument.

---

57. Krauss, *Universe From Nothing*, 174.
58. See: Copan, "Creatio Ex Nihilo A Post-Biblical Invention?"

In the face of the logically coherent answer supported by the Leibnizian cosmological argument, Krauss would dearly like to change the topic: "what is really useful is not pondering this question . . ."[59] As a result, he produces a book that's overwhelmingly devoted to questions besides the one on the front cover. Krauss's anti-philosophical prejudice leads him to embrace a verificationalist stance long ago abandoned by philosophers as self-contradictory and to toy with rejecting the ultimate question of origins as meaningless. Despite this, Krauss spends a handful of pages attempting to explain why there is something rather than nothing. The attempt leads him to beg the question against theism, to reject logic in the name of science and to embrace a double standard. This kluge of fallacies convinced Richard Dawkins to put his name to the incoherent assertion that "nothingness is unstable: something was almost bound to spring into existence from it';[60] which only goes to show just how intellectually unstable the foundations of neo-atheism are.

---

59. Krauss, *Universe From Nothing*, 178.
60. Dawkins, "Afterword" in Krauss, *Universe From Nothing*, 189.

6

A Brief Introduction to and Defence of the Modern Ontological Argument[1]

The Greek word *ontos* means "being," and the ontological argument for God (OA for short) begins with thinking about what sort of being God is supposed to be, particularly what manner of being or existence he's supposed to have if he exists. The OA was first given in 1078 by a Benedictine monk named Anselm. Philosophers have critiqued and defended many versions of the OA, but Anselm's central insight was that "God" can be defined as "a being than which nothing greater can be conceived." If one could think of a being greater than "God," then that greater being, rather than the lesser being, would deserve the title "God." Hence *if* God exists *then* he is *by definition* "the greatest possible being" or "the maximally great being;" that is, God is by definition that being with the greatest possible set of great-making properties, where a "great-making property" is *any objective property that it is* (a) *intrinsically good to have* ("which endows its bearer with some measure of value, or greatness, or metaphysical stature, regardless of external circumstances"[2]) *and which* (b) *has a logical maximum*.

Christian philosopher of religion Alvin Plantinga kick-started a philosophical re-evaluation of the traditional arguments for God in his 1974 book *The Nature of Necessity* by laying out a logically valid version of the OA. Plantinga's OA drew on Leibnitz's insight that the OA implicitly

---

1. This paper was originally published in the Forum section of Scandinavian apologetics journal *Theofilos*, Volume 7, 2015:3.

2. Morris, *Our Idea of God*, 35.

assumes that the concept of God (of "that than which nothing greater can be conceived") is logically coherent. Defining God as a "maximally great being" (a being who possesses the greatest possible set of great making properties), Plantinga argued that a maximally great being *must exist if its existence is possible*, because "necessary existence is a great making property."[3] Given the additional premise that "the existence of a maximally great being is *possible*,"[4] it follows that a maximally great being therefore "exists, and exists necessarily."[5]

Plantinga used the philosophical vocabulary of "possible worlds" (logically self-consistent descriptions of reality as a whole) and symbolic logic to lay out his argument in technical detail, but his OA can be summarised in ordinary language as follows:

1. It is possible that a maximally great being exists.
2. If it is possible that a maximally great being exists, then a maximally great being exists in at least one "possible world."
3. If a maximally great being exists in one "possible world," then it exists in every "possible world."
4. If a maximally great being exists in every "possible world," then it exists in the actual world (since the actual world is by definition a "possible world").
5. Therefore, a maximally great being exists.[6]

Indeed, the OA can be further condensed into a single logically valid syllogism as follows:

1. If it is possible that God (a "maximally great being') exists, then God exists.
2. It is possible that God exists.
3. Therefore, God exists.

---

3. Plantinga, *God, Freedom and Evil*, from Peterson *et al*, *Philosophy of Religion: Selected Readings*, 158.

4. Plantinga, *God, Freedom and Evil*, from Peterson *et al*, *Philosophy of Religion: Selected Readings*, 163.

5. Plantinga, *God, Freedom and Evil*, from Peterson *et al*, *Philosophy of Religion: Selected Readings*, 159.

6. See: Craig, "Ontological Argument," 128.

As the "greatest possible being," God is *by definition* a necessary being (since it is clearly ontologically greater to exist necessarily rather than contingently). A necessary being is *by definition* a being that must exist (i.e. which cannot not exist) if its existence is possible. Thus most philosophers agree that *if* God's existence is possible, *then*, as a necessary being, he must exist. Hence "the person who wishes to deny that God exists must claim that God's existence is impossible."[7] "God" is by definition a being whose existence is *either actual or impossible*. Therefore, *if* "God" is not impossible, *then* he must be actual.

In Defence of the Ontological Argument

Starting with Gaunilo of Marmoutiers in the eleventh century, philosophers have critiqued the Ontological Argument (OA) by suggesting that if it were logically valid then one could use it to prove the existence of all sorts of patently ridiculous things, such as "the most perfect island conceivable" (Gaunilo's example). The thought is that since these results are patently absurd, the OA must be invalid. Such "parodies" of the OA are an attempt at a *reductio ad absurdum* of the argument. However, these parodies fail to attend to the crucial role played by great-making properties (especially necessary existence), and/or the uniqueness of the concept of "the greatest possible being," in the OA. As William Lane Craig observes: "the properties that go to make up maximal excellence ... have intrinsic maximum values, whereas the excellent-making properties of things like islands do not ... Thus there cannot be a most perfect or greatest conceivable island."[8] Yujin Nagasawa agrees: "For any island it is always possible to make it greater by adding, for example, one more beautiful palm tree or one more pleasant beach. The island objection is, therefore, unsuccessful."[9]

To appreciate the OA it is crucial to understand the concept of a "great-making property" and the crucial role in the OA of the great-making property known as "necessary existence." A "great-making property" is any property that (a) *endows its bearer with some measure of objective value and which* (b) *admits of a logical maximum*. A whale isn't more valuable than you because it's bigger than you; and however big a whale we imagine, it's always possible to imagine a bigger one. Thus size isn't a great-making

---

7. Evans, *Philosophy of Religion*, 50.
8. Craig, "Ontological Argument," 129–30.
9. Nagasawa, *The Existence of God*, 31.

property. On the other hand, *power* is a great-making property, one that has a logical maximum in the quality of being "omnipotent." Likewise, *necessary being* is the maximal instantiation of the great-making property of necessary being (this just happens to be a great-making property the logical maximum degree of which is also its only possible degree). Hence, even if Immanuel Kant was right to argue that saying something "exists" doesn't add to our knowledge of its properties, to say that something "exists necessarily" certainly *does* add to our knowledge of its properties. Thus God couldn't just happen not to exist *despite his existence being possible*. To deny the existence of the Loch Ness Monster, one needn't claim that its existence is impossible. However, to deny the existence of God one *must* make the *metaphysically stronger claim* that God's existence is *impossible*. But the claim that God exists clearly isn't on a *par* with the claim that there exists a round square (this claim is obviously incoherent). Many atheists acknowledge that the idea of God is coherent. Indeed, atheist Richard Carrier warns that arguments for thinking otherwise are,

> not valid, since any definition of god (or his properties) that is illogical can just be revised to be logical. So in effect, Arguments from Incoherence aren't really arguments for atheism, but for the reform of theology.[10]

Indeed, it might be argued that at least some of God's great-making properties are in a sense identical:

> When we speak of different perfections, such as omniscience or omnipotence, we connote different things, and so the assertions have different meanings. Nevertheless, perhaps all of these different meanings have the same denotation; that is, perhaps they refer to some single capacity in God. This does not seem implausible. After all . . . perhaps being omnipotent entails being omniscient, perhaps being perfectly loving entails being perfectly just, and so forth.[11]

Nagasawa argues that "*a statement about divine omniscience can be restated in terms of a divine epistemic power.* This principle reveals a connection between divine omniscience and omnipotence . . . omniscience can be understood as God's exercising a particular part—the epistemic part—of

---

10. Carrier, *Sense and Goodness Without God*, 276.
11. Richards, "Divine Simplicity," 169.

His omnipotence."[12] If correct, this analysis of great-making properties decreases the atheist's opportunities for claiming that "God" has incompatible properties (although it still leaves open questions about the internal coherence of those properties). For example, this analysis entails that *if* necessary existence is compatible with omnipotence *then* it is necessarily compatible with omniscience, etc.

Moreover, humans exhibit non-maximal degrees of great-making properties (such as power, cognitive excellence and goodness), and this supports the hypothesis that *maximal degrees* of great-making properties can co-exist over the hypothesis that they cannot.

What if the atheist grants that *some* great-making properties can coexist in the same being, but makes a crucial exception for necessary existence? We might ask what reason the atheist has to think that the former great-making properties are compatible with one another but incompatible with necessary existence? It wouldn't do to answer by stating that while, for example, omniscience is in a sense identical to omnipotence, neither quality is identical with necessary existence. After all, properties can coexist in the same being without being identical. Given that no principled answer to our question is forthcoming, Occam's razor rules against making the atheist's proposed distinction. That is, to draw a distinction between great-making properties that can and can't coexist, and to insist without sufficient justification that necessary existence just happens to fall into the latter category, so that the OA is unsound, is an *ad hoc* leap of blind faith on the part of the atheist.

Josef Seifert argues that great-making properties "must be all compatible with each other, for it contradicts the nature of that, which it is absolutely speaking, better to possess than not to possess to exclude any other such perfection. Otherwise a logical contradiction would arise in that it would be simultaneously better to possess perfection A (a pure perfection) and not to possess it (because it would exclude another pure perfection B)."[13] The concept of "the greatest possible being" is of course the concept of the greatest possible set of great-making properties *that can coexist*. Seifert defines great-making properties as properties that it is "absolutely speaking, better to possess than not to possess." Then he argues that it is self-contradictory to make a distinction between "the set of great-making properties that *can* coexist" and "the set of great-making properties that

---

12. Nagasawa, "Omniscience and Knowledge *De Se.*"
13. Seifert in Varghese, ed. *Great Thinkers on Great Questions*, 131.

cannot coexist," since drawing this distinction means affirming the existence of properties that are *greater* than properties that it is "absolutely speaking, better to possess than not to possess."[14]

Then again, one might support the claim that God's existence is possible by arguing negatively against the coherence and/or possibility of alternative conceptions of ultimate reality (such as pantheism[15] and metaphysical naturalism)[16] and/or by supporting the theistic hypothesis via all the other arguments of natural theology. Both approaches provide independent grounds for thinking that the crucial second premise of the ontological argument is more plausibly true than its denial.

None of this implies that the OA provides us with an entirely perspicuous concept of divinity, let alone a knock-down argument for His existence. Nevertheless, for the OA to be a sound argument all that's required of its crucial second premise is that it be *more plausibly true than its denial in the light of our total available evidence*. The ontological argument thus ties together the thrust of the cumulative case for theism and has something to contribute to the project of natural theology.

---

14 Seifert, *Great Thinkers on Great Questions*, 131.

15. See: Geisler, *Baker Encyclopedia of Christian Apologetics*, 580–83; Groothuis, *Christian Apologetics*, 326–329.

16. See: Craig and Moreland, ed.'s. *Naturalism*; Goetz and Taliaferro, *Naturalism*; Menuge, *Agents under Fire*; Reppert, *Lewis' Dangerous Idea*.

7

A Beginner's Guide to the Theistic Argument from Desire[1]

The theistic "argument from desire" (AFD) is a family of arguments that move from an analysis of human desire to the conclusion that God exists (or that something like "eternal life in relationship with God" is the true human *telos*, goal or purpose). This argument was popularized in the twentieth century by C.S. Lewis, who sought to understand an "unsatisfied desire which is itself more desirable than any other satisfaction," a mystical experience to which he gave the technical label "joy"[2] (and which writers in the German Romantic tradition called *Sehnsucht*): the bitter-sweet experience of feeling drawn to a transcendent and innately desirable "something more" beyond one's worldly grasp. This experience is *occasioned but not satisfied by* various worldly "triggers" that are somewhat person-relative, but often have to do with beauty and/or natural grandeur (i.e. what the Romantics called "the sublime").

Lewis produced the preeminent literary engagement with *Sehnsucht* in English, contemplating "joy" in works of allegory, apologetics, autobiography and theology, and evoking "joy" in his fiction. He wasn't the first to explore this theme, which can be found in the Jewish scriptures (Psalm

---

1. This article was originally commissioned and published online by the Solas Centre for Public Christianity (www.solas-cpc.org/) on 31st August 2020 (www.solas-cpc.org/a-beginners-guide-to-the-theistic-argument-from-desire/) and is republished here with permission.

2. Lewis, *Surprised by Joy*, 12.

42 opens with the declaration that: "As the deer pants for pants for streams of water, so my soul pants for you, my God." *Ecclesiastes* can be read as a meditation upon this theme[3]). Nor was he the first to make a theistic AFD—something done by Boëthius, Pascal, Thomas Chalmers and G.K. Chesterton before him. Nor was he the only scholar of his era to do so (contemporaries who defended the AFD included C.E.M. Joad, Jacques Maritain and Leslie D. Weatherhead). However, it's *primarily* due to Lewis' wide-ranging discussion of the AFD that many contemporary scholars have become interested in exploring, critiquing and/or defending a variety of arguments from desire, with attention paid to the argument by Gregory Bassham, Todd Buras, Michael Cantrell, Winfried Corduan, C. Stephen Evans, Norman L. Geisler, John Haldane, Robert Hoyler, Peter Kreeft, Alister McGrath, Thomas V. Morris, Alvin Plantinga, Joe Puckett Jr., Richard Purtill, Victor Reppert, Erik Wielenberg, etc.

A Cumulative AFD

The AFD is best thought of as a cumulative argument composed of a variety of sub-arguments with different logical formulations.[4] I only have space to sketch some of these arguments here:

Prima Facie AFD

Samuel Alexander's *Space, Time and Deity* (1916–18) introduced C.S. Lewis to the distinction between "enjoyment" and "contemplation," a distinction Lewis would later illustrate in terms of looking *at* or looking *along* a beam of light. To take the experience of "joy" at face value means looking *along* it towards an innately desirable "transcendent other." Now, as Lewis points out: "As soon as you have grasped this simple distinction [between looking at and looking along], it raises a question. You get one experience of a thing when you look along it and another when you look at it. Which is the "true" or "valid" experience?"[5] Lewis observes:

> It has . . . come to be taken for granted that the external account of a thing somehow refutes or "debunks" the account given from

---

3. See: Walton, "Who Wrote Ecclesiastes?"; Kreeft, *Three Philosophies of Life*.

4. See: Bassham, ed. *C.S. Lewis' Apologetics*; Williams, "In Defence of Arguments from Desire."

5. Lewis, "Meditation in a Toolshed," 51.

inside. "All these moral ideas which look so transcendental and beautiful from inside," says the wiseacre, "are really only a mass of biological instincts and inherited taboos." And no one plays the game the other way round by replying, "If you will only step inside, the things that look to you like instincts and taboos will suddenly reveal their real and transcendental nature."[6]

Lewis argues that this reductive impulse must be resisted on at least some occasions because its generalization is incoherent: "you can step outside one experience only by stepping inside another. Therefore, if all inside experiences are misleading, we are always misled."[7] Moreover, Lewis' example of discovering that "the inside vision of the savage's dance to Nyonga may be found deceptive because we find reason to believe that crops and babies are not really affected by it"[8] illustrates the *presumption of innocence* conferred in the absence of sufficient reason for doubt upon enjoyed (i.e. looked along) experiences. Lewis concludes "we must take each case on its merits."[9]

Contemporary epistemology is well disposed to playing the game "the other way round." For example, consider the "reformed epistemology" of Alvin Plantinga, who argues for the *properly basic* status of theistic belief evoked by desire.[10]

To further motivate taking "joy" at face value, one can appeal to the epistemic principle "that we ought to believe that things are as they seem to be (in the epistemic sense) unless and until we have evidence that we are mistaken."[11] This basic principle of rationality puts the burden of proof upon the shoulders of the sceptic who claims that, despite appearances, to look along a joy is to experience a delusion rather than the insight into the nature of reality it seems to be from the inside.

Abductive AFD

Alister McGrath notes that "Lewis's reflections on desire focus on two themes . . . a general sense of longing for something . . . and a Christian

6. Lewis, "Meditation in a Toolshed," 52.
7. Lewis, "Meditation in a Toolshed," 54.
8. Lewis, "Meditation in a Toolshed," 52.
9. Lewis, "Meditation in a Toolshed," 52.
10. Plantinga, *Warranted Christian Belief*, 307.
11. Swinburne, *Is There A God?* rev. ed., 115.

affirmation that God alone is the heart's true desire . . ."[12] For McGrath, these themes form the two prongs of an *abductive* argument for the Judeo-Christian explanation of "joy:"

> Lewis saw this line of thought as demonstrating the correlation of faith with experience, exploring the "empirical adequacy" of the Christian way of seeing reality with what we experience within ourselves . . . Christianity . . . tells us that this sense of longing for God is exactly what we should expect, since we are created to relate to God. It fits in with a Christian way of thinking, thus providing indirect confirmation of its reliability.[13]

Victor Reppert likewise formulates the AFD as an *abductive* argument:

> On Christian theism God's intention in creating humans is to fit them for eternity in God's presence. As such, it stands to reason that we should find ourselves dissatisfied with worldly satisfactions. Let's put the likelihood that we should long for the infinite given theism at 0.9 . . . I wouldn't say that such desires couldn't possibly arise in an atheistic world . . . But how likely would they arise in such a world? So long as the answer is "less likely than in a theistic world," the presence of these desires confirms theism. Let's say that, if we don't know whether theism is true or not, the likelihood that these desires should arise is 0.7. Plugging these values into Bayes' theorem, we go from 0.5 likelihood that theism is true to a 0.643 likelihood that theism is true. Thus . . . the argument from desire confirms theism.[14]

Atheist Erik Wielenberg tries to explain away "joy" in terms of naturalistic evolutionary psychology (NEP).[15] Wielenberg's NEP hypothesis, which only engages with "two features of joy—the restlessness it induces and the nebulousness of its object,"[16] and thereby lacks explanatory scope, suggests that the former feature "might" be advantageous *if joy arose*: "Early humans favored with a chronic, ill-defined restlessness of heart might have outcompeted other humans who were naturally more sedentary and complacent." However, we might think that early humans afflicted with "a chronic, ill-defined restlessness of heart" would be out-competed

---

12. McGrath, *Intellectual World of C.S. Lewis*, 106.
13. McGrath, *Mere Apologetics*, 110–11.
14. Reppert, "Bayesian Argument from Desire."
15. See: Bassham ed., *Lewis' Apologetics*.
16. Wielenberg, quoted in Bassham ed., *Lewis' Apologetics*.

by humans free from such existential ennui! Again, Wielenberg suggests the somewhat nebulous nature of joy "might" be advantageous *if joy arose*: "Joy's . . . lack of a clear intentional object, might have led early humans down Lewisian 'false paths' such as the pursuit of sex, power, and adventure, that did have direct fitness advantages."[17] Wielenberg's use of "might" doesn't inspire confidence in either case, indicating that his hypothesis has a low degree of explanatory power.

Finally, Wielenberg offers *no explanation for the appearance of "joy" in our gene-pool*, only for its selection *should it appear*. As Reppert argues,

> Natural desires that are unfulfillable on earth is precisely what you should expect . . . from the point of view of theism. I seriously doubt that we can do this from the point of view of naturalism, even if a half-way-decent-looking evolutionary explanation of how such desires could arise were forthcoming . . .[18]

Inductive AFD

In *Mere Christianity* Lewis frames the AFD *inferentially*:

> Creatures are not born with desires unless satisfaction for those desires exists. A baby feels hunger: well, there is such a thing as food. A duckling wants to swim: well, there is such a thing as water . . . If I find in myself a desire which no experience in this world can satisfy, the most probable explanation is that I was made for another world.[19]

Trent Dougherty likewise presents the AFD as "a defeasible inference [wherein] the premises could be true and the conclusion yet false, but they bear *prima facie* support for the conclusion"[20]:

1. Humans have by nature a desire for the transcendent.
2. Most natural desires are such that there exists some object capable of satisfying them.
3. There is probably something transcendent.

---

17. Bassham summarizing Wielenberg in Bassham ed., *Lewis' Apologetics*, 116–17.
18. Reppert, "Bayesian Argument from Desire."
19. Lewis. *Mere Christianity*, 113.
20. Dougherty, "Argument from Desire."

Aristotelian AFD

In the preface to the third edition of *The Pilgrim's Regress*, Lewis offered a *deductive* AFD:

> If a man diligently followed this desire, pursuing the false objects until their falsity appeared and then resolutely abandoning them, he must come at last to the clear knowledge that the human soul was made to enjoy some object that is never fully given . . . in our present mode of subjective and spatio-temporal experience. This Desire was, in the soul, as the Siege Perilous in Arthur's castle–the chair in which only one could sit. And *if nature makes nothing in vain*, the One who can sit in this chair must exist.[21]

Here Lewis assumes Aristotle's (controversial) dictum that "nature makes nothing in vain."[22]

1. Nature makes nothing in vain.
2. Humans have a natural desire, joy, that would be vain unless some object that is never fully given in our present mode of existence is obtainable by humans in some future mode of existence.
3. Therefore, the object of joy must exist and be obtainable in some future mode of human existence.

One can set to one side the *universality* of Aristotle's dictum while still giving a *deductive* argument based upon *a restricted application of Aristotle's dictum to innate human desires*:

1. Nature makes no type of innate human desire in vain.
2. Humans have innate desires that would be vain if God doesn't exist.
3. Therefore, God exists.

Inductive Aristotelian arguments from desire can be mounted upon the premises that "most types of things in nature are not made in vain" or that "the majority of innate human desires are not made in vain."

We could interpret Aristotle's dictum *as a heuristic principle*.[23] A principle such as "We should assume that no [type of] natural thing exists

---

21. Lewis, *Pilgrim's Regress*, 15, emphasis mine.

22. Aristotle, *Generation of Animals*, quoted in Brodie, "Aristotle's Elusive Summum Bonum."

23. See: Mariska Leunissen's reading of Aristotle in *Explanation and Teleology in*

in vain until and unless we are shown otherwise" could serve as a premise in a *deductive heuristic* AFD:

1. Humans have natural desires that would be in vain if God doesn't exist.
2. We should assume that no [type of] natural thing exists in vain until and unless we are shown otherwise.
3. Therefore (until and unless we are shown that the relevant natural desires exist in vain) we should assume that God exists.

Reductio AFD

In *Mere Christianity* (1952), Lewis framed the AFD as a *reductio*:

> If I find in myself a desire which no experience in this world can satisfy, the most probable explanation is that I was made for another world. If none of my earthly pleasures satisfy it, that does not prove *that the universe is a fraud*. Probably earthly pleasures were never meant to satisfy it, but only to arouse it, to suggest the real thing.[24]

Various *reductio* arguments from *existentially relevant human desires* and the denial of the existential claim that human life is "absurd" can be made. For example:

1. Given an instantiated kind K possessing innate existential desires, the existence of K would be absurd to the extent that it is impossible for any member of K to have those existential desires satisfied.
2. Humans are an instantiated kind K with innate existential desires that are [probably] impossible to satisfy unless God exists.
3. Therefore, unless God exists, the existence of K is [probably] absurd (at least to a substantial extent).
4. However, the existence of K is [probably] not absurd (at least, not to any substantial extent).
5. Therefore, God [probably] exists.

Aristotle's Science of Nature.

24. Lewis, *Mere Christianity*, 113, emphasis mine.

I contend that premise 4 is an intuitively plausible belief that should be treated as innocent until proven guilty.

Conclusion

The argument from desire points to various existentially relevant desires the fulfilment of which plausibly require God's existence. The arguments from these desires are mutually consistent, are more powerful when taken together, and most powerful when considered as part of the overall case for Christian theism.

8

Natural Theology and Science in Contemporary Apologetic Context

An Overview[1]

Science, Natural Philosophy, and Natural Theology

In his "Address to the Clergy," John Wesley (1703–91) urged:

> Some knowledge of the sciences also, is . . . expedient . . . the knowledge of one . . . is even necessary . . . I mean logic. For what is this, if rightly understood, but the art of good sense, of apprehending things clearly, judging truly, and reasoning conclusively? What is it, viewed in another light, but the art of learning and teaching; whether by convincing or persuading? What is there, then, in the whole compass of science, to be desired in comparison of it? . . . Should not a Minister be acquainted too with at least the general grounds of natural philosophy? Is not this a great help to the accurate understanding of several passages of Scripture? Assisted by this, he may himself comprehend, and on proper occasions explain to others, how the invisible things of God are seen from the creation of the world; how "the heavens declare the glory of God, and the firmament showeth his handiwork;" till they cry out,

---

1. This is a slightly revised version of an essay that first appeared as an introduction to the December 2020 *Supplement* edition of the Nordic academic open access journal *Theofilos* (https://theofilos.no/) on "Science, Natural Theology, and Christian Apologetics," which I guest-edited.

The entire supplement is available online: https://theofilos.no/issues/theofilos-supplement-2020-1/.

The entire supplement is available as a pdf to download: https://theofilos.no/wp-content/uploads/2021/02/Theofilos-vol-12-nr-1-2020-Supplement-Komplett-NY-210211.pdf.

"O Lord, how manifold are thy works! In wisdom hast thou made them all."[2]

To grasp the meaning of Wesley's advice, it helps to know that the Latin word *scientia* (from which we derive the word "science") simply meant "knowledge." For scholars from classical times until the nineteenth century, *every* academic discipline that laid claim to knowledge was by definition *scientific*. This included the sciences of *theology* ('the queen of sciences') and theology's "handmaid" *philosophy*; the latter being a broad subject that included the sub-disciplines of *rhetoric* (and thus logic), *natural philosophy* (inquiry into the physical cosmos), and the making of arguments for God's existence (a discipline called *natural theology*).

The scriptures referenced by Wesley (Rom 1:18–20 and Ps 19) can be read as affirming that God can be intuitively *perceived* through contemplating the creation, rather than as affirming that discursive arguments can be constructed linking the creation to its Creator (being a matter of intuitive "general revelation" rather than "natural theology"[3]). However, there's a case for taking Rom 1:18–32 as Paul's paraphrase of anti-Gentile rhetoric (similar to that seen in *Wisdom of Solomon* 13–14) that represents the perspective of the Jewish antagonist he proceeds to critique from verse 33 (making verses 18–32 an instance of the ancient literary device of "speech-in-character").[4] As for Psalm 19, it is perhaps most plausibly read as affirming a theology of nature rather than a natural theology.[5] Another scripture worth noting in this context is Paul's speech to the Lycaonians (Acts 14:15–17), though like Psalm 19 this might be taken as a theology of nature rather than as a piece of natural theology.[6] Acts 14:15–17 and

---

2. John Wesley, "Address to the Clergy."

3. As John M. Frame observes: "For some this belief may be an immediate response to the world around them. For others it may be the result of an argument." Cowen, ed. *Five Views on Apologetics*, 80. See: Evans, *Natural Signs and Knowledge of God*; Morley, *Mapping Apologetics*, 231–32, 364.

4. See: Andrew, "Romans 1:18–32"; Wilkinson, "The Punctuation Mark that Might Change How You Read Romans."; Porter, "Romans 1.18–32." See also: Rauser, *Is the Atheist My Neighbor?*

5. Such a theology begins from faith in the divine Creator of Genesis 1 ff. and reflects "awe or wonder at the vastness, splendour and richness of nature as the handiwork of God its designer or as the self-expression of the divine artist."—Baukham, "First Steps to a Theology of Nature."

6. It seems to me that the focus in Acts 14 is on the *goodness* of God, who "makes his sun rise on the evil and on the good, and sends rain on the just and on the unjust" (Matt 5:45, ESV), rather than on arguing for God's *existence*; on a "theology of nature" rather

Psalm 19 may nevertheless be seen as laying a foundation conducive to, or at least consistent with, natural theology.[7] As Norman L. Geisler writes: "It should not seem strange to those who believe in God's manifestation in His creation (. . . Ps. 19:1) that it is possible to arrive at knowledge of God by inference from these manifestations."[8]

Natural Theology and Theology of Nature

British scientist-turned-theologian Alister McGrath advocates a "theology of nature" defined as "a Christian understanding of the natural world that reflects the core assumptions of the Christian faith."[9] He explains:

> The trajectory of thought here is from within the Christian tradition towards nature rather than from nature towards faith. This theology of nature is often expressed particularly in terms of the doctrine of creation . . . The Christian faith is here understood to provide an interpretative framework by which nature may be seen in profound and significant ways . . . like a lens bringing a vast landscape into sharp focus, or a map helping us grasp the features of the terrain around us.[10]

For McGrath, a "theology of nature" isn't opposed to "natural theology," but is a way of approaching it:

---

than "natural theology." See: Arnold, *Acts*, 134–136; Willimon, *Acts*, 126. See also: Dahle, "Acts 17:16–34: An Apologetic Model Then and Now?"

7. In his otherwise excellent essay "The Check is in The Mail: Why Darwinism Fails to Inspire Confidence" (in Dembski ed. *Uncommon Dissent*, 3–22) it seems to me that philosopher Robert C. Koons misinterprets Job 12:7-9 as teaching that "a careful study of the forms of animal life leads inescapably to the conclusion that they are creatures of God." Rather, when read in context, the point being made concerns the nature of the divine governance of creation, which is here presupposed. For commentary on Job 12:7-9, see: Longman III, *Job*, 201; Whybray, *Job*, 74–75. Likewise, when Isa 40:21 asks: "Do you not know? Do you not hear? Has it not been told you from the beginning? Have you not understood from the foundations of the earth?," I doubt the last sentence is a figurative allusion to the contingency cosmological argument, as some take it to be. Rather, the reference is to the understanding of God as the creator contained within Jewish tradition. As the Good News Bible renders the verse: "Do you not know? Were you not told long ago? Have you not heard how the world began?" Again, Jeremiah's invocation of natures' regularities (Jer 31:35–36; 33:20) is concerned with a theology of nature rather than natural theology.

8. Geisler, *Philosophy of Religion*, 208.
9. McGrath, *Enriching our Vision*, 169.
10. McGrath, *Enriching our Vision*, 169.

> The capacity of the Christian vision of reality to "fit in" so much of what we see around us and experience within us . . . can be seen as an indication of both its truth and its trustworthiness. Christianity makes sense of what we know about the history of the cosmos, especially the curious phenomenon of fine tuning. It helps make sense of the complexity of human nature, including our propensity to failure and self-delusion on the one hand and our genuine aspirations to goodness on the other.[11]

McGrath prefers this approach to natural theology over others because it's in sympathy with his preferred apologetic methodology: "My approach is more like a scientist than a philosopher,"[12] explains McGrath. "I would describe my approach as 'inductive' or 'abductive' . . ."[13] Indeed, McGrath extols "a new style of natural theology adapted to the methods of natural science rather than conforming to the conventions of the philosophy of religion."[14] However, this latter distinction rests on a caricature of "the philosophy of religion" as exclusively concerned with deductive arguments which claim "to prove the existence of God."[15]

On the one hand, contemporary philosophers of religion generally recognize that, in most contexts, including natural theology, there is no such thing as a rationally *coercive* argument. As Stephen T. Davis observes: "few arguments are intellectually coercive . . ."[16] Indeed, Alvin Plantinga comments that:

> A person might, when confronted with an argument he sees to be valid for a conclusion he deeply disbelieves from premises he knows to be true, give up (some of) those premises: in this way you can reduce someone from knowledge to ignorance by giving him an argument he sees to be valid from premises he knows to be true.[17]

In other words, the *effectiveness* of an argument is person-relative.[18]

---

11. McGrath, *Enriching our Vision*, 170.
12. McGrath, *Enriching our Vision*, 170.
13. McGrath, *Enriching our Vision*, 171.
14. McGrath, *Enriching our Vision*, 66.
15. McGrath, *Enriching our Vision*, 67.
16. Davis, *God, Reason and Theistic Proofs*, 13.
17. Plantinga, "Two Dozen (or so) Arguments for God."
18. For discussion of what makes an argument a *good* argument, see: Craig and Gorra, *Reasonable Response*; Davis, *God, Reason and Theistic Proofs*; Plantinga, "Two Dozen

On the other hand, natural theology has long incorporated arguments beyond the stereotypical "proofs" of medieval scholasticism. For example, F.C. Copleston advanced a "best explanation"[19] argument from religious experience in his 1948 debate with Bertrand Russell. F.R. Tennant made a *cumulative* argument from "cosmic teleology" in the second volume of his *Philosophical Theology*.[20] William Paley's famous "watch-maker" argument from the early nineteenth century was framed as an *inference* (though it's often incorrectly portrayed as an argument by analogy).[21] Blaise Pascal formulated an *abductive* version of the argument from desire in his seventeenth century *Pensées*.[22] Even Thomas Aquinas" "Five Ways" from *Summa Theologica* included an argument (i.e. the "fifth way') resting upon the *inference* that "natural bodies, act for an end, and this is evident from their acting always, or nearly always, in the same way, so as to obtain the best result."[23]

Moreover, twentieth century philosophers of religion explicitly imitated argumentative strategies from the natural sciences in natural theology. For example, Basil Mitchel used an analysis of scientific rationality in pursuit of *The Justification of Religious Belief* (Macmillan, 1973). Richard Swinburne's influential natural theology likewise takes its cues from scientific inferences and is famously structured using Bayes' probability theorem.[24]

In the final analysis, a preference for a given apologetic methodology cannot overrule the need to judge every purported argument for God on its individual merits, regardless of its logical form.

(or so) Arguments for God."

19. Copleston in Hick, ed. *Existence of God*, 178, 180.

20. See: Hick, ed. *Existence of God*, 120–136.

21. See: Hick, ed. *Existence of God*, 99–103; Williams, *Faithful Guide to Philosophy*, Chapter Six.

22. See: Pascal, Levi, trans., *Pensées and other writings*, 52.

23. Aquinas's fifth way from *Summa Theologica* in Hick, ed. *Existence of God*, 85.

24. See: Swinburne, "Justification of Theism;" Swinburne, "Evidence for God;" Swinburne, *The Existence of God*, second edition; Swinburne, *The Resurrection of God Incarnate*. See also: Holder, *Ramified Natural Theology*.

Natural Theology Under Fire

The project of natural theology, stretching at least as far back as the ancient Greeks,[25] came under fire in the early twentieth century from both within and without Christianity.[26]

Natural Theology Takes a Cold Bath

In the theology of Karl Barth, not only was natural theology "set against the revealed religion of Christ in Scripture" due in part to the former's historical linkage "with German national Volk-religion," but "biblical theology became isolated from rationality, presupposing its own truth . . ."[27] Barth held that knowledge of God comes only through special revelation:

> God in his sovereignty makes himself knowable. Man in his sinfulness cannot otherwise obtain any knowledge of God. A great gulf is fixed, bridged only by God in disclosing himself in Christ through the work of the Holy Spirit. Such knowledge is entirely a work of grace, unaided by human intellect.[28]

As Peter May explains, Barth,

> did not believe in arguments or evidences to proclaim Christianity, and his influence persists strongly today. Such rational approaches to belief could in his view do nothing to facilitate a personal encounter with Christ. The evidence of nature and apologetic reasoning had no role in bringing people to faith. In his view, such rational thought could only be of benefit for those who already believed in God, and such belief could only come about by God's revelation of himself.[29]

As creator, God obviously takes the initiative in making himself knowable to humanity. However, to say that human (God-given) reasoning plays no role in bringing people to knowledge of or to faith in God/Christ, flies in

---

25. See: Sedley, *Creationism And Its Critics*.
26. See: Montifiore, *Probability of God*, Chapter One.
27. May, "Karl Barth and Natural Theology?" As Wyatt Houtz writes: "Barth's protest against Natural Revelation was also a protest against the Nazi claim to be a revelation of God."—"Barth's No! to Natural Theology." See also: Barr, "Natural Theology in This Century"; Holder, *The Heavens Declare*.
28. May, "Karl Barth and Natural Theology?"
29. May, "Karl Barth and Natural Theology?"

the face of plentiful scriptural evidence to the contrary (e.g. Exod 7:5; Ezek 25:11; John 14:11, 20:29–31; Acts 1:3, 2:1–42, 9:22, 14:15–17, 17:30–31; Rom 1:17–19; 1 Pet 3:15)[30], as well as plentiful testimony from people whose belief in God and/or commitment to Christ was at least partially facilitated by Christian apologetics.[31] As a case in point, I was delighted to receive an e-mail from Venezuela some years ago offering testimony that,

> as a graduate student of philosophy, I'm a eager reader of your books and online articles, which have been instrumental in my rejection of agnosticism and naturalism and have contributed strongly to make me a new-born Christian.

Once upon a time in Vienna

There was a time, in the early twentieth century, when thinking about God was nearly banished from academia because of the many academics who thought that talk about "God" was *literally meaningless*. They thought that "God-talk" made no sense beyond its *emotive* content. "God" wasn't the only subject to suffer such banishment. Assertions about right and wrong, beauty and ugliness—*all statements that were metaphysical in nature*—were widely considered to be literally *nonsense*.

The enforcer of this philosophical dress code was the now infamous "verification principle" sponsored by a group of thinkers known as "logical positivists." Kelly James Clark explains that logical positivism "began in the early 1920s in an informal discussion group in Austria called the Vienna Circle. The original members, led by physicist Moritz Schlick, included mathematicians, physicists, sociologists and economists but no professional philosophers."[32] This omission was unfortunate, because, "united by their passionate dislike of the metaphysical . . . the group developed a unified philosophy that embraced science and attempted to destroy philosophy."[33] Attempting to develop a unified philosophy that dispenses with philosophy makes about as much sense as Groucho Marx's comment that he wouldn't belong to any club that would have him as a member. Nevertheless, the ideas of the Vienna Circle spread far and wide.

---

30. See: McGrath, *Enriching our Vision*, 56–58. See also: Craig, "Classical Apologetics," 39–43.
31. For example: "Disillusioned with Dawkins."
32. Clark, *Philosophers Who Believe*, Introduction.
33. Clark, *Philosophers Who Believe*, Introduction.

The Circle of Exclusion

Despite some disagreement among the members of the Vienna Circle, "there was an initial impulse to accept the verification theory of meaning. . ."[34] This theory held that any statement that wasn't true by definition (e.g. "all bachelors are unmarried men') was only meaningful if it could be empirically verified (at least in principle). To "empirically verify" something means to check it out with the physical senses (sight, hearing, touch, etc.) at least indirectly. In other words, the statement "this is a book" *is meaningful*, because you can verify it by seeing, hearing, touching, smelling and/or tasting the book; but a statement like "That sunset is beautiful" *is not meaningful* because you can't verify it's meaning by seeing, hearing, touching, smelling or tasting the "beauty" of the sunset. Likewise, positivists hold that the statement "God exists" cannot be verified and is therefore meaningless, a use of language on a par with nonsense poetry (like the parts of "Jabberwocky" that Lewis Carroll didn't define[35]). It may have an *emotional* resonance, but it has no *rational* content that can be understood or judged as being an accurate or inaccurate representation of reality.

The Influence of Language, Truth & Logic

The primary importer of logical positivism into Britain, and hence into Anglo-American analytic philosophy, was A.J. Ayer (1910–89). Unlike the members of the Vienna Circle, Alfred Jules Ayer (known to his friends as "Freddie") was a philosopher. Ayer studied philosophy at Oxford under Gilbert Ryle before becoming a professor himself, ending up back at Oxford for a time (1947–59).

Ayer was immersed in logical positivism during 1932 whilst studying (at Ryle's recommendation) with Moritz Schlick in Vienna. This visit filled the gap between Ayer's university finals and taking up his first lectureship. Two years later, Ayer started work on the book that would make his name: *Language, Truth, and Logic* (1936):

> Ayer's philosophical ideas were largely parasitic on those of the Vienna Circle. However, his clear, vibrant and (arguably) arrogant exposition of them makes *Language, Truth and Logic* essential

---

34. Clark, *Philosophers Who Believe*, Introduction.
35. See: Carroll, "Jabberwocky."

NATURAL THEOLOGY AND SCIENCE

reading on the tenets of logical positivism—the book is a classic and is widely read in philosophy courses around the world.[36]

Ayer proclaimed:

> The term "God" is a metaphysical term. And if "God" is a metaphysical term, then it cannot even be probable that a god exists. For to say that "God exists" is to make a metaphysical utterance which cannot be either true or false. . . . If a putative proposition fails to satisfy [the verification] principle, and is not a tautology, then. . . it is metaphysical, and . . . being metaphysical, it is neither true nor false but literally senseless.[37]

As Ayer admitted, positivism entailed that the denial of God's existence was just as meaningless as the affirmation of his existence, atheism as irrational as theism: "If the assertion that there is a god is nonsensical, then the atheist's assertion that there is no god is equally non-sensical."[38]

Likewise, according to Ayer,

> Such aesthetic words as "beautiful" and "hideous" are employed, not to make statements of fact, but simply to express certain feelings and evoke a certain response. It follows, as in ethics, that there is no sense in attributing objective validity to aesthetic judgements, and no possibility of arguing about questions of value in aesthetics . . . there is nothing in aesthetics, any more than there is in ethics, to justify the view that it embodies a unique type of knowledge. It should now be clear that the only information which we can legitimately derive from the study of our aesthetic and moral experiences is information about our own mental and physical make-up.[39]

Copleston noted that "Ayer's writings exercised a widespread influence, particularly perhaps on university students, for whom it possessed the charm of novelty and an atmosphere of daring."[40] Ayer's declaration that God-talk is nonsense has influenced generations of scholars, despite the fact that his book originally only sold "just over 1,000 copies (64 years

---

36. Wikipedia, "A.J. Ayer."
37. Ayer, *Language, Truth and Logic*, 115.
38. Ayer, *Language, Truth and Logic*, 175.
39. Ayer, *Central Questions of Philosophy*, 118–19. See Lewis, *Abolition of Man*.
40. Copleston, *Contemporary Philosophy*, 9.

later, the book still sells 2,000 a year in Britain: a 1945 reprint in the United States has sold 300,000)."[41] As Hilary Spurling observes,

> It was one of those books that galvanize a whole generation. Ambitious undergraduates commonly read it at a sitting. Their elders were appalled. When students tried to discuss the book at an Oxford seminar, the Master of Balliol flung it through the window. Ayer was denounced by a housemaster at Winchester School as the wickedest man in Oxford. Asked what came next, the young iconoclast said cheerfully: "There's no next. Philosophy has come to an end. Finished."[42]

However, within a few of decades it became clear that philosophy had *not* come to an end and that positivism was "finished," at least within academic philosophy. In 1943, E.L. Mascall observed that "the logical positivists' position seems to be crumbling from within . . ."[43] Two decades after *Language, Truth, and Logic* was published, Copleston wrote: "There are few British philosophers who willingly accept the title of 'positivists' or who make open profession of applying the principle of verifiability as a criterion of meaning . . . [Positivism] is no longer fashionable."[44] In *The Cosmological Argument: A Reassessment*, Bruce R. Reichenbach commented: "The era is past when all metaphysical statements or arguments can simply be dismissed as silly or senseless, since they do not meet a pre-established criterion of verifiability."[45] Despite being a dead issue in academic philosophy, the ghost of positivism continues to inspire uninformed attacks upon philosophy in general and natural theology in particular.

A Negative Assessment of Positivism

A number of factors explain the near total demise of positivism.

Ironically for materialists who embraced logical positivism, "materialism would have to be rejected as nonsense by a strict interpretation of logical positivism."[46] The claim that matter is objectively real is, after all, neither

---

41. Spurling, "Wickedest Man in Oxford."
42. Spurling, "Wickedest Man in Oxford".
43. Mascall, *He Who Is*, xi.
44. Copleston, *Contemporary Philosophy*, 9.
45. Reichenbach, *Cosmological Argument*, ix.
46. Reppert, *Lewis's Dangerous Idea*, 20.

true by definition nor something that can be verified by sense data (since it's the nature of what the senses perceive that's in question).

Indeed, positivism makes not only materialism, but also a realist account of science, impossible. As Copleston argued,

> If the meaning of an existential proposition consists, according to the principle, in its verifiability, it is impossible, I think, to escape an infinite regress, since the verification will still itself need verification, and so on indefinitely. If this is so, then all [existential] propositions, including scientific ones, are meaningless.[47]

In an article published in 1960, philosopher John Hick pointed out that, when made precise enough, the statement that "God exists" is, in principle at least, *indirectly* verifiable. Hick argued that:

> A set of expectations based upon faith in the historic Jesus as the incarnation of God, and in his teaching as being divinely authoritative, could be so fully confirmed in *post-mortem* experience as to leave no grounds for rational doubt as to the validity of that faith.[48]

If you were to die and then find yourself in a Christian afterlife—you are given a resurrected body and a life in a sinless community that revolves around the resurrected Jesus Christ—one could surely count this as an *indirect* verification of God's existence. Unless positivism is framed broadly enough to allow for *indirect* verification, many explanatory entities within science would count as nonsense, because they are verified indirectly. For example, scientific theories about so-called "dark matter" would count as meaningless under a verification principle that excluded indirect verification.[49] Again, just as empirical measurement of the background radiation of the universe provides *indirect* verification of the "big bang" in cosmology (to see one isn't to see the other, but to see the one is to see something

---

47. Copleston, "Logical Positivism-A Debate," 756.

48. Hick, "Theology and Verification," 69.

49. "Galaxies in our universe seem to be achieving an impossible feat. They are rotating with such speed that the gravity generated by their observable matter could not possibly hold them together; they should have torn themselves apart long ago. The same is true of galaxies in clusters, which leads scientists to believe that something we cannot see is at work. They think something we have yet to detect directly is giving these galaxies extra mass, generating the extra gravity they need to stay intact. This strange and unknown matter was called 'dark matter' since it is not visible." CERN, "Dark Matter."

from which the other can be inferred[50]), so experiencing the sort of afterlife promised in the New Testament would likewise provide indirect empirical verification of God's existence. This being so, the claim that God exists *is* open to verification, *in principle*, and therefore counts as being a meaningful claim according to any principle of verification consistent with scientific practice.

In other words, the verification principle can't be used to wall off scientific claims about the universe from religious claims about its creator, because it either lets too much metaphysics or too little science into the category of "claims that are meaningful." As Llyod Eby observes: "All attempts to solve this problem of having a version of the verification principle . . . that admits all scientific statements but excludes all metaphysical statements have met with failure."[51] Hence, as Hick concluded: "the existence or non-existence of the God of the New Testament is a matter of fact, and claims as such eventual experiential verification."[52]

In 1967 American philosopher Alvin Plantinga published *God and Other Minds*, which "applied the tools of analytic philosophy to questions in the Philosophy of Religion with an unprecedented rigour and creativity."[53] He argued by analogy with the rationality of belief in other minds (whose non-tautological existence can't be directly verified by empirical methods) that "if my belief in other minds is rational, so is my belief in God."[54] But, of course, even verificationists generally believe in other minds.

Then, with the 1974 publication of *The Nature of Necessity*, Plantinga kick-started a philosophical re-evaluation of theistic arguments by using modal logic to lay out a logically valid version of the ontological argument.[55]

Between them, *God and Other Minds* and *The Nature of Necessity* tackled both prongs of the positivist's proposed dilemma: Show that theism is either verifiable or tautologically true as a matter of definition, or else accept banishment to the outer darkness of meaninglessness. Plantinga

---

50. See: Douglas Scott and Martin White, "Cosmic Microwave Background Radiation."

51. Eby, "Viewpoint: What is Science?"

52. Hick, "Theology and Verification," 71.

53. Craig, *Philosophy of Religion*, 1.

54. Plantinga, *God and Other Minds*, 271.

55. See: Plantinga, "Ontological Argument." See also: YouTube Playlist, "Ontological Argument for God;" Williams and Millican, "Debating the Ontological Argument;" Williams, "Brief Introduction to and Defence of the Modern Ontological Argument;" Williams, *Faithful Guide to Philosophy*.

responded to the first positivist prong that a demand for direct verification renders positivism self-contradictory, thereby opening up the possibility of arguments from indirect verification. To the second prong, Plantinga responded that, even if he can't prove that God's existence is true by definition, he can prove that it is *rational to think that the possibility of God's existence entails God's existence,* and that this is sufficient to demonstrate that God-talk is meaningful, for how can a truth-claim be rational without also being meaningful?

Exploiting the openings noted by Hick and Plantinga, philosophers such as Basil Mitchell and Richard Swinburne began to argue that the God hypothesis isn't merely indirectly verifiable *in principle*, but also *in practice*, since several arguments for God can be framed using the scientific method of indirect verification (e.g. arguments from miracles or from design). As Mitchell comments,

> the Logical Positivist movement started as an attempt to make a clear demarcation between science and common sense on the one hand, and metaphysics and theology on the other. But work in the philosophy of science convinced people that what the Logical Postitivists had said about science was not true, and, by the time the philosophers of science had developed and amplified their accounts of how rationality works in science, people discovered that similar accounts applied equally well to the areas which they had previously sought to exclude, namely theology and metaphysics.[56]

Finally, as R. Douglas Geivett explains, philosophers noticed that the verification principle "was neither empirically verifiable nor tautological."[57] That is, the verification principle was itself a metaphysical claim, a claim that therefore ruled itself to be meaningless: "*it failed its own requirement* for factual meaningfulness," notes William P. Alston, "and thus was self-refuting."[58]

Ayer tried to get around this problem by admitting that the verification principle wasn't a meaningful *proposition* but saying that it was a *rule* for using language. But why pay attention to such an arbitrary rule? Ayer himself asked: "Why should anyone follow the prescription if its implications were not to his taste?'[59]

56. Mitchell, "Reflections on C.S. Lewis," 19.
57. Geivett, "Evidential Value of Religious Experience," 175.
58. Alston, "Religious Language and Verificationism," 21.
59. Ayer, *Central Questions of Philosophy*, 34.

Keith Ward reports the following conversation between Ayer and a student:

> A student once asked [Ayer] if you could make any true general statement about meaningful statements. "Yes," he replied. "You can say that all meaningful statements must be verifiable in principle." "I see what you mean," said the student. "But how can I verify that?" "I am glad you asked that," said the philosopher. "You cannot verify it. But it is not really a meaningful statement; it is just a rule for using language." "Whose rule?" "Well, it's my rule, really. But it is a very useful one. If you use it, you will find you agree with me completely. I think that would be very useful."[60]

If we adopt the rule, then of course we'll agree with Ayer, and of course he'll find that useful! But he can't provide us with a good *reason* for adopting his rule (certainly not one that doesn't implicitly contradict the rule he wants us to adopt). Instead, he recommends it on the basis of its usefulness. Usefulness for what? For insulating a worldview that excludes everything metaphysical, especially religion (as the positivist's failed attempts to produce a version of the principle able to draw a line of demarcation between science on the one hand religion on the other hand, shows). Indeed, it would seem that the motivation behind logical positivism was the desire to exclude God by excluding talk about God. Logical positivism was quite simply a form of atheistic censorship. However, philosophers who opposed this baseless peer-pressure were well within their rights to point out that the emperor of positivism had no clothes, but brazenly walked the halls of academia with nothing but a smile of fashionable popularity to disguise his embarrassingly self-contradictory ways.

James Kelly Clark describes the verification principle as a piece of "unjustifiable philosophical imperialism that, in the end, could not survive critical scrutiny."[61] William Lane Craig comments: "Fifty years ago philosophers widely regarded talk about God as literally meaningless . . . but today no informed philosopher could take such a viewpoint."[62] Ronald H. Nash concludes that positivism "is dead and quite properly so."[63] Roger Scruton observes: "Logical positivism no longer has a following, and it is

---

60. Ward, *God: A Guide for the Perplexed*, 184.
61. Clark, *Philosophers Who Believe*, 11–12.
62. Craig, "Advice to Christian Apologists."
63. Nash, *Faith and Reason*, 53.

easy to see why. The verification principle cannot be verified: it therefore condemns itself as meaningless."[64]

By 1973 Ayer himself admitted: "the verification principle is defective . . ."[65] Talking about positivism during an interview in 1978, Ayer conceded: "Nearly all of it was false."[66] He reflected: "I just stated [the verification rule] dogmatically and an extraordinary number of people seemed to be convinced by my assertion."[67] In the end, Ayer conceded: "Logical Positivism died a long time ago. I don't think much of *Language, Truth and Logic* is true. I think it is full of mistakes."[68]

The Resurrection of God-Talk

On 8 April 1966, *Time Magazine* ran a cover story about the then current "death-of-God" movement in American theology entitled "Is God Dead?" William Lane Craig explains that:

> According to the movement's protagonists, traditional theism was no longer tenable and had to be once and for all abandoned. Ironically, however, at the same time that theologians were writing God's obituary, a new generation of young philosophers was rediscovered His vitality.[69]

Only a few years later, *Time* carried a cover story asking "Is God coming back to life?" Interest in the philosophy of religion continued to grow to the point where, in 1980, *Time* ran a story about "Modernizing the case for God," describing the contemporary movement among philosophers putting new life into the arguments for God's existence:

> In a quiet revolution in thought and argument that hardly anybody could have foreseen only two decades ago, God is making a comeback. Most intriguingly, this is happening not amongst theologians or ordinary believers, but in the crisp intellectual circles of academic philosophers, where the consensus had long banished the Almighty from fruitful discourse.[70]

64. Scruton, *Guide To Philosophy*, 18.
65. Ayer, *Central Questions of Philosophy*, 22–34.
66. Ayer in *The Listener*, 2 March 1978.
67. Ayer, quoted by Ward, *Turn of the Tide*, 59.
68. Ayer in Varghese ed., *Great Thinkers on Great Questions*, 49.
69. Craig, *Philosophy of Religion*, 1.
70. "Modernizing the Case for God," 65–66.

The reference to banishing the Almighty from fruitful discourse is a reference to positivism. It's no surprise to find Tyler Burge, Professor of philosophy at UCLA, writing that the central event in philosophy during the last half-century was "the downfall of positivism and the re-opening of discussion of virtually all the traditional problems of philosophy."[71] This philosophical renaissance went hand-in-hand with a revival of interest in natural theology amongst analytic philosophers of religion. As James Brent comments: "Natural theology today is practiced with a degree of diversity and confidence unprecedented since the late Middle Ages."[72]

Defining "Natural Theology"

Thomas Aquinas famously distinguished between "revealed (dogmatic) theology and rational (philosophical) theology,"[73] writing in his *Summa Contra Gentiles* that,

> there exists a twofold truth concerning the divine being, one to which the inquiry of the reason can reach, the other which surpasses the whole ability of the human reason, it is fitting that both of these truths be proposed to man divinely for belief.[74]

Aquinas was *not* making a distinction between truths of reason in the domain of natural theology on the one hand and truths of *blind* faith on the other. Aquinas' meaning would have been clearer if he'd written that "there exists a twofold truth concerning the divine being, one to which the inquiry of the reason *unaided by special revelation* can reach, the other which surpasses the whole ability of the human reason *unaided by special revelation*." That this is what he meant becomes clear later in *Summa Contra Gentiles*, where he argues:

> Those who place their faith in this truth, however, "for which the human reason offers no experimental evidence," do not believe foolishly . . . For these "secrets of divine Wisdom" (Job 11:6) the divine Wisdom itself . . . has designed to reveal to men. *It reveals its own presence, as well as the truth of its teaching and inspiration, by fitting arguments; and in order to confirm those truths that*

71. Burge, "Philosophy of Language and Mind," 49.
72. Brent, "Natural Theology."
73. Swindal, "Faith and Reason."
74. Aquinas, *Summa Contra Gentiles*, https://dhspriory.org/thomas/english/ContraGentiles1.htm#4.

> *exceed natural knowledge, it gives visible manifestation to works that surpass the ability of all nature* . . . and what is more wonderful, there is the inspiration given to human minds, so that simple and untutored persons, filled with the gift of the Holy Spirit, come to possess instantaneously the highest wisdom . . .[75] [my italics]

In other words, human reason is enabled to reach what it otherwise would not be able to reach—truths of special revelation which surpasses the ability of human reason *unaided by special revelation*—by the divine design to reveal these truths *in such a manner that warrant is thereby provided for rational belief in them.*

For Aquinas, this warrant is provided by the Holy Spirit, either quite aside from arguments, or *in conjunction with the revelation of "fitting arguments"* and *publicly accessible evidence of "works that surpass the ability of all nature"* (that is, miracles). Aquinas argues that the latter, argumentative warrant falls into the category of "persuasive [i.e. non-deductive] reasoning" rather than that of "demonstrative reasoning" which "yields a conclusion that is undeniable for anyone who grasps the truth of the demonstration's premises."[76]

Not only does Aquinas make a principled distinction between truths of reason (i.e. truths of natural theology accessible to reason unaided by special revelation) and truths of faith (truths of revealed theology accessible to human reason with the help of special revelation), but he claims to know where the line of this distinction runs:

> Some truths about God exceed all the ability of the human reason. Such is the truth that God is triune. But there are some truths which the natural reason also is able to reach. Such are that God exists, that He is one, and the like.[77]

While it is wise to recognize that we will never *comprehend* God, I would argue that it is also wise *not* to think, with Aquinas, that we can discern *in advance of trying to understand some theological topic* that this or that topic "surpasses the whole ability of the human reason" unaided by special revelation. Indeed, not only have Christian philosophers (e.g.

---

75. Aquinas, *Summa Contra Gentiles*, https://dhspriory.org/thomas/english/ContraGentiles1.htm#6, my italics.

76. Floyd, "Aquinas: Philosophical Theology."

77. Aquinas, *Summa Contra Gentiles*, https://dhspriory.org/thomas/english/ContraGentiles1.htm#3.

Stephen T. Davies) given arguments against a Unitarian definition of God[78], some have explicitly argued for God's triunity (e.g. Richard of St Victor, Richard Swinburne and myself[79]).

Aquinas' demarcation between natural and revealed theology was highly influential, leading generations of thinkers to assume the existence of a principled division between these disciplines. For example, according to Hugh G. Gauch Jr.:

> The task of natural theology is to reach the most significant truths available to unaided reason evaluating public evidence, in contrast to the greater truths available only to faith through a genuine revelation from God.[80]

However, on the one hand, significant truths that natural theologians routinely think "available to unaided reason evaluating public evidence" can, of course, be taken on faith (treating "faith" here as a synonym for "trust"). For example, while advocates of natural theology often endorse cosmological arguments[81], the author of Hebrews writes: "By faith we understand that the universe was formed at God's command, so that what is seen was not made out of what was visible" (Heb 11:3). On the other hand, any "greater truths available only . . . through a genuine revelation from God" can only be the object of faith if human (God-given) "reason" is set to the task of "evaluating" the relevant revelation (for example, in understanding what a given scriptural passage means).

James F. Sennett and Douglas Groothuis define natural theology as:

> The attempt to provide rational justification for theism using only those sources of information accessible to all inquirers, namely, the data of empirical experience and the dictates of human reason. In other words, it is defense of theism without recourse to purported special revelation.[82]

Likewise, according to Scot MacDonald:

---

78. See: Davies, "Somewhat Playful Proof of the Social Trinity;" Moreland and Craig, *Foundations for a Christian Worldview*, 594–95.

79. See: Richard of St. Victor, *On the Trinity*; Swinburne, *Christian God*; Williams, "Understanding the Trinity."

80. Gauch Jr., "Recent Transitions in Natural Theology."

81. See: Willard, "Language, Being, God, and the Three Stages of Theistic Evidence;" Williams, "A Universe From Someone" (2012).

82. Sennett and Groothuis, "Introduction," 10.

NATURAL THEOLOGY AND SCIENCE

> Natural theology aims at establishing truths or acquiring knowledge about God (or divine matters generally) using . . . standard techniques of reasoning and facts or truths in principle available to all human beings just in virtue of their possessing reason and sense perception.[83]

However, while purported special revelation about Jesus Christ was obviously unavailable to the "empirical experience and . . . reason" of, say, stone-age humans, so too were many cosmological and biological discoveries that ground various contemporary arguments in natural theology (e.g. the "Big Bang," the precision of cosmic "fine tuning," the informational nature of life and the existence of molecular machines). Likewise, "purported special revelation" about Jesus is just as "accessible to all inquirers" today as are those cosmological and biological discoveries. And again, the purported "special revelation" available to all inquirers today is only available to them through the same "empirical experience and . . . reason" that they have to use to access the discoveries of modern science.

John Polkinghorne defines natural theology as,

> the attempt to learn something of God from the exercise of reason and the inspection of the world—in other words, from reflection on general experience.[84]

However, on the one hand, restricting natural theology to the data of "general experience" excludes much data (originating from the specialised experience of scientists) with which natural theology is traditionally concerned. On the other hand, if we allow natural theology to work with data grounded in the experience of twenty-first century scientists, why not allow natural theology to work with the apostle Paul's first century experience of encountering the resurrected Jesus?[85]

William Lane Craig defines natural theology as,

> that branch of theology which seeks to provide rational warrant for the proposition that God exists on the basis of argument and evidence independent of authoritative divine revelation.[86]

However, warrant can be provided "on the basis of argument and evidence independent of an authoritative divine revelation" *qua divine*

---

83. MacDonald, "Natural Theology."
84. Polkinghorne, "Where Is Natural Theology Today?," 169.
85. See: May, "Resurrection of Jesus;" Williams, *Getting at Jesus*.
86. Craig, "Natural Theology: Introduction," 69.

revelation without being independent of that revelation *qua* a source of potential data, as long as that data is established through the use of standard critical methods. That is, since any argument for theism that assumed the revelatory status of a purported divine revelation would be question begging, stipulating that natural theology should proceed "without recourse to purported special revelation" *qua* revelation, "on the basis of argument and evidence independent of authoritative divine revelation"[87] *as such*, is redundant.

Of course, we are free to define theological disciplines as proceeding on the assumed basis of "purported special revelation," or not, as we find it convenient. But such choices imply nothing about the legitimacy of apologetic arguments, including the arguments of natural theology. Thus the website of the famous Gifford Lecturers states that: "Traditionally natural theology is the term used for the attempt to prove the existence of God and divine purpose through observation of nature and the use of human reason."[88] While this definition leaves the question of purported special revelation to one side—as may be convenient to do in a university course of a limited duration, or a book of limited size—it doesn't try to erect a *principled* distinction between natural and revealed theology in the manner of Aquinas.

William P. Alston avoids all these problems when he simply defines natural theology as "the enterprise of providing support for religious beliefs by starting from premises that neither are nor presuppose any religious beliefs."[89] In other words, natural theology seeks to offer a non-question-begging defence of theism. As Keith Yandell put it: "Natural theology is the attempt to provide good reasons for thinking that God exists."[90]

Ramified Natural Theology

Recent developments in the philosophy of religion show that "natural theology" shouldn't be understood in too narrow or insular a manner.[91] For

87. Craig, "Natural Theology: Introduction," 69. Likewise, Colin Brown defined natural theology as "the attempt to attain an understanding of God and his relationship with the universe by means of rational reflection, without an appeal to special revelation." Ferguson and Wright, ed.'s. *New Dictionary of Theology*, 452.

88. www.giffordlectures.org/overview/natural-theology.

89. Alston, quoted by Holder, *Ramified Natural Theology*, 19.

90. Yandell, "David Hume on Meaning," 69.

91. See: Larmer, "'Argument From Miracle;'" Menuge and Taliaferro "Introduction to

one thing, as Rodney Holder writes: "the traditional division between natural theology and revealed theology breaks down as soon as we ask why we should believe in a putative revelation and how we can commend our own perceived revelation to others."[92] Then again, what Richard Swinburne has called "ramified natural theology"[93] (i.e. an expanded, more varied natural theology[94]) highlights the fact that so-called "Christian evidences" (e.g. the argument for Jesus' resurrection,[95] the "trilemma" argument for the deity of Jesus,[96] arguments about fulfilled Biblical prophecy,[97] etc.) don't merely round out the classical case for theism with reasons to believe in a specifically Christian God, but can actually do double-work as argument for God in their own right.[98]

Such arguments don't appeal to special revelation *qua* special revelation, but they often make non-question-begging appeals to evidence relating to purported acts of special revelation, including evidence contained within the historical documents that Christians call Scripture, as well as evidence outside of Scripture. As Hugh G. Gauch Jr. writes: "For natural theology's purposes, the Bible is read as historical evidence rather than authoritative scripture . . ."[99]

For example, in the course of arguing for the resurrection of Jesus, an apologist may appeal to the historical datum of the creedal material quoted by the apostle Paul in 1 Corinthians 15, as well as to archaeological evidence

---

a Special Issue of *Philosophia Christi* on Ramified Natural Theology;" Menuge, "Ramified Personalized Natural Theology."

92. Holder, *Ramified Natural Theology*, 78.

93. Swinburne, "Natural Theology, Its 'Dwindling Probabilities' and 'Lack of Rapport.'"

94. To "ramify" means "to spread and develop many parts or branches." Accordingly, "Ramified" means "having many different parts or branches" (https://dictionary.cambridge.org/dictionary/english/ramify).

95. See: Blomberg and Carl Stecher with contributions by Richard Carrier and Peter S. Williams, *Resurrection: Faith or Fact?*; Williams, "*Resurrection: Faith or Fact?* Miracle Not Required?" Williams, *Getting at Jesus*.

96. See: Williams, *Getting at Jesus*.

97. See: YouTube Playlist, "Biblical Prophecy;" Newman, ed. *Evidence of Prophecy*; Williams, *Understanding Jesus*, Chapter Six.

98. See: Menuge and Taliaferro "Introduction to a Special Issue of *Philosophia Christi* on Ramified Natural Theology."

99. Gauch Jr., "Recent Transitions in Natural Theology."

showing that it was possible for a crucified man to receive a decent burial.[100] As Robert A. Larmer observes,

> Traditionally, it has been assumed that natural theology must eschew consideration of special revelation from God and consider only data that is available to unaided reason. This, however, is to ignore the fact that a purported revelation may include content that is empirically verifiable and thus within the purview of natural theology. Miracles are publicly observable events that cry out for an explanation. One need not come to such events already accepting the interpretation placed on them by religious believers—the Bible can be read as historical evidence rather than authoritative Scripture—but neither is one prohibited from considering whether that interpretation does indeed provide the best understanding of the events. This opens up the possibility that someone who initially does not accept theism might at once accept both the claim of God's existence and the claim of God's self-disclosure.[101]

This means that natural theology is *not* restricted to the bare theism (or even deism) of what Pascal famously called "the God of the Philosophers."

The Breadth of Contemporary Natural Theology

Twenty-first century natural theology has rediscovered an emphasis upon the intuitive or "natural" nature of belief in God[102] in dialogue with what we might call "epistemologies of trust" (e.g. Richard Swinburne's defence of the principles of credulity and testimony, Alvin Plantinga's "reformed" account of warrant and properly basic beliefs,[103] and/or Michael Huemer's phenomenal conservatism[104]). These epistemologies of trust, together with the sheer *breadth* of arguments offered within contemporary natural theology,[105] helps us avoid focusing too narrowly upon the "classical"

---

100. See Williams, *Getting at Jesus*.

101. Larmer, "'Argument From Miracle.'"

102. See: Evans, *Natural Signs and Knowledge of God*; Copan and Taliaferro, ed.'s. *Naturalness of Belief*.

103. See: Plantinga, *Knowledge and Christian Belief*; Alvin Plantinga *Warranted Christian Belief*. See also: Wykstra, "'Not Done in a Corner' Revisited;" Stoke, *A Shot of Faith (to the Head)*.

104. See: CCA, "Phenomenal Conservatism;" Huemer, "Compassionate Phenomenal Conservatism;" Moretti, "Phenomenal Conservatism."

105. See: YouTube Playlist: "Natural Theology"; YouTube Playlist, "Debating God."

arguments for God discussed by ancient pagans and/or medieval thinkers (i.e. cosmological, teleological, axiological and ontological arguments),[106] although these families of argument have all been ably defended by contemporary scholars.[107]

The breadth of contemporary natural theology is demonstrated by the following half-dozen (or so) exemplars:

- Richard Swinburne's *The Existence of God* defended theistic arguments from the beauty of the natural world and from a philosophical anthropology that includes libertarian free will, conscious thoughts, sensations and desires, the conscious acquisition of warranted true beliefs and various types of religious experience (themes that have been explored in a plethora of more recent publications).[108]

- Peter Kreeft and Ronald K. Tacelli sketch nearly "Twenty Arguments For God's Existence"[109] (they actually give nineteen arguments for God's existence plus Pascal's wager) in their entry level *Handbook of Christian Apologetics*.

- *In Defense of Natural Theology: A Post-Humean Assessment* (edited by James F. Sennett and Douglas Groothuis) contains essays defending the project of natural theology from the influential but over-rated critiques of David Hume, including defences of nine theistic arguments.

- *The Blackwell Companion to Natural Theology* (edited by William Lane Craig and J.P. Moreland), contains substantial essays defending nine theistic arguments.

---

106. See: Sedley, *Creationism And Its Critics*; Copleston, *History of Philosophy: Volume 2*.

107. See: Craig, "Five Arguments for God"; Craig and Moreland, *Blackwell Companion to Natural Theology*; Moreland and Craig, *Foundations for a Christian Worldview*, second edition; Moreland, *Scaling the Secular City*; Sennett and Groothuis, ed.'s. *In Defence of Natural Theology*; Williams, *Outgrowing God?*; Williams, *Faithful Guide to Philosophy*.

108. See: Bassham ed. *Lewis's Christian Apologetics*; Dubay, *The Evidential Power Of Beauty*; Menuge, *Agents Under Fire*; Moreland, *The Recalcitrant Imago Dei*, Moreland, *Consciousness and the Existence of God*; Moreland, *Scaling the Secular City*; Plantinga, *Where The Conflict Really Lies*; Reppert, *Lewis's Dangerous Idea*; Williams, *Faithful Guide to Philosophy*; Williams, "Intelligent Design, Aesthetics and Design Arguments;" Williams "In Defence of Arguments From Desire."

109. See: Kreeft and Tacelli, "Twenty Arguments For God's Existence."

- Alvin Plantinga's famous 1986 paper on "Two Dozen (or so) Arguments for God"[110] spawned an academic conference at Baylor University in 2014[111] and a subsequent book—*The Plantinga Project: Two Dozen (Or So) Arguments For God* (edited by Jerry L. Walls and Trent Dougherty)—highlighting twenty-nine theistic arguments, including lesser known arguments such as the argument from desire,[112] play, simplicity, etc.

- *The Naturalness of Belief: New Essays on Theism's Rationality* (edited by Paul Copan and Charles Taliaferro), offers a wide-ranging collection of papers defending theism in light of the phenomena of consciousness, intentionality, beauty, human dignity, free will, rationality and knowledge; as well as looking at common-sensical, existential, psychological, and cultural reasons for theistic belief, in addition to insights from the cognitive science of religion.

- *Contemporary Arguments in Natural Theology: God and Rational Belief* (edited by Colin Ruloff and Peter Horban), presents eighteen essays discussing various arguments for the existence of God.

It bears noting that although philosophical anthropology, philosophical aesthetics, and so forth are *not the ultimate object of natural theology*, since theistic arguments can be mounted that try to make explicit relationships between certain conclusions in these different philosophical disciplines and God's existence, these different subjects are inevitably drawn into the task of elaborating a synoptic Christian worldview *through the project of natural theology*.

A Brief History of the Natural Sciences in Relation to Natural Theology

The founding assumption of Western medieval universities was that every academic discipline could be philosophically integrated into a coherent, synoptic worldview provided by Christian theology. Due to the secularizing impetus of the Enlightenment, natural philosophy became detached

---

110. Alvin Plantinga, "Two Dozen (or so) Arguments for God."

111. See: Baylor Institute for the Study of Religion, Plantinga Conference 2014.

112. See: YouTube Playlist: "Argument from Desire;" Williams, "Beginner's Guide to the Theistic Argument from Desire;" Bassham ed. *Lewis's Christian Apologetics*, 27–74; Williams "Defence of Arguments From Desire;" Puckett Jr. *Apologetics of Joy*.

from theology. In the Victorian era "natural philosophy" became known as "science." In the twentieth century, under the influence of logical positivism, "science" came to be defined as a search for the best understanding of the natural world consistent with a naturalistic worldview. This supposedly neutral "methodological naturalism" was turned into a *de facto* metaphysical naturalism via the condemnation of any dissenting understanding of science as "pseudo-science." In recent decades, these philosophical strictures have begun to loosen.[113] As Garrett J. DeWeese and J.P. Moreland report: "The inadequacy of methodological naturalism [is now] widely acknowledged by philosophers of science, even among those who are atheists ..."[114] For example, atheist philosopher of science Bradley Monton rejects methodological naturalism because it stands in tension with seeing science as a search for the truth about the natural world:

> If science really is permanently committed to methodological naturalism—the philosophical position that restricts all explanations in science to naturalistic explanations—it follows that the aim of science is not generating true theories. Instead, the aim of science would be something like: generating the best theories that can be formulated subject to the restriction that the theories are naturalistic.[115]

However one sees the relationship between science and metaphysics, it is obvious that the scientific study of the very large (cosmology) and the very small (e.g. molecular biology) has uncovered a wealth of data that gives support to key premises in various arguments for theism.

As Rodney Holder comments: "modern cosmology ... has provided a new impetus to natural theology, reviving traditional arguments but expressing them in new ways."[116] In the first place, discoveries since the 1960s have overturned the ancient pagan assumption that the cosmos exists without a beginning, thereby rejuvenating the discussion of *Kalam*-type cosmological arguments.[117] Moreover, scientists have uncovered a life-permitting

---

113. See: Williams. "Atheists Against Darwinism;" Bartlett and Holloway, eds. *Naturalism And Its Alternatives*; Gordon and Dembski, eds. *The Nature of Nature*; Moreland, ed. *Creation Hypothesis*; Ratzsch, *Science and Its Limits*.

114. DeWeese and Moreland, *Philosophy Made Slightly Less Difficult*, 146.

115. Monton, "Is Intelligent Design Science?"

116. Holder, *Ramified Natural Theology*, 4.

117. See: Copan and Craig, ed.'s. *Kalam Cosmological Argument, Volume Two*; Moreland and Craig, *Foundations for a Christian Worldview*; Williams, *Faithful Guide to Philosophy*.

"fine tuning" at the cosmic[118] (as well as the planetary[119]) levels of reality that has rejuvenated the discussion about design in both cosmology and natural theology.

Concurrently, discoveries in biology, including the complex information processing systems and intricate molecular machinery within cells, have rejuvenated discussion about design in both the biological sciences and natural theology.[120]

These scientific discoveries, coinciding with a growing disquiet amongst philosophers of science with attempts to define science as methodologically naturalistic,[121] have led to a discussion of the legitimacy of "theistic science" (a return to natural philosophy open to indirectly testable theistic hypotheses),[122] as well as the birth of the controversial scientific theory of "Intelligent Design," a scientific theory that provides material of obvious interest to natural theology. Intelligent Design theory limits itself to making inferences to design whilst heeding David Hume's point that one cannot thereby infer much about the nature of the designer or designers beyond those qualities necessary to account for the design that has been observed.[123]

Scientific contributions to natural theology are not limited to the natural sciences. For example, although it's a relatively young field of study, archaeology has yielded a wealth of data that should be taken into account by the search for the historical Jesus (and thus by ramified natural

118. See: Robin Collins' Fine-Tuning Website; Davies, *Goldilocks Enigma*; Moreland and Craig, *Philosophical Foundations for a Christian Worldview*, second edition; Williams, *Outgrowing God?*

119. See: Gonzalez and Richards, *Privileged Planet*.

120. See: Dembski and Wells, *Design of Life*; Meister, *Introducing Philosophy of Religion*. See also: Behe, *Darwin Devolves*; Behe, *The Edge of Evolution*; Behe, *Darwin's Black Box*, 10th anniversary edition; Leisola and Witt, *Heretic*; Marks II, Dembski and Ewert, *Introduction to Evolutionary Informatics*; Meyer, *Darwin's Doubt*; Meyer, *Signature in the Cell*; Thaxton et al, *Mystery of Life's Origin*; Williams, "Intelligent Designs on Science;" Williams, "Atheists Against Darwinism;" Williams, "Design Inference from Specified Complexity;" Williams, *Outgrowing God?*; Williams, *Faithful Guide to Philosophy*; Williams, *I Wish I Could Believe In Meaning*.

121. See: Ratzsch, *Science and Its Limits*.

122. See: Moreland ed., *Creation Hypothesis*; Rana and Ross, *Origins of Life*.

123. See: YouTube Playlist, "Debating Intelligent Design Theory;" Dembski and Wells, *Design of Life*; Gordon and Dembski, eds. *Nature of Nature*; Monton, *Seeking God in Science*; Williams, "Design Inference from Specified Complexity Defended by Scholars Outside the Intelligent Design Movement;" "Atheists Against Darwinism;" "Intelligent Designs on Science" (2006); "Design and the Humean Touchstone."

theology). For example, archaeologists and other scientists have recently uncovered data relevant to discussions about the historical existence of Jesus, the date from which people believed that Jesus was divine, Jesus's crucifixion and burial, etc.[124] Then again, social sciences have contributed to discussions about the reliability of oral tradition in the ancient near east.[125] Recent decades have also seen various attempts to investigate prayer for healing within the experimental scientific framework.[126] Hence Christian philosophy and/or apologetics needs to cast its net beyond the waters of the natural sciences if these disciplines are to live up to the synoptic vision of the Christian university.

Some Advice on Apologetics and Natural Theology in an Age of Science

Natural theology and ramified natural theology are sub-disciplines within both Christian apologetics and the philosophy of religion. To be a "philosopher" means to be "a lover of wisdom." As such, a philosopher is dedicated to the wise pursuit and dissemination of true answers to significant questions through the practice of good intellectual habits, "speaking the truth in love" (Ephesians 4:15).[127] Whether or not one is a professional philosopher, one's philosophical worldview[128] forms the foundation of one's way of life, that is, one's spirituality.[129] That is to say, the contents and intellectual habits of our minds, coupled with the choices, commitments and attitudes of our hearts, issue in behaviour that characterizes (and re-enforces) our spirituality or "way of life." Thus, philosophy is an integral component of any spirituality, including Christian spirituality.[130]

---

124. See: Evans, *Jesus and the Remains of His Day*; Williams, "Archaeological Evidence and Jesus;" Williams, "Archaeological Evidence and Jesus," Williams, "Defending Early High Christology;" Williams, "Digging for Evidence;" Williams, *Getting at Jesus*.

125. See: Eddy and Boyd, *Jesus Legend*.

126. See: Brown, *Testing Prayer*.

127. See: Williams, *Faithful Guide to Philosophy*.

128. See: YouTube Playlist, "Understanding Worldviews;" Sire, *Universe Next Door*, fifth edition; Williams, *Apologetics in 3D*.

129. See: Williams, "Apologetics in 3D—'Input' at Trondheim Frikirke" (2018); "Apologetics in 3D: Persuading Across Spiritualities With the Apostle Paul."

130. See: YouTube Playlist, "Discipleship & Spiritual Formation;" Comte-Sponville, *Book Of Atheist Spirituality*; Sheldrake, *Spirituality*; Williams, "Apologetics in 3D;" Williams, "Apologetics in 3D—'Input' at Trondheim Frikirke" (2018); "Apologetics in 3D:

Christian spirituality is a Christ-centred way of life, a Christ-centered way of relating to reality via one's head, heart and hands.[131] By drawing upon a range of disciplines, including natural theology, Christian apologetics aims to enable people to be persuaded that a Christ-centered spirituality is a beautiful, good, and reasonable commitment. It is the art of persuasively advocating Christian spirituality, through the responsible use of rhetoric, as being objectively beautiful, good and true or reasonable.[132] This being so, Christians should approach natural theology as a more than merely "academic" pursuit, for as Paul Copan writes,

> Philosophy should be an act of worship . . . when we undertake philosophy in Christ's name, our desk or reading chair becomes an altar, yielding "a fragrant aroma, an acceptable sacrifice, well-pleasing to God" (Phil 4:18).[133]

Apologetic appeals to scientific data, theories and/or methodology pack a strong rhetorical punch, partly because such appeals tap into a culturally accepted epistemology and partly because such appeals can undermine the mistaken belief that Christians are anti-science (especially when such appeals embrace the scientific consensus). However, it's worth bearing in mind that when making appealing to science, apologists need to avoid appearing to endorse *scientism*.[134] As McGrath comments:

> One of the most important functions of natural theology is to protest against the radically reduced visions of nature that arise from the movement sometimes known as "scientific imperialism" but now generally as simply "scientism."[135]

Although we live in a culture that encourages a degree of scientific literacy, apologists should consider how receptive non-specialist audiences

---

Persuading Across Spiritualities With the Apostle Paul"; *Understanding Jesus*.

131. See: Williams, "Discipleship in 3D: Change for head, heart and hands;" Williams, "Apologetics in 3D: Persuading across Spiritualities with the Apostle Paul."

132. To adapt a definition from the Oxford English Dictionary, to *persuade* (to be persuasive or act persuasively) is to draw the will of another to something by inclining their judgement and/or desire to it. See: Williams, "Apologetics in 3D;" Williams, "Apologetics in 3D—"Input" at Trondheim Frikirke" (2018); Williams, "Apologetics of Cultural Re-Enchantment in 3D: Makoto Fujimura's *Culture Care* & Paul M. Gould's *Cultural Apologetics;*" Williams, "Apologetics in 3D: Persuading across Spiritualities with the Apostle Paul;" Williams, *Apologetics in 3D*.

133. Copan, *Little Book for New Philosophers*, 119–20.

134. See: YouTube Playlist: "Scientism."

135. McGrath, *Enriching our Vision*, 174.

are likely to be to theistic arguments that require them to begin learning complex information about cosmology or molecular biology, etc. By comparison, other theistic arguments function at a more intuitive level, at least at a first pass.[136] For example, the meta-ethical moral argument begins with moral experiences common to, and thus readily understood by, all properly functioning humans from an early age.[137] Likewise, the argument from desire is rooted in common human experience.[138]

While Christians should continue to explore the theological fruitfulness of contemporary scientific cosmology and biology, it's worth bearing in mind both that natural theology can draw upon a broad range of scientific subjects beyond the natural sciences (e.g. archaeology and social science can both contribute to ramified natural theology) and upon a broad range of knowledge beyond the limited grasp of science (e.g. meta-ethics, aesthetics, philosophical anthropology). Indeed, making arguments that begin with mental properties such as intentionality, or with moral or aesthetic facts, helps make the point that empirical science isn't the self-justifying golden path to everything that can be known hoped for by the logical positivists.[139]

I would encourage Christians to give a higher priority to defending the *doctrine* of creation (focusing upon the creedal claim that God is the ultimate causer and intender, as well as sustainer, of the cosmos)[140] than to arguing for any particular *model* of creation (focusing upon differing interpretations of scriptural creation texts and how they can be best integrated into a synoptic Christian worldview).[141] Concerning the quest for a synoptic *model* of creation, I agree with Michael J. Murray and Michael Rea that,

---

136. See: Williams, "Arguing for God."

137. See: Williams, "Can Moral Objectivism Do Without God?"; Williams, *Outgrowing God?*, Chapter Four; Williams, *Faithful Guide to Philosophy*, Chapter Eight; Garcia and King, *Is Goodness without God Good Enough?*.

138. See: YouTube Playlist: "Argument from Desire"; Williams, "Beginner's Guide to the Theistic Argument from Desire"; "C.S. Lewis as a Central Figure in Formulating the Theistic Argument from Desire"; Bassham ed. *C.S. Lewis's Christian Apologetics*, 27–74; Williams "In Defence of Arguments From Desire"; Puckett Jr. *The Apologetics of Joy*.

139. See: Williams, *Faithful Guide to Philosophy*, Chapters Eight, Fourteen & Fifteen.

140. As C. John Collins notes: "Traditional Christian metaphysics put all these things together by describing God's initial creation — which produced all things — followed by his providential maintaining and ruling what he had made."—*Reading Genesis Well*, 267 ff. See: McGrath, *I Believe*, 29–36.

141. See: Marston, "Understanding the Biblical Creation Passages;" Barrett, Caneday and Gundry, eds. *Four Views On The Historical Adam*; Charles, ed. *Reading Genesis 1–2*;

for the religious believer, the [resolution of purported] conflicts between science and religion will involve balancing evidence against evidence: the empirical evidence favouring scientific claims against the revelatory evidence favouring theological claims. The Christian [might] conclude that the . . . evidence for an ancient earth seems quite strong, while the evidence for the naturalistic origin of life is, in fact, virtually non-existent. This then needs to be balanced against the evidence of revelation. How clear is it that the Bible teaches that the earth is young, or that God directly intervened in the cosmos to bring about life?[142]

As Plantinga reminds us:

We can't automatically assume that when there is a conflict between science and our grasp of the teaching of Scripture, it is science that is wrong and must give way. But the same holds vice versa; when there is a conflict between our grasp of the teaching of Scripture and current science, we can't assume that it is our interpretation of Scripture that is at fault. It could be that, but it doesn't have to be; it could be because of some mistake or flaw in current science.[143]

Science and theology (including natural theology) are fallible human projects. Wisdom enjoins that we do our best to follow the available evidence where it appears to lead, yet without falling into undue dogmatism.[144]

Finally, I'd encourage Christians to engage with the many challenges to and opportunities for apologetics provided by contemporary popular culture, challenges and opportunities that are often focused around science or found within science fiction.[145]

Craig, *In Quest of the Historical Adam*; Halton and Gundry, eds. *Genesis*; Stump and Gundry, eds. *Creation, Evolution, And Intelligent Design*; Swamidass, *Genealogical Adam and Eve*; Walton, *Lost World Of Genesis One*; Walton, *Lost World Of Adam And Eve*.

142. Murray and Rea, *Introduction to the Philosophy of Religion*, 211. See: Lennox, *Seven Days That Divide The World*; Meyer, *Signature in the Cell*; Thaxton et al, *Mystery of Life's Origin*.

143. Plantinga, "When Faith and Reason Clash."

144. See: Williams, "Is Christianity Unscientific?"

145. See: Dahle and Kro, "'Unraveling the Mystery;'" Williams, "Ancient Aliens;" Williams, "'Scientific Rebuttals to 'Ancient Aliens';" "A Universe From Someone;" Williams, "Carl Sagan: The Skeptic's Sceptic;" Williams, "In Search Of Innocence;" Williams, *Outgrowing God?*; Couch, Watkins and Williams, *Back In Time*; Couch, ed. *Matrix Revelations*.

Appendix A[1]

Four Dozen Key Resources on Apologetics and Natural Theology in an Age of Science

CURATED AND ANNOTATED BY PETER S. WILLIAMS
ASSISTANT PROFESSOR IN COMMUNICATION AND WORLDVIEWS
NLA UNIVERSITY COLLEGE

I was both delighted and daunted when Chief Editor Lars Dahle invited me to compile a bibliography for this special *Supplement* edition of *Theofilos* on "Science, Natural Theology, and Christian Apologetics". Of course, these days a literal interpretation of "bibliography" would preclude mentioning some of the many excellent resources available in the form of video and audio material via platforms such as the internet, and so I've chosen to provide the following list of key "resources" under several sub-headings. Each resource is followed by a brief description. The title of this list was inspired by Alvin Plantinga's famous paper on "Two dozen (or so) arguments for God", with four dozen recommendations giving room for

1. This appendix reproduces an annotated list of recommended resources I compiled for the December 2020 *Supplement* edition of the Nordic academic open-access journal *Theofilos* (https://theofilos.no/) on "Science, Natural Theology, and Christian Apologetics", which I guest-edited.
   The entire supplement is available online: https://theofilos.no/issues/theofilos-supplement-2020-1/.
   The entire supplement is available as a pdf to download: https://theofilos.no/wp-content/uploads/2021/02/Theofilos-vol-12-nr-1-2020-Supplement-Komplett-NY-210211.pdf.

covering the wide variety of issues that fall within the remit of "apologetics and natural theology in an age of science," without becoming too unwieldy.

Key Documentary Series:

The God Question: The Series/Science vs God? (Dir. Ian Morris.): www.thegodquestion.tv.

> The website for the series provides study guides, leaders guides, and materials for schools.
> See also: Peter S. Williams and Lars Dahle, "Turning Back the Tide of Atheism with the God Question" https://youtu.be/wBWYvCBRYYw.
> https://foclonline.org/talk/turning-back-tide-atheism-god-question.

Key Websites:

Reasonable Faith website: www.reasonablefaith.com.

> This leading Christian apologetics website showcases the work of William Lane Craig.

Peter S. Williams' YouTube channel, curated playlists: www.youtube.com/user/peterswilliamsvid/playlists?flow=grid&view=1.

> Over one hundred and twenty-five curated YouTube playlists on a wide variety of apologetic and philosophical subjects.

Key Podcasts:

Reasonable Faith Podcast: www.reasonablefaith.org/media/reasonable-faith-podcast/.

> William Lane Craig's interview-style podcast.

Unbelievable? www.premierchristianradio.com/Shows/Saturday/Unbelievable.

> In this program from Premier Christian Radio, Justin Brierley ably hosts discussion between guests with differing ideas about important issues.

The Peter S. Williams Podcast: http://podcast.peterswilliams.com.

This apologetics podcast often covers issues related to science, natural theology, and Christian apologetics.

Key Texts:

Barrett, Matthew, Ardel B. Caneday, and Stanley N. Gundry eds. *Four Views On The Historical Adam* (Zondervan, 2013).

> Denis O. Lamoureux, John H. Walton, C. John Collins, and William D. Barrick have a four-way discussion about how to understand the biblical figure of Adam.

Bassham, Gregory ed. *C.S. Lewis's Christian Apologetics: Pro and Con* (Brill/Rodopi, 2015).

> A series of short debates over arguments drawn from the works of C.S. Lewis. The debate between Bassham and Peter S. Williams over the argument from desire is continued by the latter in "In Defence of Arguments From Desire" (2016) www.peterswilliams.com/2016/11/02/in-defence-of-arguments-from-desire/.

Blomberg, Craig and Carl Stecher, with contributions by Richard Carrier and Peter S. Williams, *Resurrection: Faith or Fact? A Scholars' Debate Between a Skeptic and a Christian* (Pitchstone, 2019).

> This written debate on the resurrection is the only such volume published by a non-Christian publisher. See also: Peter S. Williams, "Resurrection: Faith or Fact? Miracle Not Required?" *Theofilos* 11.2 (2019) https://theofilos.no/wp-content/uploads/2020/03/Theofilos-vol.-11-nr.-2-2019-Forum-3-Arkiv.pdf.

Copan, Paul and William Lane Craig, eds. *The Kalam Cosmological Argument, Volume Two: Scientific Evidence for the Beginning of the Universe* (Bloomsbury Studies in Philosophy of Religion, 2019).

> This collection of papers reviews and assesses the latest scientific evidences for the universe's beginning and ends with an examination of the kalam argument's conclusion that the universe has a cause—a personal cause with properties of theological significance.

Copan, Paul and Charles Taliaferro, eds. *The Naturalness of Belief: New Essays on Theism's Rationality* (Lexington, 2018).

Beginning with naturalist Graham Oppy's own account of the naturalness of a naturalistic worldview, this wide-ranging collection of papers defends the naturalness of theism in light of consciousness, intentionality, beauty, human dignity, free will, rationality, and knowledge; as well as looking at common-sensical, existential, psychological, and cultural reasons, in addition to insights from the cognitive science of religion.

Copan, Paul et al. eds. *Dictionary of Christianity and Science* (Zondervan, 2017).

Billing itself as "the definitive reference for the intersection of Christian faith and contemporary science", this multi-author work by over one hundred and forty leading international scholars includes "multiple-view essays on controversial topics" and entries on over four hundred and fifty key terms, theories, individuals and subjects of debate.

Copan, Paul and Paul Moser, eds. *The Rationality of Theism* (Routledge, 2003).

A good collection of introductory/intermediate level papers. Part One addresses foundational issues about religious language and epistemology. Part Two focuses on arguments for God's existence, including the ontological argument, the cosmological argument, the teleological argument, and miracles. Part Three examines arguments against theism from the divine attributes and the existence of evil.

Cowen, Steven B. ed. *Five Views on Apologetics* (Zondervan, 2000).

Brings leading exponents of five different apologetic methodologies into dialogue.

Craig, William Lane. *On Guard for Students: A Thinker's Guide to the Christian Faith* (David C. Cooke, 2015).

The foremost apologist of our times writes an accessible book aimed at non-Christian readers.

Craig, William Lane and J.P. Moreland eds. *The Blackwell Companion to Natural Theology* (Wiley-Blackwell, 2009).

Substantial essays on different aspects of natural theology written by leading philosophers.

Craig, William Lane and J.P. Moreland eds. *Naturalism: A Critical Analysis* (Routledge, 2014).

> A stellar collection of papers that put the debate about theism in the context of arguments against metaphysical naturalism.

Dembski, William A. and Jonathan Wells. *The Design of Life: Discovering Signs of Intelligence in Biological Systems* (ISI, 2007).

> An engaging intermediate level introduction to intelligent design theory within the biological sciences.

Gordon, Bruce L and William A. Dembski, eds. *The Nature of Nature: Examining the Role of Naturalism in Science* (ISI, 2010).

> A large collection of papers, from different perspectives, on naturalism in science.

Gundry, Stanley N. and J.B. Stump eds. *Four Views on Creation, Evolution, and Intelligent Design* (Zondervan, 2017).

> Representatives from Answers in Genesis, Reasons to Believe, BioLogos and the Discovery Institute dialogue over their different models of origins.

Hannam, James. *The Genesis of Science: How the Christian Middle Ages Launched the Scientific Revolution* (Regnery, 2011).

> Sets straight the record about the relationship between Christianity and science in the middle ages.

Holder, Rodney. *Ramified Natural Theology in Science and Religion: Moving Forward from Natural Theology* (Routledge, 2021).

> Uses Bayesian confirmation theory to defend a "ramified natural theology" in dialogue with both science and historical-critical study of the Bible.

Kitchen, K.A. *On the Reliability of the Old Testament* (Eerdmans, 2006).

> A robust defence of the historical reliability of the Old Testament by an eminent Egyptologist.

Larmer, Robert A. *The Legitimacy of Miracle* (Lexington, 2014).

> A brilliant philosophical defense of miracles.

APPENDIX A

Lennox, John C. *God's Undertaker: Has Science Buried God?* Second edition (Lion, 2009).

> A winsome rejection of the popular idea that modern science has "buried" God.

Licona, Michael R. *The Resurrection of Jesus: A New Historiographical Approach* (IVP/Apollos, 2010).

> This substantial monograph by a protégé of Gary R. Habermas leans over backwards to avoid confirmation bias and is noteworthy for its careful discussion of historical methodology.

Menuge, Angus. *Agents under Fire: Materialism and The Rationality of Science* (Rowman & Littlefield, 2004).

> Philosopher Menuge relates intelligent design theory to the philosophy of mind, arguing that irreducible complexity challenges reductionist accounts of human psychology as well as reductionism in biology.

Meyer, Stephen C. *The Return of The God Hypothesis: Three Scientific Discoveries Revealing the Mind Behind The Universe* (HarperOne, 2021).

> Philosopher of science and leading intelligent design theorist Stephen C. Meyer mounts an argument for theism.

Miller, Corey and Paul Gould, ed.'s. *Is Faith in God Reasonable?* (Routledge, 2014).

> Begins with the transcription of a debate between William Lane Craig and Alex Rosenberg, adds several commenting papers, and gives the debaters the opportunity to respond.

Monton, Bradley. *Seeking God in Science: An Atheist Defends Intelligent Design Theory* (Broadview Press, 2009).

> Atheist philosopher of science Bradley Monton defends the scientific status of intelligent design theory and explains why its arguments make him less certain of his atheism.

Moreland, J.P. *The Recalcitrant Imago Dei: Human Persons and the Failure of Naturalism* (SCM, 2009).

> A leading Christian philosopher, Moreland mounts a wide-ranging argument against naturalistic accounts of human beings.

Moreland, J.P. *Consciousness and the Mind of God* (Routledge, 2008).

> Moreland is a leading proponent of the theistic argument from mind.

Moreland, J.P. *Scaling the Secular City: A Defence of Christianity* (Baker, 1987).

> One of the finest one-volume apologetics of the twentieth century.

Moreland, J.P. and William Lane Craig. *Philosophical Foundations for a Christian Worldview*, second edition (IVP, 2017).

> Moreland and Craig join forces to write a high-level "introduction" to philosophical issues relevant to forming a synoptic Christian worldview. Includes chapters on arguments for God.

Moreland, J.P. and Kai Nielsen et al. *Does God Exist?: The Debate Between Theists and Atheists* (Prometheus, 1993).

> An interesting if somewhat frustrating debate between Moreland and Nielsen. On the atheist side, there are also contributions from atheists Antony Flew and Keith Parsons; but the real value of this collection lies in William Lane Craig's incisive debate analysis, Dallas Willard's classic "Language, Being, God, and the Three Stages of Theistic Evidence" and Peter Kreeft's introduction, concluding chapter and appendix—all designed to help readers decide for themselves whether God is fact or fantasy.

Nagasawa, Yujin. *The Existence of God: A Philosophical Introduction* (Routledge, 2011).

> Leading philosopher of religion Yujin Nagasawa takes the arguments for God seriously in this well written introductory work suitable for undergraduates.

Nagel, Thomas. *Mind and Cosmos: Why the Materialist Neo-Darwinian Conception Of Nature Is Almost Certainly Wrong* (Oxford, 2012).

> A leading atheist philosopher of mind, Nagel made waves with this short book in which he critiques the orthodox naturalistic worldview of contemporary Western culture, says nice things about the proponents of Intelligent Design theory, discusses the problems of fitting consciousness into a naturalistic ontology, and hopes vaguely for a non-theistic teleological alternative.

APPENDIX A

Plantinga, Alvin. *Where the Conflict Really Lies: Science, Religion, and Naturalism* (Oxford University Press, 2012).

> Leading Christian philosopher Alvin Plantinga argues that science and theistic religion are in concord, whereas science and naturalistic atheism are in conflict.

Polkinghorne, John C. *Belief in God in an Age of Science* (Yale, 2003).

> Quantum-physicist-turned-theologian John Polkinghorne's Terry Lectures focus on the collegiality between science and theology.

Ratzsch, Del. *Science and Its Limits: The Natural Sciences in Christian Perspective.* Second edition (IVP, 2000).

> An accessible introduction to the philosophy of science.

Sennett, James F. and Douglas Groothuis, eds. *In Defence of Natural Theology: A Post-Humean Assessment* (IVP, 2005).

> Collection of papers written in the light of David Hume's influential critique of natural theology.

Smart, J.J.C. and J.J. Haldane. *Atheism & Theism*, second edition (Blackwell, 2003).

> A wide-ranging written debate between two noted philosophers.

Swinburne, Richard. *The Existence of God*, second edition (2004).

> A pioneering inductive approach to natural theology from a leading Christian philosopher of religion.

Swinburne, Richard. *The Resurrection of God Incarnate* (Clarendon Press, 2003).

> Swinburne applies his inductive approach to defending the resurrection of Jesus.

Walls, Jerry L. and Trent Dougherty ed.'s, *The Plantinga Project: Two Dozen (Or So) Arguments for God* (Oxford University Press, 2018).

> Papers from an academic conference inspired by Alvin Plantinga's seminal 1986 paper "Two Dozen (Or So) Arguments for God", highlighting the breadth of contemporary natural theology.

Williams, Peter S. *Outgrowing God? A Beginner's Guide to Richard Dawkins and the God Debate* (Cascade, 2020).

Written in dialogue form, this response to atheist Richard Dawkins' book *Outgrowing God* encourages critical thinking about Professor Dawkins' arguments concerning God, Jesus, and the Bible. Several chapters interact with Dawkins on issues of science and natural theology, covering the moral argument, arguments from design in biology and cosmology, and the *kalam* cosmological argument.

Williams, Peter S. *Getting at Jesus: A Comprehensive Critique of Neo-Atheist Nonsense about the Jesus of History* (Wipf and Stock, 2019).

This "comprehensive critique" of New Atheist views on the historical Jesus and the historical testimony concerning his life, death and resurrection draws on philosophy, history, archaeology and other scientific evidence to make a positive case for the Christian understanding of Jesus. It also shows how statements from neo-atheists can be used to defend the major elements of this understanding.

Williams, Peter S. *A Faithful Guide to Philosophy: A Christian Introduction to the Love of Wisdom*, reprint edition (Wipf and Stock, 2019).

This well-received Christian introduction to philosophy includes an unusually broad range of material on natural theology and a chapter on the relationship between science and theology. This reprint edition includes a new author's preface and a foreword by Angus Menuge.

Appendix B

Recommended Resources

My website has a page dedicated to this book containing various resources, including videos and podcasts: www.peterswilliams.com/publicationsbooks/a-universe-from-someone-essays-on-natural-theology/

Peter S. Williams

Website: www.peterswilliams.com
Podcast: http://peterswilliams.podbean.com/?source=pb
YouTube channel playlists: www.youtube.com/user/peterswilliamsvid/playlists?view=1&flow=grid
Acedemia.edu profile with links to published papers: https://mediehogskolen.academia.edu/PeterSWilliams
Twitter: @Williams_PeterS

Websites

BeliefMap: www.beliefmap.org
BeThinking: www.bethinking.org
Discovery Institute Centre for Science & Culture: www.discovery.org/id/
Evangelical Philosophical Society: www.epsociety.org/
Faith and Philosophy: https://place.asburyseminary.edu/faithandphilosophy/
Forum of Christian Leaders: https://foclonline.org/

J.P. Moreland: www.jpmoreland.com/
Joshua L. Rasmussen's "Worldview Design" YouTube channel: www.youtube.com/c/WorldviewDesignChannel/videos
Last Seminary: www.lastseminary.com/
Paul Copan: www.paulcopan.com/
Robin Collins' Fine-Tuning Website: http://home.messiah.edu/~Collin's/Fine-tuning/FT.HTM
Stephen C. Meyer: https://stephencmeyer.org/
The God Question: www.thegodquestion.tv/
Theofilos: https://theofilos.no/
Unbelievable?: www.premierradio.org.uk/shows/saturday/unbelievable.aspx?mod_page=0
William Lane Craig - Reasonable Faith: www.reasonablefaith.org

Watch

YouTube channel playlists: www.youtube.com/user/peterswilliamsvid/playlists?view=1&flow=grid
Against the Tide: Finding God In An Age Of Science. Pensmore Films, 2021.
The God Question. www.thegodquestion.tv/

Online Papers

Beck, W. David. "God's Existence" https://digitalcommons.liberty.edu/cgi/viewcontent.cgi?article=1086&context=sor_fac_pubs.
Craig, William Lane. "Five Arguments for God" http://christianevidence.org/docs/booklets/five_arguments_for_god.pdf.
Evans, C. Stephen. "The Mystery of Persons and Belief in God" www.lastseminary.com/cumulative-arguments/The%20Mystery%20of%20Persons%20and%20Belief%20in%20God.pdf.
Kreeft, Peter and Ronald K. Tacelli. "Twenty Arguments For God's Existence" www.peterkreeft.com/topics-more/20_arguments-gods-existence.htm.
Plantinga, Alvin. "Two Dozen (Or So) Arguments for God" https://appearedtoblogly.files.wordpress.com/2011/05/plantinga-alvin-22two-dozen-or-so-theistic-arguments221.pdf.
Swinburne, Richard. "Evidence for God" (1986) http://christianevidence.org/docs/booklets/evidence_for_god.pdf.

Willard, Dallas. "Language, Being, God, and the Three Stages of Theistic Evidence" https://dwillard.org/articles/language-being-god-and-the-three-stages-of-theistic-evidence.

Books

Amazon List: "Recommended Reading for Aspiring Apologists" www.amazon.co.uk/hz/wishlist/genericItemsPage/1OU3I7M8DYEEP.

Amazon List: "Debating God and Jesus" www.amazon.co.uk/hz/wishlist/genericItemsPage/FZUMMTM9145Z.

Bassham, Gregory ed. *C.S. Lewis' Apologetics: Pro and Con.* Leiden: Rodolpi-Brill, 2015.

Beck, W. David. *Does God Exist? A History of Answers to the Question.* Downers Grove, IL: IVP Academic, 2021.

Beckwith, Francis J. ed. *To Everyone an Answer: A Case for the Christian Worldview.* Downers Grove, IL: IVP, 2004.

Behe, Michael J. *Darwin Devolves: The New Science About DNA That Challenges Evolution.* New York: Harper One, 2020.

———. *The Edge of Evolution: The Search for the Limits of Darwinism.* New York: Free Press, 2007.

———. *Darwin's Black Box: The Biochemical Challenge to Evolution,* second edition. New York: Free Press, 2006.

Bignon, Guillaume. *Confessions of a French Atheist: How God Hijacked My Quest to Disprove the Christian Faith.* Carol Stream, IL: Tyndale House, 2022.

Blomberg, Craig, and Carl Stecher with contributions by Richard Carrier and Peter S. Williams. *Resurrection: Faith or Fact? A Scholars' Debate Between a Skeptic and a Christian.* Durham, NC: Pitchstone, 2019.

Cowen, Steven B., and James S. Spiegel. *The Love Of Wisdom: A Christian Introduction To Philosophy.* Nashville: B&H, 2009.

Copan, Paul, and William Lane Craig, eds. *The Kalam Cosmological Argument: Volume One – Philosophical Arguments for the Finitude of the Past.* London: Bloomsbury, 2019.

———, ed.'s. *The Kalam Cosmological Argument: Volume Two – Scientific Evidence for the Beginning of the Universe.* London: Bloomsbury, 2019.

RECOMMENDED RESOURCES

Copan, Paul, and Paul K. Moser, ed.'s. *The Rationality of Theism*. London: Routledge, 2003.

Copan, Paul, and Charles Taliaferro, eds. *The Naturalness of Belief: New Essays on Theism's Rationality*. Lanham, Maryland: Lexington, 2019.

Cottingham, John. *Why Believe?* London: Continuum, 2009.

Craig, William Lane. *Does God Exist?* Pine Mountain, Georgia: Impact 360, 2019.

———. *On Guard - For Students: A Thinker's Guide to the Christian Faith*. Colorado Springs, CO: David C. Cook, 2015.

———. ed. *Philosophy of Religion: A Reader and Guide*. Edinburgh: Edinburgh University Press, 2002.

Craig, William Lane, and J.P. Moreland, ed.'s. *The Blackwell Companion To Natural Theology*. Oxford: Wiley-Blackwell, 2009.

———, ed.'s. *Naturalism: A Critical Analysis*. London: Routledge, 2014.

Dennett, Daniel C., and Alvin Plantinga. *Science and Religion: Are They Compatible?* Oxford: Oxford University Press, 2011.

Drew Jr., James K., and Paul M. Gould. *Philosophy: A Christian Introduction*. Grand Rapids, MI: Baker Academic, 2019.

Evans, C. Stephen. *Why Christian Faith Still Makes Sense: A Response To Contemporary Challenges*. Grand Rapids, MI: Baker Academic, 2015.

———. *Natural Signs and Knowledge of God: A New Look at Theistic Arguments*. Oxford University Press, 2010.

———. *The Historical Christ & The Jesus of Faith: The Incarnational Narrative as History*. Oxford: Clarendon, 2004.

———. *Why Believe?: Reason and Mystery as Pointers to God*. Grand Rapids, MI: Eerdmans, 1996.

———. *Despair: A Moment Or A Way Of Life?* Downers Grove, IL: IVP, 1973.

Ganssle, Gregory E. *A Reasonable God: Engaging the New Face of Atheism*. Waco, Texas: Baylor University Press, 2009.

———. *Our Deepest Desires: How The Christian Story Fulfils Human Aspirations*. Downers Grove, IL: IVP Academic, 2017.

Geisler, Norman L. *Christian Apologetics*, 2nd edition. Grand Rapids, MI: Baker Academic, 2013.

Geivett, R. Douglas, and Gary R. Habermas ed.'s. *In Defence of Miracles: A Comprehensive Case for God's Action in History*. Leicester: Apollos, 1997.

Gellman, Jerome I. *Experience of God and the Rationality of Theistic Belief*. Ithica, New York: Cornell University Press, 1997.

Glass, David H. *Atheism's New Clothes: Exploring and Exposing the Claims of the New Atheists*. Nottingham: Apollos, 2012.

Gundry, Stanley N. ed. *Creation, Evolution And Intelligent Design*. Grand Rapids, MI: Zondervan, 2017.

Goetz, Stewart, and Charles Taliaferro. *Naturalism*. Grand Rapids, MI: Eerdmans, 2008.

Holder, Rodney D. *God, The Multiverse, And Everything*. London: Routledge, 2016.

———. *Big Bang, Big God: A Universe Designed For Life?* Oxford: Lion, 2013.

Hunter, James Davison, and Paul Nedelisky. *Science And The Good: The Tragic Quest For The Foundations Of Morality*. New Haven: Yale University Press/Templeton, 2018.

Kreeft, Peter. *Heaven: The Heart's Deepest Desire*, expanded edition. San Francisco: Ignatius, 1989.

Larmer, Robert A. *The Legitimacy of Miracle*. Lanham, Maryland: Lexington, 2014.

Lennox, John C. *God and Stephen Hawking: Whose Design Is It Anyway?* Second edition. Oxford: Lion, 2021.

———. *God's Undertaker: Has Science Buried God?* 2nd edition. Oxford: Lion, 2009.

Lewis, C.S. *Miracles*. New York: Collins, 2012.

Licona, Michael R. *The Resurrection of Jesus: A New Historiographical Approach*. Downers Grove, IL: IVP/Apollos, 2010.

Lo, Thomas Y. et al. *Evolution And Intelligent Design In A Nutshell*. Seattle: Discovery Institute, 2020.

Markham, Ian. *Truth and the Reality of God: An Essay in Natural Theology*. Edinburgh: T&T Clark, 1998.

Menuge, Angus. *Agents Under Fire: Materialism And The Rationality Of Science*. Rowman & Littlefield, 2004.

Meyer, Stephen C. *The Return of the God Hypothesis*. New York: HarperCollins, 2021.

———. *Darwin's Doubt: The Explosive Origin of Animal Life and the Case for Intelligent Design*, revised edition. Bravo, 2014.

———. *Signature in the Cell: DNA and the Evidence for Intelligent Design*. New York: HarperOne, 2010.

Miller, Corey and Paul Gould, ed.'s. *Is Faith in God Reasonable?* London: Routledge, 2014.

Monton, Bradly. *Seeking God in Science. An Atheist Defends Intelligent Design*. Peterborough, Ontario: Broadview, 2009.

Moreland, J.P. *Scientism and Secularism: Learning to Respond to a Dangerous Ideology*. Wheaton, IL: Crossway, 2018.

———. *Consciousness and the Existence of God: A Theistic Argument*. London: Routledge, 2009.

———. *The Recalcitrant Imago Dei: Human Persons and the Failure of Naturalism*. London: SCM, 2009.

———. *Scaling the Secular City: A Defence of Christianity*. Grand Rapids, MI: Baker, 1987.

Moreland, J.P. and Kai Nielson et al. *Does God Exist?: The Debate Between Theists and Atheists*. Amherst, New York: Prometheus, 1993.

Moreland, J.P., and Garrett J. DeWeese. *Philosophy Made Slightly Less Difficult: A Beginner's Guide to Life's Big Questions*. Second edition. Downers Grove, IL: IVP Academic, 2021.

Moreland, J.P., and William Lane Craig. *Philosophical Foundations for a Christian Worldview*. Second edition. Downers Grove, IL: IVP, 2017.

Nagasawa, Yujin. *The Existence of God: A Philosophical Introduction*. London: Routledge, 2011.

Nagel, Thomas. *Mind and Cosmos: Why the Materialist Neo-Darwinian Conception of Nature Is Almost Certainly False*. Oxford: Oxford University Press, 2012.

———. *Secular Philosophy and the Religious Temperament*. Oxford: Oxford University Press, 2010.

Plantinga, Alvin. *Knowledge and Christian Belief*. Grand Rapids, MI: Eerdmans, 2015.

Polkinghorne, John. *Science & Christian Belief: Theological reflections of a bottom-up thinker*. London: SPCK, 1994.

Puckett Jr., Joe. *The Apologetics of Joy: A Case for the Existence of God from C.S. Lewis's Argument from Desire*. Cambridge: Lutterworth, 2013.

Rasmussen, Joshua and Kevin Vallier, ed.'s. *A New Theist Response To The New Atheism*. London: Routledge, 2020.

Ratzsch, Del. *Science & Its Limits: The Natural Sciences in Christian Perspective*. Nottingham: Apollos, 2000.

Reppert, Victor. *C.S. Lewis's Dangerous Idea: In Defence of the Argument from Reason*. Downers Grove, IL: IVP, 2003.

Rosenberg, Alex. *The Atheist's Guide to Reality: Enjoying Life Without Illusions*. W.W. Norton, 2011.

Ruloff, Colin and Peter Horban, ed.'s. *Contemporary Arguments in Natural Theology: God and Rational Belief*. London: Bloomsbury Academic, 2021.

Sennett, James F. and Douglas R. Groothuis, ed.'s. *In Defence of Natural Theology: A Post-Humean Assessment*. Downers Grove, IL: IVP, 2005.

Smith, Christian. *Atheist Overreach: What Atheism Can't Deliver*. Oxford: Oxford University Press, 2019.

Stokes, Mitch. *A Shot of Faith (to the Head): Be a Confident Believer in an Age of Cranky Atheists*. Nashville: Thomas Nelson, 2012.

Strobel, Lee. *The Case for Christ*, second edition. Grand Rapids, MI: Zondervan, 2016.

———. *In Defence of Jesus*. Grand Rapids, MI: Zondervan, 2016.

Swinburne, Richard. *The Existence of God*. Second edition, Oxford, Clarendon, 2004.

———. *Was Jesus God?* Oxford: Oxford University Press, 2008.

———. *The Resurrection of God Incarnate*. Oxford: Clarendon, 2003.

Tan, Change Laura and Rob Stadler. *The Stairway To Life: An Origin-of-Life Reality Check*. Evorevo, 2020.

Thaxton, Charles B. et al. *The Mystery Of Life's Origin: The Continuing Controversy*. Seattle: Discovery Institute, 2020.

Thomas, Neil. *Taking Leave of Darwin: A Longtime Agnostic Discovers The Case For Design*. Seattle: Discovery Institute, 2021.

Walls, Jerry L., and Trent Dougherty ed.'s. *Two Dozen (or so) Arguments for God: The Plantinga Project*. Oxford: Oxford University Press, 2018.

West, John G. ed. *The Magician's Twin: C.S. Lewis on Science, Scientism, and Society*. Seattle: Discovery Institute, 2012.

Willard, Dallas. *Knowing Christ Today: How We Can Trust Spiritual Knowledge*. New York: HarperOne, 2009.

RECOMMENDED RESOURCES

Williams, Peter S. *Apologetics in 3D: Essays On Apologetics and Spirituality*. Eugene, OR: Wipf and Stock, 2021.

———. *Outgrowing God? A Beginner's Guide to Richard Dawkins and the God Debate*. Eugene, OR: Cascade, 2020.

———. *A Faithful Guide to Philosophy: A Christian Introduction to the Love of Wisdom*. Eugene, OR: Wipf and Stock, 2019.

———. *Getting at Jesus: A Comprehensive Critique of Neo-Atheist Nonsense About the Jesus of History*. Eugene, OR: Wipf and Stock, 2019.

———. *C.S. Lewis vs. the New Atheists*. Milton Keynes: Paternoster, 2013.

———. *Understanding Jesus: Five Ways to Spiritual Enlightenment*. Milton Keynes: Paternoster, 2011.

———. *A Sceptic's Guide to Atheism*. Milton Keynes: Paternoster, 2009.

———. *I Wish I Could Believe In Meaning: A Response to Nihilism*. Southampton: Damaris, 2005.

———. *The Case for Angels*. Milton Keynes: Paternoster, 2002.

———. *The Case for God*. Tunbridge Wells: Monarch, 1999.

Wright, N.T. *The Resurrection of the Son of God*. London: SPCK, 2017.

Bibliography

Abel, David L., ed. *The First Gene*. New York: Long View Academic, 2011.
———. *Primordial Prescription: The Most Plaguing Problem of Life Origin Science*. London: Long View Academic, 2015.
Adler, Mortimer J. *Great Books of the Western World*. Encyclopedia Britannica, 1991.
Aeschliman, Michael D. *The Restoration of Man: C.S. Lewis and the Continuing Case Against Scientism*. 3rd ed. Seattle: Discovery Institute, 2019.
Albert, David. "On the Origin of Everything." *The New York Times*. www.nytimes.com/2012/03/25/books/review/a-universe-from-nothing-by-lawrence-m-krauss.html.
Alston, William P. "Religious Language and Verificationism." In *The Rationality of Theism*, edited by Paul Copan and Paul K. Moser, 17–34. London: Routledge, 2003.
Anscombe, G.E.M. "Modern Moral Philosophy." In *Virtue Ethics*, edited by Roger Crisp and Michael Slote, 26–44. Oxford: Oxford University Press, 1997.
Aquinas, Thomas. Quoted by Robert E. Maydole. "The Third Ways Modalized." www.bu.edu/wcp/Papers/Reli/ReliMayd.htm.
———. "The Five Ways." *Summa Theologica*. www.faculty.umb.edu/adam_beresford/courses/phil_100_11/reading_five_ways.pdf.
———. *Summa Contra Gentiles*. https://isidore.co/aquinas/ContraGentiles.htm.
Arnold, Clinton E. *Acts*. Grand Rapids, MI: Zondervan, 2002.
Atkins, Peter vs. William Lane Craig. "Does God Exist?" www.bethinking.org/who-are-you-god/advanced/does-god-exist-bill-craig-debates-peter-atkins.htm.
Atkins, Peter. YouTube video. "Calum Miller vs. Peter Atkins "Does God Exist?" Debate—Oxford 2012" 2:00:28. http://youtu.be/NhIr9OQBsto.
———. *On Being*. Oxford: Oxford University Press, 2011.
Augustine. *Confessions*. Translated by R.S. Pine-Coffin. London: Penguin, 1981.
Ayer, A.J. "Sir Alfred Ayer." In *Great Thinkers on Great Questions*, edited by Roy Abraham Varghese, 48. Oxford: OneWorld, 1998.
———. *Language, Truth and Logic*. 2nd edition. London: Victor Gollancz, 1946.
———. *The Central Questions of Philosophy*. London: Penguin, 1991.
———. "Men of Ideas," *The Listener*, 2 March 1978.
Baggett, David, and Jerry L. Walls. *Good God: The Theistic Foundations of Morality*. Oxford: Oxford University Press, 2011.
Baggini, Julian. *Atheism: A Very Short Introduction*. Oxford: Oxford University Press, 2003.

BIBLIOGRAPHY

Bannister, Andy. *The Atheist Who Didn't Exist*. Oxford: Monarch, 2015.

Barr, James. "Natural Theology in This Century: Concepts and Approaches." Gifford Lectures, 1994. www.giffordlectures.org/books/biblical-faith-and-natural-theology/1-natural-theology-century-concepts-and-approaches.

Barthes, Roland. "The Death of the Author." https://sites.tufts.edu/english292b/files/2012/01/Barthes-The-Death-of-the-Author.pdf.

Bartlett, Jonathan and Eric Holloway, eds. *Naturalism And Its Alternatives In Scientific Methodologies*. Broken Arrow, OK: Blyth Institute, 2017.

Bassham, Gregory, ed. *C.S. Lewis's Christian Apologetics: Pro and Con*. Leiden: Brill, 2015.

Bauckham, Richard. "First Steps to a Theology of Nature." *The Evangelical Quarterly* 58 (1986) 229–44. https://biblicalstudies.org.uk/pdf/eq/1986-3_bauckham.pdf.

Baylor Institute for the Study of Religion, Plantinga Conference 2014. YouTube videos. www.youtube.com/playlist?list=PLoJmtbsEea3gcN5eNq-0JXq2qTwDg7L_Q.

Beck, W. David. "God's Existence." In *In Defence Of Miracles: A Comprehensive Case for God's Action in History*, edited by R. Douglas Geivett and Gary R. Habermas, 149-62. Leicester: Apollos, 1997. https://digitalcommons.liberty.edu/cgi/viewcontent.cgi?article=1086&context=sor_fac_pubs.

———. *Does God Exist? A History of Answers to the Question*. Downers Grove, IL: IVP Academic, 2021.

Beckwith, Francis J. "Why I Am Not a Moral Relativist." www.coursehero.com/file/80654567/Beckwithpdf/.

Beckwith, Francis J. and Gregory Koukl. *Moral Relativism: Feet Firmly Planted in Mid-Air*. Grand Rapids, MI: Baker, 1998.

Behe, Michael J. *A Mousetrap for Darwin: Michael J. Behe Answers His Critics*. Seattle: Discovery Institute, 2020. Kindle.

———. "Irreducible Complexity: Obstacle to Darwinian Evolution." www.lehigh.edu/~inbios/Faculty/Behe/PDF/Behe_chapter.pdf.

———. *Darwin Devolves: The New Science about DNA That Challenges Evolution*. New York: HarperOne, 2019.

———. *Darwin's Black Box: The Biochemical Challenge to Evolution*, 10th anniversary edition. New York: Free, 2006.

———. *The Edge of Evolution: The Search for the Limits of Darwinism*. New York: Free, 2007.

———. *The Edge of Evolution: The Search for the Limits of Darwinism*. New York: Free, 2007.

Blomberg, Craig and Carl Stecher. *Resurrection: Faith or Fact? A Scholars' Debate Between a Skeptic and a Christian*. Durham, NC: Pitchstone, 2019.

Bradshaw, David. "Introduction." In *Natural Theology in the Eastern Orthodox Tradition*, edited by David Bradshaw and Richard Swinburne, 1–22. St. Paul, MN: Iota, 2021.

Brent, James. "Natural Theology." *Internet Encyclopedia of Philosophy*. www.iep.utm.edu/theo-nat/#H4.

Brodie, Sarah. "Aristotle's Elusive Summum Bonum." https://lucian.uchicago.edu/blogs/objects/files/2014/05/Broadie.pdf.

Brown, Candy Gunther. *Testing Prayer*. Cambridge, MA: Harvard University Press, 2012.

Burge, Tyler. "Philosophy of Language and Mind." *Philosophical Review* 101 (1992) 3–51.

Bracht, John. "Natural Selection as an Algorithm: Why Darwinian Processes Lack the Information Necessary to Evolve Complex Life" *Perspectives On Science And*

Christian Belief 54.4 (2002) www.lastseminary.com/against-darwinism/Natural%20 Selection%20as%20an%20Algorithm.pdf.
Byrom, Peter. "Disillusioned with Dawkins: My Journey from Atheism to Christianity: Peter Byrom." *Solas*. www.solas-cpc.org/disillusioned-with-dawkins-my-journey-from-atheism-to-christianity-peter-byrom/.
Lewis, C.S. *Mere Christianity*. London: Fount, 1997.
Carnap, Rudolph. "Psychology in Physical Language." https://web.stanford.edu/~paulsko/papers/Carn.pdf.
Caroll, William E. "The Science of Nothing." *Catholic World Report*. www.catholicworldreport.com/2012/04/10/the-science-of-nothing/.
Carrier, Richard. *Sense and Goodness Without God*. Bloomington, IN: Author House, 2005.
Carroll, Lewis. "Jabberwocky." *Interesting Literature*. https://interestingliterature.com/2016/01/22/a-short-analysis-of-jabberwocky-by-lewis-carroll/.
Carroll, Sean. *The Big Picture: On the Origins of Life, Meaning, and the Universe Itself*. Oxford: OneWorld, 2017.
Carson, D.A. *The Gagging of God: Christianity Confronts Pluralism*. Grand Rapids, MI: Zondervan Academic, 2009. Kindle.
Cave, Peter. *Humanism*. Oxford: OneWorld, 2009.
CCA. "Phenomenal Conservatism, Evidentialism, and Religious Epistemology (Dr. Chris Tucker)." YouTube video. Streamed live August 17, 2020. 59:50. https://youtu.be/LgBlLnT3h38.
Cerebral Faith. "Why The Divisibility Of Time Is Irrelevant To The Kalam Cosmological Argument." https://cerebralfaith.net/why-the-divisibility-of-time-is-irrelevant-to-the-kalam-cosmological-argument/.
CERN. "Dark Matter" https://home.cern/science/physics/dark-matter.
Chalmers, D. J. "Facing up to the Problem of Consciousness." *Journal of Consciousness Studies*, 2.3 (1995) 200–19.
Chalmers, David. "Hard Problem of Consciousness." YouTube video. www.youtube.com/watch?v=C5DfnIjZPGw.
Chapman, Allan. *Slaying the Dragons: Destroying Myths in the History of Science and Faith*. Oxford: Lion, 2013.
Charles, J. Daryl, ed. *Reading Genesis 1–2: An Evangelical Conversation*. Peabody, MA: Hendrickson, 2013.
Cicero, Lucilius. *On the Nature of the Gods*. Translated by H. Rackham. Loebs Classical Library. Cambridge, MA: Harvard University Press, 1986.
Clark, Kelly James. *Philosophers Who Believe: The Spiritual Journeys Of 11 Leading Thinkers*. Downers Grove, IL: InterVarsity, 1997.
Collins, John. *Reading Genesis Well*. Grand Rapids, MI: Zondervan, 2018.
Collins, Robin. "Modern Cosmology and Anthropic Fine-Tuning: Three Approaches." In *George Lemaitre: Life, Science and Legacy*, edited by Rodney D. Holder and Simon Mitton, 173–91. New York: Springer, 2013.
———. "The Argument from Physical Constants: The Fine Tuning for Discoverability." In *Two Dozen (Or So) Arguments For God*, edited by Jerry L. Walls and Trent Dougherty, 89–107. Oxford: Oxford University Press, 2018.
———. "The Teleological Argument: An Exploration of the Fine-Tuning of the Universe." In *The Blackwell Companion to Natural Theology*, edited by William Lane Craig and J.P. Moreland, 202–81. Oxford: Wiley-Blackwell, 2009.

———. "The Teleological Argument." In *The Rationality of Theism*, edited by Paul Copan and Paul K. Moser, 132–48. London: Routledge, 2003.

———. "Fine-Tuning Website." http://home.messiah.edu/~Collin's/Fine-tuning/FT.HTM.

Comte-Sponville, André. *The Book Of Atheist Spirituality: An Elegant Argument For Spirituality Without God*. London: Bantam, 2007.

Copan, Paul and Charles Taliaferro, eds. *The Naturalness of Belief: New Essays on Theism's Rationality*. London: Lexington, 2018.

Copan, Paul and Paul K. Moser, eds. *The Rationality of Theism*. London: Routledge, 2003.

Copan, Paul and William Lane Craig, eds. *The Kalam Cosmological Argument: Volume One – Philosophical Arguments for the Finitude of the Past*. London: Bloomsbury, 2019.

———, eds. *The Kalam Cosmological Argument: Volume Two – Scientific Evidence for the Beginning of the Universe*. London: Bloomsbury, 2019.

Copan, Paul. "God, Naturalism, and the Foundations of Morality." In *The Future of Atheism*, edited by Robert B. Stewart, 141–61. London: SPCK, 2008.

———. "Hume and the Moral Argument." In *In Defence Of Natural Theology: A Post-Humean Assessment*, edited by in James F. Sennett and Douglas Groothuis, 200–25. Downers Grove, IL: InterVarsity, 2005.

———. "Is Creatio Ex Nihilo A Post-Biblical Invention? An Examination of Gerhard May's Proposal." *EarlyChurch.org*. www.earlychurch.org.uk/article_exnihilo_copan.html.

———. "Is the Trinity a Logical Blunder? God as Three-in-One." www.paulcopan.com/articles/pdf/is-the-Trinity-a-logical-blunder_God-as-three-and-one.pdf.

———. "The Naturalists Are Declaring the Glory of God: Discovering Natural Theology in the Unlikeliest Places." In *Philosophy And The Christian Worldview: Analysis, Assessment and Development*, edited by David Werther and Mark D. Linville, 50–70. New York, NY: Continuum, 2012.

———. *A Little Book for New Philosophers*. Downers Grove, IL: IVP Academic, 2016.

———. *True For You, But Not For Me*. Minneapolis, Minnesota: Bethany House, 1998.

Copleston, F.C. "Commentary on the Five Ways." In *The Existence of God*, edited by John Hick, 86–93. New York: Macmillan, 1964.

———. "Logical Positivism—A Debate." In *A Modern Introduction to Philosophy, 2nd edition*, edited by Paul Edwards and Arthur Pap, 276–756. New York: Free, 1965.

———. *A History of Philosophy: Volume 2, Medieval Philosophy*. New York: Continuum, 2003.

———. *Contemporary Philosophy: Studies of Logical Positivism and Existentialism*. London: Burns and Oates, 1957.

Cottingham, John. "Philosophers Are Finding Fresh Meanings in Truth, Goodness and Beauty." *The Times*, 17 June 2006.

Couch, Steve, ed. *Matrix Revelations: A Thinking Fan's Guide to the Matrix Trilogy*. Southampton: Damaris, 2003.

Couch, Steve, Tony Watkins and Peter S. Williams. *Back In Time: A Thinking Fan's Guide to Doctor Who*. Southampton: Damaris, 2005.

Cowan, Steven B. "The Question of Moral Values." In *The Big Argument: Does God Exist?*, edited by John Ashton and Michael Westacott, 165–77. Green Forest, AR: Master, 2006.

BIBLIOGRAPHY

Cowen, Steven B. and James Spiegel. *The Love Of Wisdom*. Nashville, Tennessee: Broadman & Holman, 2009.

Cowen, Steven B., ed. *Five Views on Apologetics*. Grand Rapids, MI: Zondervan, 2000.

Coyne, Jerry. "David Alberts Pans Lawrence Krauss' New Book." http://whyevolutionistrue.wordpress.com/2012/04/02/david-albert-pans-lawrence-krausss-new-book/.

Craig, William Lane. "A Formulation and Defence of the Doctrine of the Trinity." *Reasonable Faith*. www.reasonablefaith.org/writings/scholarly-writings/christian-doctrines/a-formulation-and-defense-of-the-doctrine-of-the-trinity/.

———. "Advice to Christian Apologists." www.bethinking.org/apologetics/advice-to-christian-apologists.

———. "Atheist Physicist's Repudiation of Logic and Probability Theory." *Reasonable Faith*. www.reasonablefaith.org/atheistic-physicists-repudiation-of-logic-and-probability-theory

———. "Can the Universe Exist Without God?" *Reasonable Faith*. www.reasonablefaith.org/media/craig-vs-enqvist-helsinki.

———. "Classical Apologetics." In *Five Views On Christian Apologetics*, edited by Steven B. Cowen, 39–43. Grand Rapids, MI: Zondervan, 2000.

———. "Does God Exist?" *Philosophy Now*. https://philosophynow.org/issues/99/Does_God_Exist.

———. "Five Arguments for God." *Christian Evidence*. http://christianevidence.org/docs/booklets/five_arguments_for_god.pdf.

———. "In Defence of Rational Theism." In *Does God Exist? The Debate Between Theists and Atheists*, edited by J.P. Moreland and Kai Nielson, et al., 139–61. Amherst, NY: Prometheus, 1993.

———. "Natural Theology: Introduction." In *Philosophy of Religion: A Reader and Guide*, edited by William Lane Craig, 69–81. Edinburgh: Edinburgh University Press, 2002.

———. "Opening Speech" *Reasonable Faith*. www.reasonablefaith.org/media/debates/does-god-exist/.

———. "The Kalam Cosmological Argument." In *The Blackwell Companion To Natural Theology*. ed. William Lane Craig and J.P. Moreland; Oxford: Wiley-Blackwell, 2009.

———. "The Ontological Argument." In *To Everyone An Answer: A Case For The Christian Worldview*, edited by Francis J. Beckwith et al., 124–37. Downers Grove, IL: InterVarsity, 2004.

———. "The Resurrection of Theism." *Reasonable Faith*. www.reasonablefaith.org/writings/popular-writings/existence-nature-of-god/the-resurrection-of-theism.

———. "The Sam Harris Debate (part 2)." Reasonable Faith Podcast (12 June 2011). www.reasonablefaith.org/media/reasonable-faith-podcast/the-sam-harris-debate-part-2.

———. "Theism Defended." In *The Nature of Nature: Examining the Role of Naturalism in Science*, edited by Bruce L. Gordon and William A. Dembski, 101–19. Wilmington, DE: ISI, 2011.

———. "Why Does Anything at All Exist?" *Reasonable Faith*. www.reasonablefaith.org/media/why-does-anything-at-all-exist-nflc-north-carolina.

———. *Does God Exist?* Pine Mountain, GA: Impact 360 Institute, 2019.

———. ed. *Philosophy of Religion: A Reader and Guide*. Edinburgh: Edinburgh University Press, 2002.

———. *God, Are You There?* Milton Keynes: RZIM, 1999.

Craig, William Lane and Walter Sinnott-Armstrong. *God? A Debate Between A Christian And An Atheist*, edited by James P. Sterba. Oxford: Oxford University Press, 2004.

———. *In Quest of the Historical Adam: A Biblical and Scientific Exploration*. Grand Rapids, MI: Eerdmans, 2021.

———. "William Lane Craig." In *Science and Religion: 5 Questions*, edited by Gregg D. Caruso. New York: Automatic/VIP, 2014.

———. *On Guard: Defending Your Faith with Reason and Precision*. Colorado Springs: David C. Cook, 2010.

———. *Reasonable Faith: Christian Truth and Apologetics*. 3rd edition. Wheaton, IL: Crossway, 2009.

———. *The Kalam Cosmological Argument*. Eugene, OR: Wipf and Stock, 2000.

Craig, William Lane and J.P. Moreland, eds. *Naturalism: A Critical Analysis*. London: Routledge, 2000.

———. eds. *The Blackwell Companion to Natural Theology*. Oxford: Wiley-Blackwell, 2009.

Craig, William Lane and Joseph E. Gorra. *Reasonable Response*. Chicago, IL: Moody, 2013.

Dahle, Lars. "Acts 17:16-34: An Apologetic Model Then and Now?" *Tyndale Bulletin* 53.2 (2002) 313-16.

Dahle, Margunn Serigstad and Ingvild Thu Kro. "'Unraveling the Mystery' Assessing The Big Bang Theory as a Secular Fictional Universe." In *Theofilos* 12.1 (2020) 112-37.

Davies, Brian, ed. *Philosophy of Religion: a guide and anthology*. Oxford: Oxford University Press, 2000.

Davies, Paul. "The Birth of the Cosmos." In *God, Cosmos, Nature and Creativity*, edited by Jill Gready, 1-9. Edinburgh: Scottish Academic, 1995.

———. *The Cosmic Blueprint*. New York: Touchstone, 1989.

———. *The Goldilocks Enigma*. London: Penguin, 2007.

———. *The Origin of Life*. London: Penguin, 2003.

Davies, Stephen T. "A Somewhat Playful Proof of the Social Trinity in Five Easy Steps." *Philosophia Christi* 2.1 (1999) 105.

———. *God, Reason and Theistic Proofs*. Edinburgh: Edinburgh University Press, 1997.

Dawkins, Richard. "God's Utility Function." *Scientific American*, November 1995.

———. *The God Delusion*. London: Bantam, 2006.

———. *The Magic of Reality: How We Know What's Really True*. London: Bantam, 2011.

Deane, David R.C. "Is Science the Only Means for Acquiring Truth?" In *The Comprehensive Guide to Science and Faith*, edited by William A. Dembski et al., 415-27. Eugene, OR: Harvest House, 2021. Kindle.

"Delusion." *Stanford Encyclopedia of Philosophy*. http://plato.stanford.edu/entries/delusion/#DefDel.

Dembski, William A. "Specification: The Pattern That Signifies Intelligence." https://billdembski.com/documents/2005.06.Specification.pdf.

———. "Irreducible Complexity Revisited." *Design Inference*. www.designinference.com/documents/2004.01.Irred_Compl_Revisited.pdf.

———. *No Free Lunch: Why Specified Complexity Cannot Be Purchased Without Intelligence*. Lanham, MD: Rowman and Littlefield, 2002.

Dembski, William A. and Jonathan Wells. *The Design of Life: Discovering Signs of Intelligence in Biological Systems*. Richardson, TX: Foundation for Thought and Ethics, 2008.

Dennett, Daniel C. and Alvin Plantinga. *Science and Religion*. Oxford: Oxford University Press, 2011.

Denton, Michael. *Nature's Destiny: How The Laws Of Biology Reveal Purpose In The Universe*. New York: Free, 1998.

DeWeese, Garrett J. and J.P. Moreland. *Philosophy Made Slightly Less Difficult: A Beginner's Guide to Life's Big Questions*. 2nd Edition. Downers Grove, IL: IVP Academic, 2021.

———. *Philosophy Made Slightly Less Difficult: A Beginner's Guide to Life's Big Questions*. Downers Grove, IL: IVP Academic, 2005.

Dougherty, Trent. "Argument from Desire." http://prosblogion.ektopos.com/archives/2005/11/argument_from_d.html.

"Dr. Angus Menuge: Models of Consciousness (Part II)." *Mind Matters*. https://mindmatters.ai/podcast/ep134/.

Dubay, Thomas. *The Evidential Power Of Beauty: Science And Theology Meet*. San Francisco: Ignatius, 1999.

Eby, Lloyd. "Viewpoint: What is Science? Part I." *World Peace Herald*, December 16th, 2005. www.wpherald.com/storyview.php?StoryID=20051216-041328-8321r.

Eddy, Paul Rhodes and Gregory A. Boyd. *The Jesus Legend: A Case for the Historical Reliability of the Synoptic Jesus Tradition*. Grand Rapids, MI: Baker Academic, 2007.

Edwards, Rem B. "Behaviorism: II. Philosophical Issues." *Encyclopedia of Bioethics* (1995). www.encyclopedia.com/science/encyclopedias-almanacs-transcripts-and-maps/behaviorism-ii-philosophical-issues.

Enqvist, Karl and William Lane Craig. "Can the Universe Exist Without God?" *Reasonable Faith*. www.reasonablefaith.org/media/craig-vs-enqvist-helsinki.

Evans, C. Stephen. *Despair: A Moment Or A Way Of Life?* Downers Grove, IL: InterVarsity, 1973.

———. "The Mystery of Persons and Belief in God." www.lastseminary.com/cumulative-arguments/The%20Mystery%20of%20Persons%20and%20Belief%20in%20God.pdf.

———. *Natural Signs and Knowledge of God: A New Look at Theistic Arguments*. Oxford: Oxford University Press, 2012.

———. *Philosophy of Religion*. Downers Grove, IL: InterVarsity, 2001.

Evans, Craig A. *Jesus and the Remains of His Day: Studies in Jesus and the Evidence of Material Culture*. Peabody, MA: Henderickson, 2015.

Everist, Randy. "Can Science Explain Everything?" http://randyeverist.blogspot.com/2011/04/can-science-explain-everything.html

Ewing, A.C. *The Fundamental Questions of Philosophy*. London: Routledge, 1985.

———. *Value and Reality: The Philosophical Case for Theism*. London: George Allen & Unwin, 1973.

Ferguson, Sinclair B. and David F. Wright, eds. *New Dictionary of Theology*. Leicester: InterVarsity, 1988.

Flannagan, Matthew. "Is Naturalism Simpler Than Theism? Some Reflections on Graham Oppy's 'Best Argument Against God.'" www.mandm.org.nz/2018/10/is-naturalism-simpler-than-theism-some-reflections-on-graham-oppys-best-argument-against-god.html.

Flew, Antony. "Response to Lewis, Professor Antony Flew." In *Cosmos, Bios, Theos: Scientists Reflect on Science, God, and the Origins of the Universe, Life, and Homo sapiens*, edited by Henry Margenau and Roy Abraham Varghese, 241. Chicago: Open Court, 1994.

———. In Craig J. Hazen, Gary R. Habermas and Antony Flew, "My Pilgrimage from Atheism to Theism: An Exclusive Interview with Former British Atheist Professor Antony Flew." www.apologitis.com/gr/ancient/symp/flew-interview.pdf.

Floyd, Shawn. "Aquinas: Philosophical Theology." *Internet Encyclopedia of Philosophy*. www.iep.utm.edu/aq-ph-th/#SH3c.

Foster, John. *The Divine Lawmaker: Lectures on Induction, Laws of Nature, and the Existence of God*. Oxford: Oxford University Press, 2004.

Francis J. Beckwith, "Moral Law, the Mormon Universe, and the Nature of the Right We Ought to Choose." In *The New Mormon Challenge*, edited by Francis J. Beckwith et al., 219–41. Grand Rapids: Zondervan, 2002.

Fuller, Steve. *Dissent Over Descent*. London: Icon, 2008.

Gage, Logan Paul. "Is The God Hypothesis Improbable?" In *A New Theist Response To The New Atheism*, edited by Joshua Rasmussen and Kevin Vallier, 59–76. London: Routledge, 2020.

Garcia, Robert K. and Nathan L. King, eds. *Is Goodness without God Good Enough? A Debate on Faith, Secularism, and Ethics*. Lanham, MD: Rowman & Littlefield, 2009.

Gauch Jr., Hugh G. *Recent Transitions in Natural Theology: The Emergence of a Bolder Paradigm*. Interdisciplinary Biblical Research Institute, 2012.

Geisler, Norman L. *Baker Encyclopedia of Christian Apologetics*. Grand Rapids: Baker, 1999.

———. *Christian Apologetics*. Grand Rapids: Baker, 1988.

———. *Philosophy of Religion*. Grand Rapids, MI: Zondervan, 1974.

Geivett, R. Douglas and Brendan Sweetman, eds. *Contemporary Perspectives on Religious Epistemology*. Oxford: Oxford University Press, 1992.

Geivett, R. Douglas and Gary R. Habermas, eds. *In Defence of Miracles: A Comprehensive Case For God's Action In History*. Leicester: Apollos, 1997.

Geivett, R. Douglas. "The Evidential Value of Religious Experience." In *The Rationality of Theism*, edited by Paul Copan and Paul K. Moser, 175–203. London: Routledge, 2003.

Göcke, Benedikt Paul, ed. *After Physicalism*. South Bend, IN: University of Notre Dame Press, 2012.

Goetz, Stewart and Charles Taliaferro. *Naturalism*. Grand Rapids, MI: Eerdmans, 2008.

Gonzalez, Guillermo and Jay W. Richards. *The Privileged Planet: How Our Place in The Cosmos Is Designed For Discovery*. Washington, DC: Regnery, 2004.

Gordon, Bruce L. and William A. Dembski, eds. *The Nature of Nature: Examining the Role of Naturalism in Science*. Wilmington, DE: ISI, 2011.

Gordon, Bruce L. "Balloons on a String: A Critique of Multiverse Cosmology." In *The Nature of Nature: Examining the Role of Naturalism in Science*, edited by Bruce L. Gordon and William A. Dembski, 558–601. Wilmington, Delaware: ISI, 2011.

———. "Is Intelligent Design Science? The Scientific Status and Future of Design-Theoretic Explanations." In *Signs of Intelligence: Understanding Intelligent Design*, edited by William A. Dembski and James M. Kushiner, 193–216. Grand Rapids, MI: Brazos, 2001.

Graham, George. "Behaviorism." https://plato.stanford.edu/entries/behaviorism/.

Grant, Edward. *A History of Natural Philosophy: From the Ancient World to the Nineteenth Century*. Cambridge: Cambridge University Press, 2007.

Groothuis, Douglas. *Christian Apologetics: A Comprehensive Case for Biblical Faith*. Downers Grove, IL: InterVarsity, 2011.

―――. *Truth Decay*. Downers Grove, IL: InterVarsity, 2000.

Grossman, Lisa. "Death of the eternal cosmos." *New Scientist* (January 2012).

Habermas, Gary R. and J.P. Moreland. *Beyond Death: Exploring the Evidence for Immortality*. Wheaton, IL: Crossway, 1998.

Hackett, Stuart C. *The Resurrection of Theism: Prolegomena to Christian Apology*. Eugene, OR: Wipf and Stock, 2009.

Halton, Charles and Stanley N. Gundry, eds. *Genesis: History, Fiction, or Neither? Three Views On The Bible's Earliest Chapters*. Grand Rapids, MI: Zondervan, 2015.

Hannam, James. *The Genesis of Science: How the Christian Middle Ages Launched the Scientific Revolution*. Washington, DC: Regnery, 2010.

Harman, Gilbert and Judith Jarvis Thomson. *Moral Relativism and Moral Objectivity*. Oxford: Blackwell, 1996.

Harris, Sam. *The Moral Landscape: How Science Can Determine Human Values*. Bantam, 2011.

Hartley, Donald E. "Heb 11:6 – A Reassessment Of The Translation 'God Exists.'" *Trinity Journal* 27:2 (2006) 289–307.

Hasker, William. "Objections to Social Trinitarianism." *Religious Studies* 46 (2010) 421–39.

Hawking, Stephen and Leonard Milodinov. *The Grand Design*. London: Bantam, 2010.

Hawking, Stephen. *A Brief History of Time*. New York: Bantam, 2017.

Hawthorne, Tim. *Windows on Science and Christian Faith*. InterVarsity, 1986.

Heil, John. *Philosophy of Mind: A Contemporary Introduction*. London: Routledge, 1998.

Hemple, Carl. *Philosophy of Natural Science*. Englewood Cliffs, NJ: Prentice-Hall, 1966.

Hick, John, ed. *The Existence of God*. New York: Macmillan, 1964.

―――. "Theology and Verification." In *The Philosophy of Religion*, edited by Basil Mitchell, 53–71. Oxford: Oxford University Press, 1971.

Himma, Kenneth Einar. "Christian Faith Without Belief That God Exists: A Defense of Pojman's Conception of Faith." *Faith and Philosophy* 23.1 (2006) 65–79.

Hitchens, Christopher. "Christopher Hitchens Makes a Shocking Confession." YouTube video. 01:58. www.youtube.com/watch?v=E9TMwfkDwIY.

Holder, Rodney D. *Big Bang, Big God: A Universe Designed For Life?* Oxford: Lion, 2013.

―――. *God, The Multiverse, And Everything*. London: Routledge, 2016.

―――. *Ramified Natural Theology in Science and Religion: Moving Forward from Natural Theology*. London: Routledge, 2021.

―――. *The Heavens Declare: Natural Theology and the Legacy of Karl Barth*. West Conshohocken, PA: Templeton, 2012.

Houtz, Wyatt. "Karl Barth's No! to Natural Theology: Secular Parables of the Kingdom." *PostBarthian*. https://postbarthian.com/2016/07/22/karl-barths-no-natural-theology-secular-parables-kingdom/.

Howard-Snyder, Daniel. "Does Faith Entail Belief?" *Faith and Philosophy* 33.2 (2016) 133–42.

Hoyle, Fred. "The Universe: Past *and* Present Reflections." *Engineering and Science*, November 1981. https://calteches.library.caltech.edu/527/2/Hoyle.pdf.

Huemer, Michael. "Compassionate Phenomenal Conservatism." *Philosophy and Phenomenological Research* 74.1 (2007) 30–55.

Hunter, James Davidson and Paul Nedelisky. *Science and the Good: The Tragic Quest for the Foundations of Morality*. New Haven: Yale University Press, 2018.

Iredale, Matthew. "Putting Descartes Before the Horse." *The Philosophers' Magazine* 42 (2008) 40.

Joad, C.E.M. *Guide to Modern Thought*. London: Faber and Faber, 1942.

———. *Guide To Philosophy*. London: Victor Gollancz, 1946.

Johnson, Donald C. *Programming of Life*. Sylacauga, AL: Big Mac, 2010.

Keas, Michael Newton. *Unbelievable: 7 Myths About the History and Future of Science and Religion*. Wilmington, DE: ISI, 2019.

Klinghoffer, David, ed. *Debating Darwin's Doubt: A Scientific Controversy that Can No Longer Be Denied*. Seattle: Discovery Institute, 2015.

———, ed. *Signature of Controversy: Responses to Critics of Signature in the Cell*. Seattle: Discovery Institute, 2010.

Kojonen, Rope. "Methodological Naturalism and the Truth Seeking Objection." *International Journal for Philosophy of Religion* 81.3 (2017) 335–55.

Koons, Robert C. "Science and Theism: Concord not Conflict." In *The Rationality of Theism*, edited by Paul Copan and Paul Moser, 72–91. London: Routledge, 2003.

———. "The Check Is In The Mail: Why Darwinism Fails to Inspire Confidence." In *Uncommon Dissent: Intellectuals Who Find Darwinism Unconvincing*, edited by William A. Dembski, 3–22. Wilmington, Delaware: ISI, 2004.

Koons, Robert C. and George Bealer, eds. *The Waning of Materialism*. Oxford University Press, 2010.

Krauss, Lawrence M. "The Consolation Of Philosophy." *Scientific American*, April, 2012. www.scientificamerican.com/article/the-consolation-of-philos/.

———. "The Consolation of Philosophy." *Scientific American*. www.scientificamerican.com/article.cfm?id=the-consolation-of-philos&page=3.

———. *A Universe From Nothing: Why There Is Something Rather Than Nothing*. London: Free, 2012.

———. "Audio and Video from the Debate between William Lane Craig and Lawrence Krauss." Wintery Knight. http://winteryknight.wordpress.com/2011/03/30/audio-and-video-from-the-debate-between-william-lane-craig-and-lawrence-krauss/.

———. "Unbelievable: A Universe From Nothing? Lawrence Krauss vs. Rodney Holder." *Premier Radio*. www.premierradio.org.uk/listen/ondemand.aspx?mediaid=%7B02949395-E52F-4784-BF29-3A3138738B0B%7D.

———. "Everything and Nothing: An Interview with Lawrence M. Krauss." *Richard Dawkins Foundation*. http://richarddawkins.net/articles/644472-everything-and-nothing-an-interview-with-lawrence-krauss.

Kreeft, Peter and Ronald K. Tacelli. "Twenty Arguments For God's Existence." www.peterkreeft.com/topics-more/20_arguments-gods-existence.htm.

Kreeft, Peter. "A Refutation of Moral Relativism." www.peterkreeft.com/audio/05_relativism.htm.

———. "The Thomistic Cosmological Argument." www.youtube.com/watch?v=wefohtJBnN8.

———. *Three Philosophies of Life*. San Francisco: Ignatius, 1990.

Küppers, Bernd-Olaf. *Information and the Origin of Life*. Cambridge, MA: MIT, 1990.

Kurtz, Paul. *Forbidden Fruit*. Amherst, New York: Prometheus, 1988.

Larmer, Robert A. "The 'Argument From Miracle:' An Example of Ramified Natural Theology." www.epsociety.org/userfiles/art-Larmer%20(ArgumentFromMiracle-ExampleOfRamified).pdf.

———. "Science, Methodological Naturalism, and Question-Begging." In *The Naturalness of Belief: New Essays on Theism's Rationality*, edited by Paul Copan and Charles Taliaferro, 85–103. Lanham: Lexington, 2019.

Latham, Antony. *The Enigma of Consciousness: Reclaiming the Soul.* Cambridge: Janus, 2012.

Lehe, Robert T. *God, Science, and Religious Diversity: A Defense of Theism.* Eugene, OR: Cascade, 2018.

Leisola, Matti and Jonathan Witt. *Heretic: One Scientist's Journey from Darwin to Design.* Seattle: Discovery Institute, 2018.

Lennox, John C. *Seven Days That Divide The World: The Beginning According To Genesis And Science.* Grand Rapids, MI: Zondervan, 2011.

———. *God's Undertaker: Has Science Buried God?*, Second Edition. Oxford: Lion, 2009.

Leunissen, Mariska. *Explanation and Teleology in Aristotle's Science of Nature.* Cambridge: Cambridge University Press, 2010.

Levin, Margarita Rosa. "A Defence of Objectivity." In *Classics of Philosophy* Volume III – *The Twentieth Century*, edited by Louis J. Pojman, 549–59. Oxford: Oxford University Press, 2001.

Lewis, C.S. *First and Second Things.* London: Fount, 1985.

———. *The Weight of Glory and other addresses.* New York: HarperOne, 2001.

———. *Pilgrim's Regress.* 3rd ed. London: Fount, 1977.

———. *Surprised by Joy.* London: Fount, 1998.

———. *The Abolition of Man.* London: Fount, 1978.

Lewis, Geraint F. and Luke A. Barnes. *A Fortunate Universe: Life in a Finely Tuned Cosmos.* Cambridge: Cambridge University Press, 2016.

Lockwood, Michael. "Consciousness and the Quantum World: Putting Qualia on the Map." In *Consciousness: New Philosophical Perspectives*, edited by Q. Smith and A. Jokic, 447–67. Oxford: Clarendon, 2003.

Løkhammer, Espen. "The Fine-Tuning Argument for God's Existence: Does the Multiverse Objection Undermine the Fine-Tuning Argument for God's existence?" Master's thesis. Vitenskapelig Høyskole, 2020.

Longman III, Tremper. *Job.* Grand Rapids, MI: Baker Academic, 2012.

Luskin, Casey. "Atheists Who Defend Intelligent Design: Interview With Bradley Monton." YouTube video. IDQuest. 1:01:55. http://youtu.be/Et2VTJ1UBC4.

MacDonald, Scott. "Natural Theology" *Routledge Encyclopedia of Philosophy.* www.rep.routledge.com/articles/thematic/natural-theology/v-1.

Mackie, J.L. *Ethics: Inventing Right and Wrong.* London: Penguin, 1990.

———. *The Miracle of Theism.* Oxford: Oxford University Press, 1982.

Marks II, Robert J., William A. Dembski and Winston Ewert. *Introduction to Evolutionary Informatics.* Singapore: World Scientific, 2017.

Marks, Joel. "An Amoral Manifesto: Part I." www.philosophynow.org/issue80/An_Amoral_Manifesto_Part_I?vm=r.

Marston, Paul. "Understanding the Biblical Creation Passages." www.asa3.org/ASA/topics/Bible-Science/understanding_the_biblical_creation_passages.pdf.

Martin, Michael and Peter S. Williams. "Is there a personal God? Head to Head Debate. Atheist Michael Martin and Christian Peter S. Williams debate the existence of a unitary, personal god." *The Philosopher's Magazine* 8 (1999) 19–23.

Mascall, E.L. *He Who Is.* New York: Longmans, 1954.

BIBLIOGRAPHY

Matthew Barrett, Ardel B. Caneday and Stanley N. Gundry, eds. *Four Views On The Historical Adam*. Grand Rapids, MI: Zondervan, 2013.

May, Peter. "Karl Barth and Natural Theology?" *BeThinking*. www.bethinking.org/is-christianity-true/karl-barth-and-natural-theology.

———. "The Resurrection of Jesus and the Witness of Paul." *BeThinking*. www.bethinking.org/did-jesus-rise-from-the-dead/the-resurrection-of-jesus-and-the-witness-of-paul.

McGinn, Colin. *Ethics, Evil and Fiction*. Oxford: Clarendon, 1999.

McGrath, Alister. "John Polkinghorne (1930–2021): The pre-eminent voice on science and religion." www.premierchristianity.com/home/john-polkinghorne-1930-2021-the-pre-eminent-voice-on-science-and-religion/4010.article.

———. *Enriching our Vision of Reality: Theology and the Natural Sciences in Dialogue*. West Conshohocken, PA: Templeton, 2017.

———. *Enriching our Vision of Reality*. London: SPCK, 2016.

———. *I Believe: Exploring the Apostle's Creed*. Leicester: InterVarsity, 1997.

———. *Mere Apologetics*. Grand Rapids, MI: Baker, 2012.

———. *The Intellectual World of C. S. Lewis*. Oxford: Wiley-Blackwell, 2014.

McKaughan, Daniel and Daniel Howard-Snyder. "Faith." In *The Encyclopedia of Philosophy of Religion, Volume III*, edited by Stewart Goetz and Charles Taliaferro. Oxford: Wiley-Blackwell, 2021.

McKaughn, Daniel J. "On the Value of Faith and Faithfulness." *International Journal of the Philosophy of Religion* 81 (2017) 7–29.

Meister, Chad. *Introducing Philosophy of Religion*. London: Routledge, 2009.

Menuge, Angus and Charles Taliaferro. "Introduction to a Special Issue of Philosophia Christi on Ramified Natural Theology." www.epsociety.org/philchristi/tocs/philchristi_15-2.pdf.

Menuge, Angus J. *Agents Under Fire: Materialism and the Rationality of Science*. Lanham, MD: Rowman & Littlefield, 2004.

———. "Ramified Personalized Natural Theology: A Third Way?" *Evangelical Philosophical Society*. www.epsociety.org/userfiles/art-Menuge%20(Ramified%20Personalized%20Natural%20Theology).pdf.

Meyer, Stephen C. "DNA and the Origin of Life." *Discovery*. www.discovery.org/a/2184.

———. "Evidence of Intelligent Design in the Origin of Life" In Charles Thaxton et al, *The Mystery Of Life's Origin: The Continuing Controversy*, 424–28. Seattle: Discovery Institute, 2020.

———. "Sauce For The Goose: Intelligent Design, Scientific Methodology, and the Demarcation Problem." In *The Nature of Nature: Examining the Role of Naturalism in Science*, edited by Bruce L. Gordon and William A. Dembski, 95–131. Wilmington, Delaware: ISI, 2011.

———. "Teleological Evolution: The Difference it Doesn't Make." www.arn.org/docs/meyer/sm_teleologicalevolution.htm.

———. *Darwin's Doubt: The Explosive Origin Of Animal Life And The Case For Intelligent Design*. New York: HarperOne, 2013.

———. *Signature in the Cell: DNA and the Evidence For Intelligent Design*. New York: HarperOne, 2009.

———. *The Return of the God Hypothesis: Three Scientific Discoveries That Reveal the Mind Behind the Universe*. New York: HarperOne, 2021.

Midgley, Mary. *Are You An Illusion?* Durham: Acumen, 2014.

BIBLIOGRAPHY

Miller, Calum and Peter Atkins. www.premierunbelievable.com/unbelievable/does-god-exist-calum-miller-vs-peter-atkins-unbelievable-31-may-2012/12348.article.

Mitchell, Basil. "Reflections on C.S. Lewis, Apologetics, And the Moral Tradition: Basil Mitchell in Conversation with Andrew Walker." In *Rumours of Heaven: Essays in Celebration of C.S. Lewis*, edited by Andrew Walker and James Patrick, 7–26. Guildford: Eagle, 1998.

"Modernizing the Case for God." *Time*, April 7th, 1980.

Montifiore, Hugh. *The Probability of God*. London: SCM, 1985.

Monton, Bradley. "Is Intelligent Design Science? Dissecting the Dover Decision." www.arn.org/docs/monton/is_intelligent_design_science.pdf.

———. *Seeking God in Science: An Atheist Defends Intelligent Design*. Ontario: Broadview, 2009.

Moreland, J.P. "Intelligent Design and the Nature of Science." In *Intelligent Design 101*, edited by H. Wayne House, 43–65. Grand Rapids: Kregel, 2008.

———. "Physicalism, Naturalism and the Nature of Human Persons." In *To Everyone an Answer: A Case for the Christian Worldview*, edited by Francis J. Beckwith et al., 224–37. Downers Grove, IL: InterVarsity, 2004.

———. *Consciousness and the Existence of God: A Theistic Argument*. London: Routledge, 2008.

———. ed. *The Creation Hypothesis: Scientific Evidence for an Intelligent Designer*. Downers Grove, IL: InterVarsity, 1994.

———. *Scaling the Secular City: A Defence of Christianity*. Grand Rapids: Baker, 1987.

———. *Scientism and Secularism: Learning to Respond to a Dangerous Ideology*. Wheaton, IL: Crossway, 2018.

———. *The Recalcitrant Imago Dei: Human Persons and the Failure of Naturalism*. London: SCM, 2009.

Moreland, J.P. and Kai Nielson, ed. *Does God Exist? The Debate Between Theists and Atheists*. Amherst, NY: Prometheus, 1993.

Moreland, J.P. and William Lane Craig. *Philosophical Foundations for a Christian Worldview*. 2nd ed. Downers Grove, IL: InterVarsity, 2017.

———. eds. *The Blackwell Companion To Natural Theology*. Oxford: Wiley-Blackwell, 2009.

Morley, Brian K. *Mapping Apologetics: Comparing Contemporary Approaches*. Downers Grove, IL: InterVarsity, 2015.

Morris, Thomas V. *Making Sense of it All: Pascal and the Meaning of Life*. Grand Rapids: Eerdmans, 1992.

———. *Our Idea of God*. Notre Dame: University of Notre Dame Press, 1991.

Mosteller, Timothy M. and Gayne John Anacker, eds. *Contemporary Perspectives on C.S. Lewis' "The Abolition of Man:" History, Philosophy, Education, and Science*. London: Bloomsbury Academic, 2018.

Murray, Michael J. and Michael Rea. *An Introduction to the Philosophy of Religion*. Cambridge: Cambridge University Press, 2008.

Nagasawa, Yujin. "Divine Omniscience and Knowledge *De Se*." *Divine Conspiracy*. www.thedivineconspiracy.org/Z3214A.pdf.

———. *The Existence of God: A Philosophical Introduction*. London: Routledge, 2011.

Nagel, Thomas. *Secular Philosophy and the Religious Temperament*. Oxford: Oxford University Press, 2010.

———. *Mind and Cosmos: How The Materialist Neo-Darwinian Conception Of Nature Is Almost Certainly False*. Oxford: Oxford University Press, 2012.

Nash, Ronald H. *Faith and Reason*. Grand Rapids, MI: Zondervan, 1988.

National Academy of Sciences. *Teaching about Evolution and the Nature of Science*. Washington DC: National Academy, 1998.

Newman, Robert C., ed. *The Evidence of Prophecy: Fulfilled Prediction as a Testimony to the Truth of Christianity*. Hatfield, PA: IBIR, 1998.

Nielsen, Kai. "Why Should I Be Moral?" *American Philosophical Quarterly* 21.1 (1984) 81–91.

Nietzsche, Friedrich. "The Parable of the Madman." https://sourcebooks.fordham.edu/mod/nietzsche-madman.asp.

———. *Beyond Good and Evil*. Translated by Helen Zimmern. Project Gutenberg Ebook, 2013. www.gutenberg.org/files/4363/4363-h/4363-h.htm.

"Obituaries: Michael Durrant." www.cardiff.ac.uk/obituaries/obituary/michael-durrant.

O'Hear, Anthony. *Philosophy*. London: Continuum, 2001.

O'Leary-Hawthorn, John. "Arguments for Atheism." In *Reason for the Hope Within*, edited by Michael J. Murray, 116–34. Grand Rapids, MI: Eerdmans, 1999.

Overman, Dean L. *A Case Against Accident and Self-Organization*. Lanham: Rowman & Littlefield, 1997.

Pascal, Blaise. *Pensées and other writings*. Translated by Honor Levi. Oxford: Oxford University Press, 1995.

Pearcey, Nancy R. and Charles B. Thaxton. *The Soul of Science*. Wheaton, IL: Crossway, 1994.

Peterson, Derick. *Flat Earths and Fake Footnotes: The Strange Tale of How The Conflict of Science and Christianity Was Written Into History*. Eugene, OR: Cascade, 2021.

Peterson, Michael, et al. *Philosophy of Religion: Selected Readings*. Oxford: Oxford University Press, 1996.

Pigliucci, Massimo. "Lawrence Krauss: another physicist with an anti-philosophy complex." *Rationally Speaking*. http://rationallyspeaking.blogspot.co.uk/2012/04/lawrence-krauss-another-physicist-with.html.

Plantinga, Alvin. "Should Methodological Naturalism Constrain Science?" *Perspectives on Science and Christian Faith* 49 (1997) 143–54.

———. "The Ontological Argument." *Last Seminary*. www.lastseminary.com/ontological-argument/Plantinga%20-%20The%20Ontological%20Argument.pdf.

———. "When Faith and Reason Clash: Evolution and the Bible." *Christian Scholar's Review* 21.1 (1991) 8–33.

———. *God and Other Minds*. Ithaca, NY: Cornell University Press, 1967.

———. *God, Freedom and Evil*. Grand Rapids, MI: Eerdmans, 1977.

———. *Knowledge and Christian Belief*. Grand Rapids, MI: Eerdmans, 2015.

———. *Warranted Christian Belief*. Oxford: Oxford University Press, 2000.

———. *Where The Conflict Really Lies: Science, Religion, & Naturalism*. Oxford: Oxford University Press, 2011.

Plato. *The Collected Dialogues of Plato*. Translated by Lane Cooper. Edited by Edith Hamilton and Huntingdon Cairns. Princeton: Princeton University Press, 1961.

Pojman, Louis. "Faith Without Belief?" *Faith and Philosophy: Journal of the Society of Christian Philosophers* 3.2 (1986) 157–76.

Polanyi, Michael. "Life Transcending Physics and Chemistry." *Chemical Engineering News* 45.35 (1967) 54–66.

BIBLIOGRAPHY

Polkinghorne, John. "Where Is Natural Theology Today?" *Science and Christian Belief* 18 (2006) 169.

———. *The Case For God*. Tunbridge Wells: Monarch, 1999. Endorsement.

Porter, Calvin L. "Romans 1.18–32: Its Role in the Developing Argument." *New Testament Studies* 40.2 (1994) 210–28.

Pray, Leslie A. "Discovery of DNA Structure and Function: Watson and Crick." *Nature Education* 1.1 (2008) 100.

Pruss, Alexander R. "Christian Faith and Belief." *Faith and Philosophy*. http://alexanderpruss.com/papers/FaithAndBelief.html.

Puckett Jr., Joe. *The Apologetics of Joy: A Case for the Existence of God from C.S. Lewis's Argument from Desire*. Cambridge: Lutterworth, 2013.

Pullen, Stuart. *Intelligent Design or Evolution? Why the Origin of Life and the Evolution of Molecular Knowledge Imply Design*. Raleigh, NC: Intelligent Design, 2005.

"Ramified." *Dictionary.com*. https://dictionary.cambridge.org/dictionary/english/ramify.

Ramm, Bernard. *The Christian View of Science and Scripture*. Milton Keynes, UK: Paternoster, 1967.

Rana, Fuzz and Hugh Ross. *Origins of Life: Biblical and Evolutionary Models Face Off*. Colorado Springs: NavPress, 2004.

Rasmussen, Joshua. "An argument for a supreme foundation." In *A New Theist Response To The New Atheism*, edited by Joshua Rasmussen and Kevin Vallier, 21–32. London: Routledge, 2020.

Ratcliffe, Susan, ed. *Oxford Essential Quotations*. 4th edition. www.oxfordreference.com/view/10.1093/acref/9780191826719.001.0001/q-oro-ed4-00002890.

Ratzsch, Del. *Science and Its Limits: The Natural Sciences in Christian Perspective*. 2nd edition. Downers Grove, IL: InterVarsity, 2000.

Rauser, Randal. *Is the Atheist My Neighbor? Rethinking Christian Attitudes toward Atheism*. Eugene, OR: Cascade, 2015.

Reichenbach, Bruce R. *The Cosmological Argument: A Reassessment*. Springfield, IL: Charles C. Thomas, 1972.

Reppert, Victor. "The Bayesian Argument from Desire." *Dangerous Idea*. http://dangerousidea.blogspot.com/2006/09/bayesian-argument-from-desire.html#comments.

———. *C.S. Lewis' Dangerous Idea: In Defence of the Argument from Reason*. Downers Grove, IL: InterVarsity, 2003.

Richard of St Victor. *On the Trinity*. Eugene, OR: Cascade, 2011.

Richards, Jay Wesley. "Divine Simplicity: The Good, the Bad, and the Ugly." In *For Faith and Clarity: Philosophical Contributions to Christian Theology*, edited by James K. Beilby, 157–77. Grand Rapids: Baker Academic, 2006.

Robinson, Howard. "Qualia, Qualities, and Our Conception of the Physical World." In *After Physicalism*, edited by Benedikt Paul Göcke, 231–63. Notre Dame: University of Notre Dame Press, 2012.

"Romans 1:18–32 and Wisdom of Solomon." *TheoGeek*. July 22, 2008. http://theogeek.blogspot.com/2008/07/romans-118-32-and-wisdom-of-solomon.html.

Russell, Bertrand and F. C. Copleston. "A Debate on the Existence of God." In *The Existence of God*, edited by John Hick, 167–191. New York: Macmillan, 1964.

Russell, Bertrand. "A Free Man's Worship." *Bertrand Russell Society*. http://bertrandrussellsocietylibrary.org/br-pe/br-pe-ch2.html.

———. *Why I Am Not A Christian*. London: Routeldge, 1996.

Ryle, Gilbert. *The Concept of Mind*. Chicago: University of Chicago Press, 1949.

Sadowsky, James A. "Can There be an Endless Regress of Causes?" In *Philosophy of Religion: a guide and anthology*, edited by Brian Davies, 239–41. Oxford: Oxford University Press, 2000.

Sartre, Jean-Paul. *Existentialism Is a Humanism*. Yale University Press, 2007.

Scott, Douglas and Martin White. "Cosmic Microwave Background Radiation." www.astro.ubc.ca/people/scott/cmb_intro.html.

Scruton, Roger. *An Intelligent Person's Guide To Philosophy*. London: Duckworth, 1997.

Sedley, David. *Creationism And Its Critics In Antiquity*. Berkeley: University of California Press, 2007.

Sennett, James F. and Douglas Groothuis, eds. *In Defence Of Natural Theology: A Post-Humean Assessment*. Downers Grove, IL: InterVarsity, 2005.

Shaefer-Landau, Russ. *Whatever Happened to Good and Evil?* Oxford: Oxford University Press, 2004.

Shalkowski, Scott A. "Atheological Apologetics." In *Contemporary Perspectives on Religious Epistemology*, edited by R. Douglas Geivett and Brendan Sweetman, 58–73. Oxford: Oxford University Press, 1992.

Sheldrake, Philip. *Spirituality: A Very Short Introduction*. Oxford: Oxford University Press, 2012.

Sire, James W. *The Universe Next Door: A Basic Worldview Catalogue*. 5th edition. Downers Grove, IL: InterVarsity, 2009.

Smith, Quentin. "The Uncaused Beginning of the Universe." *Philosophy of Science* 55 (1988) 39–57.

Sorley, W.R. *Moral Value And The Idea Of God, Second Edition*. Cambridge: Cambridge University Press, 1921.

Spitzer, Robert J. "The Curious Metaphysics of Dr Stephen Hawking." *Catholic Education Resource Centre*. www.catholiceducation.org/en/science/faith-and-science/the-curious-metaphysics-of-dr-stephen-hawking.html.

Spurling, Hilary. "The Wickedest Man in Oxford." *The New York Times*. www.nytimes.com/books/00/12/24/reviews/001224.24spurlit.html.

Stenger, Victor J. *The New Atheism: Taking a Stand for Science and Reason*. Amherst, NY: Prometheus, 2009.

Stoke, Mitch. *A Shot of Faith (to the Head): Be a Confident Believer in an Age of Cranky Atheists*. Nashville, TN: Thomas Nelson, 2012.

Stump, J.B. and Stanley N. Gundry, eds. *Creation, Evolution, and Intelligent Design*. Grand Rapids, MI: Zondervan, 2017.

Swamidass, Joshua. *The Genealogical Adam and Eve: The Surprising Science Of Universal Ancestry*. Downers Grove, IL: IVP Academic, 2019.

Swinburne, Richard. "Evidence for God" (1986). *Christian Evidence*. http://christianevidence.org/docs/booklets/evidence_for_god.pdf.

———. "Natural Theology, Its 'Dwindling Probabilities' and 'Lack of Rapport.'" *Faith and Philosophy* 21.4 (2004) 533–46.

———. "The Justification of Theism." www.leaderu.com/truth/3truth09.html.

———. *Faith and Reason*. 2nd edition. Oxford: Clarendon, 2005.

———. *Is There A God?* rev. ed. Oxford: Oxford University Press, 2010.

———. *Mind, Brain, and Free Will*. Oxford: Oxford University Press, 2013.

———. *The Christian God*. Oxford: Oxford University Press, 1995.

———. *The Existence of God*. 2nd edition. Cambridge: Clarendon, 2004.

———. *The Resurrection of God Incarnate*. Cambridge: Clarendon, 2003.
Swindal, James. "Faith and Reason." *Internet Encyclopedia of Philosophy*. www.iep.utm.edu/faith-re/#SH4e.
Taliaferro, Charles. "Where Do Thoughts Come From?" In *The Big Argument: Does God Exist?*, edited by John Ashton and Michael Westcott, 155–63. Green Forest, AR: Master Books, 2006.
———. *Aesthetics: A Beginner's Guide*. Oxford: OneWorld, 2011.
———. *Consciousness and the Mind of God*. Cambridge: Cambridge University Press, 1994.
———. *Contemporary Philosophy of Religion*. Oxford: Blackwells, 2001.
Tallis, Raymond. *Aping Mankind: Neuromania, Darwinitis and the Misrepresentation of Humanity*. London: Routledge, 2014.
Tallon, Philip. "The Theistic Argument from Beauty and Play." In *Two Dozen (Or So) Arguments For God*, edited by Jerry L. Walls and Trent Dougherty, 321–40. Oxford: Oxford University Press, 2018.
Tan, Change Laura and Rob Stadler. *The Stairway To Life: An Origin-of-Life Reality Check*. Evorevo, 2020.
Taylor, A.E. *Does God Exist?* London: Fontana, 1961.
Taylor, Richard. "The Cosmological Argument: A Defence." http://mind.ucsd.edu/syllabi/02-03/01w/readings/taylor.pdf
———. *Ethics, Faith, and Reason*. Englewood Cliffs, NJ: Prentice-Hall, 1985.
Thaxton, Charles B. *The Mystery of Life's Origin: The Continuing Controversy*. Seattle: Discovery Institute, 2020.
Trigg, Roger. *Does Science Undermine Faith?* London: SPCK, 2018.
Varghese, Roy Abraham, ed. *Great Thinkers on Great Questions*. Oxford: OneWorld, 1998.
Vilenkin, Alexander. "Did the Universe Have a Beginning?" http://youtu.be/NXCQelhKJ7A.
Vining, Teresa Turner. *Making Your Faith Your Own*. Downers Grove, IL: InterVarsity, 2001.
Walls, Jerry L. and Trent Dougherty, eds. *Two Dozen (Or So) Arguments For God*. Oxford: Oxford University Press, 2018.
Waltham, David. *Lucky Planet: Why Earth Is Exceptional – And What It Means For Life In The Universe*. London: Icon, 2014.
Walton, John H. *The Lost World Of Adam And Eve: Genesis 2-3 and the Human Origins Debate*. Downers Grove, IL: IVP Academic, 2015.
———. "Who Wrote Ecclesiastes and What Does It Mean?" Zondervan. https://zondervanacademic.com/blog/who-wrote-ecclesiastes-and-what-does-it-mean/.
Ward, Keith. *God: A Guide for the Perplexed*. Oxford: OneWorld, 2002.
———. *The Turn of the Tide*. London: BBC, 1986.
Ward, Michael. *After Humanity: A Guide to C.S. Lewis' "The Abolition of Man."* Park Ridge, IL.: Word on Fire Academic, 2021.
Ward, Peter D. and Donald Brownlee. *Rare Earth: Why Complex Life Is Uncommon in the Universe*. New York: Copernicus, 2000.
Wesley, John. "An Address to the Clergy." *Wesley Center Online*. http://wesley.nnu.edu/john_wesley/10clergy.htm.
West, John G., ed. *The Magician's Twin: C.S. Lewis on Science, Scientism, and Society*. Seattle: Discovery Institute, 2012.

"What is Natural Theology?" *The Gifford Lectures.* www.giffordlectures.org/overview/natural-theology.

Whybray, Norman. *Job.* Sheffield: Phoenix, 2008.

Wilkinson, Dan. "The Punctuation Mark that Might Change How You Read Romans." *Above All, Love.* www.patheos.com/blogs/unfundamentalistchristians/2015/09/the-punctuation-mark-that-might-changehow-you-read-romans/.

Willard, Dallas. "Language, Being, God, and the Three Stages of Theistic Evidence." https://dwillard.org/articles/language-being-god-and-the-three-stages-of-theistic-evidence.

———. "Knowledge And Naturalism." https://dwillard.org/articles/knowledge-and-naturalism.

———. "The Three-Stage Argument for the Existence of God." In *Contemporary Perspectives on Religious Epistemology*, edited by Douglas Geivett and Brendan Sweetman, 212–24. Oxford: Oxford University Press, 1992.

Williams, Peter S. "Ancient Aliens: Rebutting Alien Conspiracy Theories." Forum of Christian Leaders. YouTube video, 29:20. www.youtube.com/watch?v=d7OUXOfI0-g.

———. "A Beginner's Guide to the Theistic Argument from Desire." *Solas.* www.solas-cpc.org/a-beginners-guide-to-the-theistic-argument-from-desire/.

———. "A Brief Introduction to and Defence of the Modern Ontological Argument." *Theofilos* 7.3 (2015) 339–44. https://theofilos.no/wp-content/uploads/2019/09/3d_Forum_Williams_A-Brief-Introduction-to-and-Defence-of-the-Modern-Ontological-Argument.pdf.

———. "A Christian Worldview and Science in Apologetic Perspective: Introduction." *The Peter S. Williams Podcast*, October 25, 2021. Podcast. http://podcast.peterswilliams.com/e/a-christian-worldview-and-science-in-apologetic-perspective-introduction/

———. "A Universe From Someone – Against Lawrence Krauss." *BeThinking.* www.bethinking.org/is-there-a-creator/a-universe-from-someone-against-lawrence-krauss.

———. "The Design Inference from Specified Complexity Defended by Scholars Outside the Intelligent Design Movement: A Critical Review." *Philosophia Christi* 9.2 (2007) 407–28. www.discovery.org/scripts/viewDB/filesDB-download.php?command=download&id=1491.

———. "Apologetics in 3D – 'Input' at Trondheim Frikirke." *The Peter S. Williams Podcast*, March 12. 2018. Podcast. http://podcast.peterswilliams.com/e/apologetics-in-3d-input-at-trondheim-frikirke/.

———. "Apologetics in 3D: Persuading Across Spiritualities with the Apostle Paul." *Theofilos* 1 (2012) 3–24. www.bethinking.org/apologetics/apologetics-in-3d.

———. "Apologetics in 3D." www.youtube.com/watch?v=hiUHeaEaPLA.

———. "The Apologetics of Cultural Re-Enchantment in 3D: Makoto Fujimura's *Culture Care* & Paul M. Gould's *Cultural Apologetics*." *Theofilos* 1 (2019), 79–88. https://theofilos.no/wp-content/uploads/2020/03/3e_Forum_Williams_The-Apologetics-of-Cultural-Re-Enchantment-in-3D.pdf.

———. "Archaeological Evidence and Jesus." *The Peter S. Williams Podcast*, May 27, 2020. 46:56. http://podcast.peterswilliams.com/e/elf-2020-archaeological-evidence-and-jesus/.

———. "Archaeological Evidence and Jesus." Forum of Christian Leaders. YouTube video, October 12, 2020. 47:13. https://youtu.be/ZaGlKZqED1k.

BIBLIOGRAPHY

———. "Arguing for God." *The Peter S. Williams Podcast.* http://podcast.peterswilliams.com/e/arguing-for-god/.

———. "Atheists Against Darwinism: Johnson's Wedge Breaks Through." *Evangelical Philosophical Society.* http://epsociety.org/library/articles.asp?pid=66.

———. "C.S. Lewis as a Central Figure in Formulating the Theistic Argument from Desire." *Linguaculture* 10.2 (2019) http://journal.linguaculture.ro/images/2019-2/Linguaculture%202_2019_11_Peter%20S%20Williams.pdf.

———. "Can Moral Objectivism Do Without God?" *Theofilos* (2011) www.peterswilliams.com/wp-content/uploads/2022/07/Can-Moral-Objectivism-Do-Without-God-v3.pdf.

———. "Carl Sagan: The Skeptic's Sceptic." *BeThinking.* www.bethinking.org/atheism/carl-sagan-the-skeptics-sceptic.

———. "Cosmic Fine Tuning: Design or Multiverse?" *The Peter S. Williams Podcast.* http://podcast.peterswilliams.com/e/cosmic-fine-tuning-design-or-multiverse/.

———. "Debate: Does God Exist? Peter S. Williams vs. Einar Bohn at the Norwegian University of Science and Technology in Trondheim" *The Peter S. Williams Podcast.* http://peterswilliams.podbean.com/mf/feed/e5dvj8/Trondheim_2018_Debate.mp3arguments-from-desire/.

———. "Defending Early High Christology with Archaeology and New Testament Letters" www.youtube.com/watch?v=vUha7-4Puy8.

———. "Design and the Humean Touchstone." www.arn.org/docs/williams/pw_humeantouchstone.htm.

———. *Digging for Evidence: Archaeology and the Historical Reliability of the New Testament.* London: Christian Evidence Society, 2016. http://christianevidence.org/docs/booklets/digging_for_evidence.pdf.

———. "Discipleship in 3D: Change for head, heart and hands." Damaris Norge. YouTube video, April 29, 2020. 45:26. https://youtu.be/QTyEooJgIBI.

———. "Hebrews 11 and faith in the new atheism." *The Peter S. Williams Podcast.* http://podcast.peterswilliams.com/e/hebrews-11-faith-in-the-new-atheism/.

———. "In Defence of Arguments From Desire." www.peterswilliams.com/2016/11/02/in-defence-of-arguments-from-desire/.

———. "In Search Of Innocence: Ghost in a Shell 2." www.peterswilliams.com/2016/02/09/in-search-of-innocence/.

———. "Intelligent Design, Aesthetics and Design Arguments." www.arn.org/docs/williams/pw_idaestheticsanddesignarguments.htm.

———. "Intelligent Designs on Science." (2006) www.peterswilliams.com/2016/02/09/intelligent-designs-on-science/.

———. "Intelligent Designs on Science." www.peterswilliams.com/2016/02/09/intelligent-designs-on-science/.

———. "Is Christianity Unscientific?" Forum of Christian Leaders. YouTube video, July 24, 2014. 50:26. https://youtu.be/mWiU2p_PIE8.

———. "Is Christianity Unscientific?" *Theofilos* 3 (2010) 4–15. www.peterswilliams.com/wp-content/uploads/2013/07/Is-Christianity-Unscientific-Theofilos-Paper.pdf.

———. "*Resurrection*: Faith or Fact? Miracle Not Required?" *Theofilos* 11.2 (2020). https://theofilos.no/wp-content/uploads/2020/03/Theofilos-vol.-11-nr.-2-2019-Forum-3-Arkiv.pdf.

BIBLIOGRAPHY

———. "Scientific Rebuttals to 'Ancient Aliens' as Popular Alternatives to Biblical History." *Theofilos* 12.1 (2020). https://theofilos.no/wp-content/uploads/2020/12/Theofilos-vol-12-nr-1-2020-Supplement-academia-6.pdf.

———. "Sermon: Revelation 1:1–8 (On Revealing the Trinity)." Sermon preached at Highfield Church, Southampton, February, 2017. https://mcdn.podbean.com/mf/web/3w9cgh/Rev_1.mp3.

———. "Understanding the Trinity." *BeThinking*. www.bethinking.org/god/understanding-the-trinity / www.peterswilliams.com/wp-content/uploads/2016/02/Trinity.pdf.

———. "Who Made God?" *BeThinking*. www.bethinking.org/god/who-made-god.

———. *A Faithful Guide to Philosophy: A Christian Introduction to the Love of Wisdom*. Eugene, OR: Wipf and Stock, 2019.

———. *Apologetics in 3D: Essays on Apologetics and Spirituality*. Eugene, OR: Wipf and Stock, 2021.

———. *C.S. Lewis vs. the New Atheists*. Milton Keynes: Paternoster, 2013.

———. *Getting at Jesus: A Comprehensive Critique of Neo-Atheist Nonsense About the Jesus of History*. Eugene, OR: Wipf & Stock, 2019.

———. *I Wish I Could Believe In Meaning: A Response To Nihilism*. Southampton: Damaris, 2004.

———. *Outgrowing God? A Beginner's Guide to Richard Dawkins and the God Debate*. Eugene, OR: Cascade, 2020.

———. *The Case For God*. Monarch, 1999.

———. *Understanding Jesus: Five Ways to Spiritual Enlightenment*. Milton Keynes: Paternoster, 2011.

Williams, Peter S. and Peter Millican. "Debating the Ontological Argument." *Unbelievable*. https://unbelievable.podbean.com/e/debating-the-ontological-argument-peter-s-williams-peter-millican/.

Willimon, William H. *Acts*. Louisville, KY: Westminster John Knox, 2010.

Wright, N.T. "Jesus' Resurrection and Christian Origins." In *Passionate Conviction*, edited by Paul Copan and William Lane Craig, 123–37. Nashville, TN: B&H Academic, 2007.

Wykstra, Stephen. "'Not Done in a Corner' Revisited: Becoming a More Sensible Evidentialist about Jesus." Baylor Institute for Studies of Religion. YouTube video, September 23, 2017. 1:14:15. https://youtu.be/7Tmngq3ZR1w.

Yandell, Keith E. "Theology, Philosophy, And Evil." In *For Faith And Clarity*, edited by James K. Beilby, 219–42. Grand Rapids: Baker, 2006.

———. "David Hume on Meaning, Verification and Natural Theology." In *In Defence of Natural Theology: A Post-Humean Account*, edited by James F. Sennett and Douglas Groothuis, 58–81. Downers Grove, IL: InterVarsity, 2005.

YouTube Playlist. "Beauty." www.youtube.com/playlist?list=PLQhh3qcwVEWiL488-SGbfODhf6kLPSZbJ.

———. "Biblical Prophecy." www.youtube.com/playlist?list=PLQhh3qcwVEWgq_Hba52LXvmcUHR4T010a.

———. "Christianity and Science." www.youtube.com/playlist?list=PLQhh3qcwVEWjeYJfOKB1YYXsInZ5GIPL_.

———. "Cosmic Fine Tuning." www.youtube.com/playlist?list=PLQhh3qcwVEWj4aeE76A1vjLvPqWieH8tE.

BIBLIOGRAPHY

———. "Cosmological Arguments for God." www.youtube.com/playlist?list=PLQhh3qcwVEWjEXjiEjnCCbr_Qnu-1UbAa.

———. "Debating God." www.youtube.com/playlist?list=PLQhh3qcwVEWiY3UmTAiRdj2OW4SBGoy_W.

———. "Debating Intelligent Design Theory." www.youtube.com/playlist?list=PLQhh3qcwVEWhO4mPNzA-K41C7VfvSvkQW.

———. "Discipleship & Spiritual Formation." www.youtube.com/playlist?list=PLQhh3qcwVEWhGSK1x6H3qeqzefB8hmvvM.

———. "Introduction to Intelligent Design Theory." www.youtube.com/playlist?list=PLQhh3qcwVEWhNWeZ2LxPUa5j2afVcG-B6.

———. "Irreducible Complexity." www.youtube.com/playlist?list=PLQhh3qcwVEWh3orLA2I3KySSxUoIXAdZ3.

———. "Mind-Body Dualism, Free Will and Related Issues." www.youtube.com/playlist?list=PLQhh3qcwVEWhoMdW-hlHBPyLRWgFjzhPT.

———. "Natural Theology." www.youtube.com/playlist?list=PLQhh3qcwVEWiDA8QN4h8wLrrbm49fLzPN.

———. "Problems with Materialism/Metaphysical Naturalism." www.youtube.com/playlist?list=PLQhh3qcwVEWgolWsfZnhQvzNfRT_jHLJA.

———. "Scientism" www.youtube.com/playlist?list=PLQhh3qcwVEWiIgrCwkM8Y-RoqU1TmYK8R.

———. "Specified Complexity." www.youtube.com/playlist?list=PLQhh3qcwVEWiQrIEmUwrpyxVxVaZMc4i_.

———. "The Moral Argument For God." www.youtube.com/playlist?list=PLQhh3qcwVEWhOfs_uQrFceuBRfMF1asf4.

———. "The Nature of Faith." https://youtube.com/playlist?list=PLQhh3qcwVEWgaKjEEuPC-ziv9pbReCFHD.

———. "The Ontological Argument for God." www.youtube.com/playlist?list=PLQhh3qcwVEWjE7hqAz3D6jp7MWjChVYKn.

———. "The Origin of Life." www.youtube.com/playlist?list=PLQhh3qcwVEWggFeEP9H7k1LyccfxzvoSr.

———. "The Problem of Evil." www.youtube.com/playlist?list=PLQhh3qcwVEWjSOz8xsGXuS_VahByzSzhe.

———. "The Scientific Status of Intelligent Design Theory." www.youtube.com/playlist?list=PLQhh3qcwVEWhq9Tl1f9UdqL6ZFNPLsc8P.

———. "The Theological Roots of Science." www.youtube.com/playlist?list=PLQhh3qcwVEWh3jDVYqFFzWSnTbtlUeCg3.

———. "The Trinity." www.youtube.com/playlist?list=PLQhh3qcwVEWhlDMYNYyenLkqdEQMMtMY0.

———. "Understanding Worldviews." www.youtube.com/playlist?list=PLQhh3qcwVEWhCn7rqlW7UsvFNRjQ9wxoH.

———. "Natural Theology." YouTube playlist: www.youtube.com/playlist?list=PLQhh3qcwVEWiDA8QN4h8wLrrbm49fLzPN.

———. "Scientism" www.youtube.com/playlist?list=PLQhh3qcwVEWiIgrCwkM8Y-RoqU1TmYK8R.

———. "The Argument from Desire." www.youtube.com/playlist?list=PLQhh3qcwVEWj3nK3TBydEVAFRtdqfrpW2.

Zacharias, Ravi. *Can Man Live Without God*. Milton Keynes: Word, 1994.

www.ingramcontent.com/pod-product-compliance
Lightning Source LLC
Chambersburg PA
CBHW050809160426
43192CB00010B/1695